D0215984

TRANSNATIONAL BUSINESS AND CORPORATE CULTURE

PROBLEMS AND OPPORTUNITIES

edited by

STUART BRUCHEY
ALLAN NEVINS PROFESSOR EMERITUS
COLUMBIA UNIVERSITY

A GARLAND SERIES

TRANSFORMATION TO AGILITY

MANUFACTURING IN THE MARKETPLACE OF UNANTICIPATED CHANGE

JEFFREY AMOS

GARLAND PUBLISHING, INC.
A MEMBER OF THE TAYLOR & FRANCIS GROUP
NEW YORK & LONDON / 1998

Library of Congress Cataloging-in-Publication Data

Amos, Jeffrey, 1965–
    Transformation to agility : manufacturing in the marketplace
of unanticipated change / Jeffrey Amos..
        p.   cm. — (Transnational business and corporate cul-
ture)
    Includes bibliographical references and index.
    ISBN 0-8153-3347-1 (alk. paper)
    1. Production planning. 2. International business enter-
prises—Case studies. 3. Aerospace industries—Case studies. I.
Title. II. Series.
TS176.A46 1998
658.5—dc21
                                                    98-46666

Printed on acid-free, 250-year-life paper
Manufactured in the United States of America

The author wishes to dedicate this book to his family and friends who have supported him greatly throughout his effort.

Contents

Figures

Tables

Acknowledgments

The author wishes to thank all members of the Aerospace Agile Manufacturing Research Center Team at the IC^2 Institute for their support and advice during this research effort including: Dr. David Gibson, Jennifer Kodish, Kurt Hoover, Dr. Sheila Kearns, Alf Steiner Saetre, and Sunil Tankha. Dr. Amos would like to extend special thanks to Dr. George Kozmetsky for the vision and encouragement to pursue a non-traditional interdisciplinary degree. Without Dr. Kozmetsky's firm belief in applying engineering knowledge and background to business topics, the barriers and special approvals required for the interdisciplinary degree would not have been possible. The author would also like to thank the interdisciplinary committee members: Dr. Tapley, Director, Center for Space Research, Aerospace Engineering, College of Engineering; Dr. Fowler, Aerospace Engineering, College of Engineering; Dr. Gibson, Assistant to Director of the IC^2 Institute, MSIS Department, School of Business; Dr. Kozmetsky, Chairman of the IC^2 Institute, Management Department, School of Business; Dr. Srivastava, Senior Associate Dean for Academic Affairs, Chairman of Marketing Science, School of Business; and Dr. Fossum, Director, Quality Management Consortia, Management Department, School of Business.

Transformation to Agility

CHAPTER 1

Introduction

History is replete with examples of one theology overtaking another, one political system replacing a former, one scientific discovery invalidating a host of old theories. This cycle has occurred repeatedly in the production of goods and products for society. Sometimes there are those who recognize years or even decades ahead that a certain way of "doing things" is changing, hopefully, for increased effectiveness and efficiency. Now is one of those times where a massive transition can be observed first hand.

Various global changes in American business and manufacturing have forced a review of accepted thinking. The last great change in business paradigms was the move from the American System to the system of Mass Manufacturing (Hounshell, 1984). For many years now, multiple scholars, industry researchers and business executives have been working on pieces of a replacement paradigm to the well-accepted thinking and philosophy of mass manufacturing.

A few scholars foresaw the decline of the system of mass manufacturing early, "we have begun the painful process of replacing the . . . already outdated concept of production, which I shall call, for want of a better name, 'mass production'," from "Production Under Pressure," by Wickham Skinner, 1966 (qtd in Pisano, 1995, p. xv). Later in 1971, Skinner declared that the "conventional factory is fast becoming an anachronism" (qtd in Pisano, 1995, p. xv). By the late 1970s, it became painfully obvious to most that there were problems with the very structure of the American mass manufacturing production system. Scholars and practitioners began to try to find causes and solutions to the changes that were occurring. Some looked at the "emergence of a technology gap in manufacturing" (MSB/NRC, 1984, p.1). Others looked at the perceived excessive separation between companies and their customers. Many looked abroad and hoped to emulate the success of some foreign nations particularly the Japanese and the Germans. Hayes and Wheelwright (1984) concluded that the secret weapon of international competitors was manufacturing superiority (foreign companies were simply better at *making* products. The critical change factor, these scholars claimed, was that the U.S. had relinquished its manufacturing focus and leadership. This is an unacceptable situation. Manufacturing research experts Giffi, Roth and Seal assert, "manufacturing is vital for the economic health of the nation and for North American world leadership" (Giffi, Roth et al., 1990, p 1).

In response to the apparent decline of American industrial dominance, a multitude of programs and initiatives were developed that helped some companies while doing nothing for others. Many "rational analytical plans" have been found to be the source of an "attribution error." Scholars and consultants have prematurely linked these plans with competitive success when they may have contributed very little to that success (Pascale, 1984; Mintzberg, 1989). The overuse of these uncorrelated plans led to the declaration that

> ... there is a crises of failing competition and in our desperation to survive and recover we are grabbing at anything new that offers hope to do better on any single criterion of performance. As a result, productivity and quality are up, inventories are down and we are still losing market shares in dozens of industries. Why? (Skinner, 1992, p. 25).

After more than a decade of individual programs with sporadic successes, there is a boisterous consensus that it is the mass manufacturing paradigm itself that is untenable. Industry is in the midst of a major transition. Multiple sources declare that manufacturing and business in general must be reconsidered from an entirely new perspective.

- the [manufacturing] 'mind set' since the beginning of the Industrial Revolution is now dysfunctional (Skinner, 1985).

- It's undeniable that such practices as TQM, benchmarking, rightsizing, and just-in-time have helped many companies improve their operations. But such devices are limited and incremental. [New management systems] will require an entirely different focus and effort (one that is strategic and unending (Want, 1993, p. 28).

- What is needed are new manufacturing strategies which innovate entirely new integrated structures and create a true manufacturing enterprise (Skinner, 1992, p. 25).

- Manufacturing in the 1990s and beyond . . . is no longer based on huge accumulations of capital, standardization of products, mass production, and mass consumption (Kozmetsky, 1993).

- A new American paradigm for competitive manufacturing is essential in order to create wealth, economic stability and maintain world leadership (Roe, Fossum et al., 1993, p.xviii).

- Most manufacturing people in the U.S. now know we need a new theory of manufacturing (Drucker, 1990).

RESEARCH STATEMENT

This dissertation examines and helps refine a proposed manufacturing framework that is purported to be the replacement of mass manufacturing, namely Agile Manufacturing. Indeed, the concepts under investigation actually extend beyond manufacturing into the most fundamental aspects of business. The objective of this effort is to provide a comprehensive description and theoretical formulation for 'Agile Manufacturing' and 'Agility'.[1] At this time, there is a virtual absence of academically rigorous investigations of Agility.

The approach is to develop a systemic, normative model based upon an analysis and interpretation of manufacturers at various stages of Agility. The experiences of these manufacturers are supplemented by data collected through in-depth interviews, personal observation, and correspondence, and through a thorough review of literature on Agility and related sub-topic issues. This research provides a step towards the generation of an Agile implementation methodology. The research also builds on previous studies to provide a basis for increased understanding of the transition from mass manufacturing processes and practices to agile manufacturing processes and practices.

CONTRIBUTIONS

This dissertation makes the following specific contributions:

Conceptual Definition

*   Compilation and review of existing models and definitions,

*   Development of definition of Agility that lends itself to testing,

*   Development of a conceptual model for Agility that lends itself to empirical verification,

*   Presentation of postulates of antecedent factors leading to Agility and expected results,

*   Revision of model and postulates that are analyzed based upon grounded theory data.

Analysis and Interpretation of Data

*   Proposes criteria for the identification of Agile attributes and characteristics,

*   Identifies ways in which manufacturers characterize success and failure and measure process improvement,

*   Presents a comprehensive description of the status of Agile technology and barriers and enablers to its implementation,

*   Presents and initial review of the application of Data Envelop Analysis as a possible candidate for the creation of a metric of Agility.

Implications of Research

*   Presentation of elements addressing the required focus of organizational change for Agility,

*   Presentation of guidelines and recommendations addressing factors important to an creating and maintaining and Agile organizational infrastructure,

- Presentation of guidelines and recommendations addressing Agility implementation through Agile implementation projects,

- Relation of propositions and guidelines in a conceptual framework for Agile implementation,

- Presentation of links to other research areas critical to Agility.

OVERVIEW OF DISSERTATION FORMAT

This dissertation is broken down as follows: an analysis of manufacturing history, the theory of Agility, presentation of an antecedent model of Agility, case study analyses, and the testing of a particular measure for Agility. Chapter 2 begins with a presentation of manufacturing development throughout history divided into stages. The drivers, attributes and consequences are identified in each stage. Following the stage presentation is an overview of the drivers both economic and in the businessplace that are forcing changes in the status quo. Chapter 3 identifies concepts and theories that are closely related to Agility, some of which form basic building blocks for the Agile framework. The early development and critical theoretical concepts of agility are then presented. After the completion of this literature review basis for agility, Chapter 4 provides the methodology for the current research. In Chapter 5 the proposed preliminary model for agility is presented which builds into the presentation of the two major case studies. Each case study is analyzed individually in Chapters 6 and 7 and then a cross study examination is provided in Chapter 8. Chapter 9 provides additional supporting case studies which focus on individual specific individual variables. Chapter 10 shifts the flow of the research and presents the work and conclusions on the attempt to determine an effective global metric of Agility. Finally, research results, summarized conclusions and areas identified for future research are provided in Chapter 11.

NOTE

1. The definition of Agility will be formally reviewed in Chapter 5, but at this point business Agility refers to the nimbleness of a company to quickly assemble its technology, employees, and management via a communication and information infrastructure in a deliberate, effective, and coordinated response to

changing customer demands in a market environment of continuous and unanticipated change.

CHAPTER 2

Stages of Manufacturing

As a prerequisite for an effective presentation of Agility it is necessary to first recount some key events in the progression of manufacturing (Figure 2.1). This presentation is based upon the Stage Model theories (Kuznets, 1965) which have been applied in many fields (e.g. economic development, Marx, 1932; Information systems, Nolan, 1973; 1979, etc.). Presentation of stages of manufacturing helps provide a framework for the theory formulation of Agile Manufacturing. Multiple stages and transitions identified by many well-respected authors will be presented. An effort is made to show the attributes of each stage and the forces driving its evolutionary process. The stage models compiled in this chapter are loosely based upon the models of Skinner (1985), Jaikumar (1986), Goldman (1993), Shapiro (1987), Doll and Vonderembse (1992) and Rostow (1993).

MANUFACTURING / PRODUCTION HISTORY

Humankind began producing items long before recorded history. Over time knowledge began to grow and be passed down to others concerning the "best" methods for producing a particular jar, bow, or shelter. The great monuments of the past stand as testament to the integration of activities that must have been achieved. The Great Pyramids, the Colossus of Rhodes, the Temple of Artemis required much more than architects, slaves, bricks and sweat. Someone *made* the bricks. Someone *made* the carts that carried the bricks. Someone *made* the wheels that rolled the carts. Someone *built* the platforms, hoists and levers that allowed for the building of ever greater things (Cowan, 1977).

400's	600's	1784	1800's	1900's	1910	1950's	1960's	1970's	1980's	1990'

Craft: Master/Apprentice
Craft: Guild
Craft: Entrepreneurial
Adam Smith
"Wealth of Nations"
Factory Manufacturing
American Production System
Mass Manufacturing
Scientific Management (Taylorism)
Ford
Rockerfeller
Sloan
Participative Management
Japan Lean Mfg.
Quality Circles (US 1965)
Lean US (1972)
TQM (1985)
SQC
JIT
Reengineering
TBC (1988)
Innovation
Learning
World Class
Agile Mfg.

Figure 2.1 Some Highlights of Manufacturing History

Craft System: Master/Apprentice

For hundreds even thousands of years learning about "making" was accomplished the same way. A master would teach an apprentice who would eventually replace the master. Some masters would look for new ways to do things that might be easier or perhaps safer. New ideas (technologies (might come along and help their work, change it significantly or even render it irrelevant. However, the process of *making* remained generally the same. Items were created by hand from a set of the most basic raw materials with few components. Communities often sprung up around marketplaces. These communities had a few "craftsman" who were considered knowledgeable in building chairs, working iron, or forming pottery. Some craftsmen traveled from town to town, others became well known for their products because of particular high quality or workmanship. They consisted of individuals or small families who carried their expertise with them through life (Bowyer, 1973).

Craft System: Guilds

This craft system was the fundamental form of manufacturing for all of ancient history. A slightly modified version of this system appeared in Northern Europe in the twelfth century: the craft guild. Someone realized that teams of craftsmen could produce much more work than individuals. Guilds were formed around every known area of production: glass blowing, metalworks, woodworking, etc. The optimum methods in construction or production were shared and easily transmitted between masters within the guild. However, the masters lost the ability to control their products. The guild leaders comprised a tiny minority of wealthy individuals who used their guilds in economic contests between city states. Guilds impacted the economic and social structure of the day. They controlled the markets. The techniques were influential and quickly spread throughout Europe. This era of manufacturing multiplied the limited capabilities of the past. It is defined as the "first form" (Goldman, 1994).

Craft System: Entrepreneurs

The second form broke the growing strangle hold of the craft guilds returning power to the actual craftsmen. It was enabled primarily by the fast expanding cities occurring in the sixteenth century. Producers were able to reach distant markets and were able to elude the control of the guilds. The second form was reminiscent of the past since once again single masters or families were able to gain fame and prominence in their individual work. To have a crest or signature that was considered the best became the goal of these entrepreneurial craftsmen. The knowledge enhancements of the guilds were applied in the knew era of expansion. However, the entrepreneurial craftsmen soon found that they could not keep up with demand. The rate of change demanded faster and cheaper solutions.

Factory System

These changes ushered in the third era of manufacturing. In order to meet rising demand, the lead craftsmen wanted to regain the production benefits of the guilds yet retain control of their craft. They created the factory. The factory system born in the early 1700s brought an emphasis on production, quality and financial controls (Shapiro and Cosenza, 1987). Changes in technology began to build on one another more quickly than before, and the young United States was piecing together many of the manufacturing advantages of multiple countries and developing its own interpretation of manufacturing. Technical revolutions as described by Rostow (1989, 1990) and Abetti (1987) can more easily be identified as drivers towards new eras of manufacturing.

As mentioned most products throughout history until the 1700s consisted of a minimum of component parts. If a part broke or wore out, it was generally replaced with another hand crafted part. As the factory developed, a key objective was to make component parts as similar as possible. Ultimately, interchangeable parts were introduced in the 1780s. As in the past, businesses in this era were basically one-man or one-family affairs. Factories were considered to be reaching their pinnacle when the first concepts of mass production were introduced in England in 1813 by Francis Cabot Lowell in the first cotton textile plant (Rostow, 1990). Also in the same year, the Waltham system of steel manufacturing introduced the world to the first "modern" large-scale, integrated corporate manufacturing facility (Shapiro and Cosenza, 1987).

Overlapping these structural changes in manufacturing were economic issues and social concerns that began to be investigated with vigor in the 1700s. The guild system with its sometimes harsh economic holds on politics and people had evolved into the still restrictive spirit of Mercantilism. Some interesting concepts clearly guided the manufacturing development of the time. Governments clearly supported monopolies, there were significant subsidies, burdensome taxes, and public spending was often extravagantly directed towards a select few beneficiaries (West, 1969). Sir James Steuart was a leading scholar in England in the 1700s. In 1767, he published *The Principals of Political Economy*. This summarized many economic ideas, primarily protectionism, that were prevalent in England, France, Spain and elsewhere throughout Europe. According to Steuart, "no competition should be allowed to come from abroad, . . . no domestic competition should be encouraged upon articles of superfluity, . . . when [certain pricing standards] cannot be preserved . . . public money must be thrown into the scale" (qtd. in West, 1969, p. 167).

A contemporary of Sir Steuart was a Scottish professor at Glasgow, Adam Smith. He published an extensive body of work on economics, business, and lifestyle that profoundly impacted the western world. On March 9, 1776, Smith published *An Inquiry into the Nature and Causes of the Wealth of Nation's*. He cited cases where the division of labor succeeded in improving productivity but was inhibited by government and current business policies. He argued for the then very unpopular idea of accumulation of capital as a necessary condition for economic progress. He discussed the importance of free trade both domestically and especially internationally. Smith wrote that when "two men trade between themselves it is undoubtedly for the advantage of both . . . The case is exactly the same betwixt any two nations" (Smith, 1776, p. 204). He warned against the destructive effects of excessive taxation as well as "scandalously wasteful and unnecessary public expenditure" which could reduce the whole country to the "lowest pitch of misery" (p. 205).

It is hard to overestimate the impact of Smith's work on the future of manufacturing, especially in the fledgling United States. In fact, while many Europeans became sidetracked trying to apply Smith's concepts to justify social divisions, the American's adopted the philosophy into their newly forming sensibilities of economics and business. Today, Smith is considered the pioneer in supply side wage theory. He believed that reward should be based upon only five criterion: attractiveness of work, cost of acquiring skill, regularity of employment, degree of responsibility, and probability of success. Smith's invisible hand methodology is now credited as a pioneering use of the idea of cybernetics and free market prices (West, 1969).

American Manufacturing System

Adding a technological revolution to a revolution in economic ideology, the railroad was introduced in 1830. Companies could now obtain raw material from the cheapest sources and gain access to most distant customers. This miracle of transportation allowed the growth of the large hierarchical organization. By the 1860s, the form of the factory system in the United States became so distinctive that the British were desperately studying it to learn how to emulate the "American System" (Rosenberg, 1969, p. 128-129). In 1916, Joseph Wickham Roe defined the critical distinguishing attribute of the American System as the "system of interchangeable manufacture" (Roe, 1916). The American System dominated the economy in the U.S. between 1875 and 1899 (Pine and Davis, 1993, p.10).

A new social revolution occurred in the mid-1800s that also impacted the progress of manufacturing: the Protestant Movement. Particularly in the U.S., Calvinists, Baptists, etc. began to believe that how they behaved and produced at work reflected how they were working for God (Shapiro and Cosenza, 1987). The Protestant faiths encouraged the pursuit of material wealth and social status as a sign of God's grace. The grandchildren of the Puritans pushed their way into occupations in which they could be their own masters and demonstrate their success (Shapiro and Cosenza, 1987). This individual social dynamism impacted manufacturing significantly creating new entrepreneurs and a driving labor force to propel the next era of manufacturing.

Mass Manufacturing

By the last decade of the 1800s the factory was 200 years old and ideas of mass production were nearly 100 years old. Steam engines were fairly efficient and the telegraph was the latest in communication. The American Production System was a force in the world economy. Like suddenly seeing where the last few puzzle pieces fit, forward thinkers began to connect how they could use these social, technical and structural changes to their advantage. Swift, Morgan, Rockefeller, Singer and others saw the possibility of integrating *existing* production, transportation, and information technologies into a new organizational structure: a centrally administered, vertically integrated, hierarchically managed corporation (Wandmacher, 1994).

Much like agility today, the concepts that made mass manufacturing possible were not new. It was the combined impact of the new structure and operating paradigm that allowed unprecedented competitive power (Goldman, 1994).

Mass production manufacturing systems soon became a necessary condition for survival. Mass production utilized the manufacturing interchangeability aspects of the American System applied to a design and assembly process that allowed production on an enormous scale (Ford, 1926). Between 1898 and 1903 critical periods of consolidation and centralization took place (Shapiro and Cosenza, 1987). Factories that did not recognize and join the new paradigm were quickly enveloped by the weight of change (Shapiro and Cosenza, 1987; Goldman, Nagel et al., 1995). *Just as it is anticipated for the 21st century, the competitive advantage came not from the newest technologies, but from systematic coordination of the latest technologies of communication, transportation, and mass production* (Goldman and Nagel, 1993; Kozmetsky, 1994; Rostow, 1992; Limerick, 1994).

Even while Ford was experimenting with his version of mass production, new concepts of management and organizational thinking appeared. In 1911, much like Adam Smith before him, Frederick W. Taylor built upon the ideas of the past in arguably one of the most influential works of the 20th century, *The Principles of Scientific Management* (1911). Taylor applied the premise of Smith's division of labor into a scientific and measurable pursuit. He noted that some companies were using practices that seem to make them especially productive. The Protestant Movement notwithstanding, an early goal of Taylor's work was to resolve the problem of workers "who were unwilling or unable to perform to their potential." As he described his work initially, he was simply looking to determine a rationale and logic behind time-honored work methods (Shapiro and Cosenza, 1987). Some aspects of Taylor's theories were ignored while others were fully embraced. The heart of accepted Taylorism was the separation of organizations into strictly distinct functions. This idea, appropriated from the Catholic Church in turn appropriated from the Roman Army among others was a simple idea. That is, the best performance could be obtained from breaking up tasks into their smallest components, specializing functional components through the application of technology or experts and then recombining the components into a whole piece that is more efficient. Many during his time and since have accused him of treating people like machines. However, a portion of Taylor's theory that remains largely unrecognized was the concept that knowledge was to be obtained from the average workman or laborer. He wrote that the critical knowledge that the workers obtained through day-to-day activities was the best source for specialization (Taylor, 1911). However, the managers and engineers of the time (like many today) resisted this concept. They believed the average workman was unintelligent and unskilled and unable to contribute significantly concerning their work other than following orders of those more capable (Shapiro and Cosenza, 1987).

As "fourth form manufacturing" became de facto, the field of management studied as a science became firmly entrenched in the US. Furthermore, the division of labor concepts that Taylor presented so effectively became so strongly engraved in the American Business psyche that they hinder our movement into another era of manufacturing (Shapiro and Cosenza, 1987).

Much that is now attributed to "Taylorism" was not built by Taylor alone. Max Weber defined rigid ideas concerning bureaucracy which became prevalent around 1910. Building on both Weber and Taylor, Robert K. Merton described bureaucracy as a system based on strict formality between workers with a strongly enforced social hierarchy among persons occupying different positions within a public or private sector group (Shapiro and Cosenza, 1987). Also during this time, William C. Durant worked as a key innovator as an organizer of finance and people in diversifying markets. Ford better defined his manufacturing processes throughout the 1910s putting clear boundaries on "Fordism." The Frenchman, Henri Fayol redefined the concept of bureaucratic management into fourteen principles and is considered the "father of functional management" (qtd in Shapiro, 1987, p. 17). These individuals formed a core group that is credited with developing what is now called "classical management."

Classical Management was moderated during the twenties, thirties and forties, first by unions and then by the human relations movement. The automation aspects of Taylorism began to be rebelled against in the workplace. Elton Mayo conducted studies in the 1920s that demonstrated that people liked to be treated as "human beings, not as appendages to machines" (Shapiro and Cosenza, 1987). The high growth era of the 1950s brought a twist to the classical management ideas by emphasizing ideas of organizing manufacturing around profit centers where decentralized, multidivision companies would have coordinated, centralized corporate control. Leading the way in this was Alfred P. Sloan who effectively separated divisions of General Motors Company into four key profit center groups.[1] Pierre du Pont successfully implemented similar concepts at Du Pont. The management era of the 1950s and 1960s, referred to as the "neoclassical school," evolved somewhat into what might be termed as the modern organizational industrial format. This is a combination of past philosophies that working during their time. Somewhat mechanistic with humanistic overtones partially based on statistical scientific principles, the current industrial format is clearly evident at the operative or working levels of American corporations (Shapiro, 1987).

Becoming increasingly rigid, the ideas of the last 80 years have become more entrenched. More and more information and instruction of management comes through filters. These filters are divisions and departments that were at first separated functionally and then often physically from the production site (Chase and Garvin, 1989). Industrial systems became more systematic in the physical processes, methods, tools and equipment. This systematic approach generally improved efficiency, but the more efficient systems became more inflexible and rigid resulting in non-effective response to customer needs (Doll and Vonderembse, 1992). Unable or unwilling to heed the warnings from business scholars such as Skinner (1958, 1974), Wheelwright (1978), etc., manufacturing became in most cases a secondary concern of top business management. Some key principles are still prevalent today even in the face of dynamic change: workers work, staff provides ideas, managers are in charge, evaluation is based upon quantity of work produced and direct costs, and operations are maintained by strong centralized coordination (Buzacott, 1995).

What can be defined as the fourth technology revolution has been occurring since the 1970s with the innovations of micro-electronics, new industrial material, information, communications, and genetic engineering. This technological revolution may hold significant sway over global industry for the next 50 years if extrapolated from the duration of the past three technical revolutions (Rostow, 1991).

In summary, the past shapes today's accepted norms. An analysis of why things are done the current way must be considered before an effective vision of alternate solutions can be created. The next section presents the drivers that have led many to think of new solutions and review possible sources for improvement. Following that will be a discussion of many of the techniques that have been applied to meet the observed changes.

FACTORS FORCING THIS MOST RECENT PARADIGM CHANGE

Before continuing with the historical development, a review is presented of some of the many factors that experts consider critical which are forcing recent change in the manufacturing paradigm. The theme of manufacturing in the 20th century and particularly after World War II was that company success generally correlated with bigger. Also, as wages rose companies determined that they could only survive through extensive automation and precision. If companies couldn't do either of those, they could only compete by shifting to low wage sources still focusing on minimizing cost of manufacturing even though labor is less and less a critical piece of the production cost (Pisano and Hayes, 1995).

In *Manufacturing Renaissance*, Pisano and Hayes (1995) describe first availability and later price as the basis of competition in the first half of the century. The authors then document a changing emphasis on reliability and defect reduction. The more recent focus has been on flexibility and speed. It is important to investigate why these changes are occurring. What is changing the marketplace and the basis for competition?

There are a number of underlying forces provided in the literature, yet it is difficult to show precisely how these forces actually change the basis of the economic environment. Rostow (1991) takes a global perspective and lists these underlying forces as the wide ranging technological revolution, the movement of new groups of nations to technical maturity, and the international recognition (in many cases by default) of the need to rely more on market forces than direct bureaucratic control of economies. Shapiro (1987) notes the movement of the first world countries from economies based upon manufacturing to those based upon service. Pisano and Hayes (1995) look to the end of fixed exchange rates in the early 70s as a principle contributor to fundamental change in ground rules for international competition. Merrifield (1987) adds the US perspective by claiming that the monetary and fiscal policies since the 1970s have had a destructive affect on "smokestack America" forcing our move to the service industry. Jay Forester of MIT uses systems dynamics models to draw parallels to the Kondratieff long wave theory promoted in the 1920s. In this theory changing technology forces a destructive change of competitive bases every 50 years. Extending this theory, Merrifield (1987) holds that technologies are changing so fast that they now cycle through industry such that an overall long wave effect remains hidden.

Bowen (1994) states a commonly held opinion that the development of a new product is relatively easy in a stable environment. However, when markets are dynamic or turbulent, anticipating how customers will perceive and evaluate products in five, ten or one year can seem nearly impossible. That is the clearest description of the marketplace for the foreseeable future, turbulent and dynamic. Certainly the explosion of technology has a root part in this new marketplace. Figure 2.2 shows that the scientific knowledge has been growing exponentially and when viewed over human history is just a spike (Kiechel, 1993). Over 90% of all that we know has been developed in the last 30 years (Merrifield, 1987). However, it must be understood that "technological innovation alone [is] insufficient" to achieve economic success and leadership in a hypercompetitive global world market. "[Technological innovations] must be accompanied by a . . . manufacturing infrastructure" (Kozmetsky, 1993).

These changes in technology have created increasing complexity. These factors have led to changes in organizational structures and the disintegration of traditional labor management relationships (Shapiro,

1987). Doll and Vonderembse (1992) and others look at the rapid spread of manufacturing capabilities worldwide and the increasing competition that occurs with an ever growing number of players entering niche markets. Indeed, Kozmetsky (1993) declares that future manufacturing will be "driven by niches in technology, product design and markets." Customers are themselves driving significant change by becoming increasingly impatient while at the same time more knowledgeable about products and choices. These customers are demanding increased quality and reliability at the lowest prices.

Globalization is certainly changing the competitive environment, but this factor has been present for a number of centuries. Adam Smith's studies were focused on how international competition and trade was changing the environment in the 1700s. The significant change in the past 15 years has been to virtually destroy the traditional limits of how responsive suppliers and manufacturing companies could be using traditional forms of communication. This leads to the heart of what is different about today's competition. *Greater communication and networking capabilities place companies in direct contact with suppliers and customers.* This fact combined with the powerful computers that collect, store and assimilate increasingly great volumes

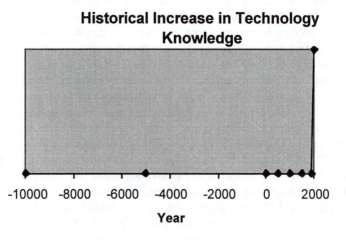

Figure 2.2. Technology Explosion

Intensifying Competition	Rapidly Changing Markets Decreasing Cost of Information Increasing Capable Communication Technologies Increasing Pressure on Costs/Productivity High rate of Innovation Decreasing New Product Time-to-Market Global Competitive Pressures
Fragmentation of of Mass Markets	Growth of Niche Markets High Rate of Model Change Shrinking Product Lifetimes Shrinking Product "Windows" Declining Niche Market Entry Costs
Cooperative Business Relationships	Increasing Inter-Enterprise Cooperation Interactive Value-Circle Relationships Increasing Inter-Enterprise Cooperation Interactive Value-Circle Relationships Increasing Outsourcing Global Sourcing/Marketing/Distribution Shifting Resource Constraints Interactive Labor-Management Relationships
Evolving Customer Expectations	Individualized Products and Services Life Cycle Product Support Rapid Time-to-Market Rapid Delivery Changing Quality Expectations Increasing Value of Information/Services
Increasing Societal Values Pressures	Regulatory Environment Workplace/Workforce Expectations Legal/Political/Cultural Pressures Workforce Education Changing Social Contract

Figure 2.3. Market Forces Driving Business Change

Source: Knowledge Base, The Agility Forum, Lehigh Institute

of data are critical drivers behind the agile environment (Asava and Engwall, 1994). Nation states are less and less significant competitive entities when compared with networks of globally diverse companies competing with one another across vaguely relevant international boundaries (Kozmetsky, 1988). These networks use information technology to make agile environments possible.

The Agility Forum has summarized what it sees as the critical market forces that are driving business change today (Figure 2.3). These driving forces are broken down into five areas: *intensifying competition, fragmentation of mass markets, cooperative business relationships, evolving customer expectations, increasing societal values and pressures.* While the exact interrelations between international economies and market dynamics remains unclear and while there multiple solutions are offered to address these conditions, there is consensus that the turbulent and dynamic environment is forcing a revision of business thought (Kozmetsky, 1988; Gibson and Rogers, 1994; Hayes and Pisano, 1994; Preiss and Goldman, 1994; Rostow, 1994).

MEETING THE CHALLENGES OF CHANGING REQUIREMENTS

Since the 1950s the key precepts of mass manufacturing have been sometimes challenged, dismissed, and replaced while at other times reinforced, refocused and strengthened. A dizzying array of philosophies has been investigated, offered and practiced by the business community (Table 2.1). Each "buzz word" had its methods for improving business.

During the period of business theory development through all of the 1900s and especially since the 1970s two distinct patterns of business organization emerged in practice that might be most relevant to the concepts under investigation in Agility. In some industries (agriculture, food processing, electricity/electronics, chemical), research and development was moved intimately into day-to-day operations and executive planning. In another set of industries (steel, machine tools, automotive), research and development was separated out of day-to-day operations and effective links between the two failed especially as manufacturing became formally identified as a "separate" business function. Blamed as a critical factor in the US trade deficit and contributing to a lack of technological dynamism, the linkage between creative R&D and reasonable bureaucratic order is essential to future competitive success (Rostow, 1993).

The following sections review activities offered for meeting the forces changing the world of manufacturing. Some ideas that are considered early components of Agility are presented here with more detail.

Quality Circles and TQM (1970s, 1980s, 1990s)

After World War II, business became so large that they were forced to decentralize. In this largely negatively motivated decentralization, management was forced to relinquish and distribute control because they were unable to keep up with size and technology (Leavitt and Whisler, 1958). Many concepts of the past 40 years have attempted to try correct the vulnerabilities introduced by decentralization through some version of localized control. Companies began to believe that the only way to create new forms of decision systems was to completely "know" or map out the organizational structure (Forrester, 1958). Great effort was place on determining where delays in decisions occurred and how actions were implemented. Research was focused on the creation of detailed procedures for purchasing and inventory. The emphasis was to find out the details and measure them scientifically. Similar to the Gant charts and time and motion studies of the 1920s, the time-study man became the efficiency expert trying to help firms further maximize some detailed Taylorized process component (Skinner, 1969). This scientific / statistical approach was held in such high esteem that in 1958, John Kenneth Galbraith declared that the US had "solved the problem of production" (Galbraith, 1958).

It is interesting that into this environment was the early introduction of quality circles. The statistician W. Edwards Deming promoted quality control concepts and methodology as a way to operate more effectively in an increasingly complex environment. Unfortunately for the US, the concepts were not adequately understood in the US and hardly attempted until the 1980s. Generally, such "quality" work programs revolved around control charts which were seen as methods to obtain secure statistical control over processes and activities in manufacturing (Shapiro, 1987). It was not until the

Table 2.1. Business Solution Pieces From the Past

1950s	1960s	1970s	1980s	1990s
Theory Y	T Groups	Zero Based Budgeting	Theory Z	Reengineering
Management by Objectives	Managerial Grid	Portfolio Management	One-Minute Management	Mass Customization
Diversification	Matrix Management	Experience Curve	MRP I	Virtual Organizations
Statistical Process Control	Queuing theory	Quality of Life Work Groups	MRPII	Process Innovation
Work Simplification	Simulation	Unit Management	Just In Time	
	Heuristic Algorithms	Quality Circles	Flexible Manufacturing System	
	Economic Order Quantity		Computer Integrated Manufacturing	
			Computer Aided Design	
			Management for Time	
			Quality Circles	
			Total Quality Management	

introduction and acceptance of Total Quality Management that a more effective adoption occurred of Deming's concepts. In addition to these statistically ideas, there was a need to focus on long-term commitment to fundamentals. As described by Garvin of Motorola these critical fundamentals to TQM success included: working with vendors, educating and training the workforce, developing accurate and responsive quality information systems, setting targets for quality improvement, demonstrating commitment and interest at the highest levels of management (Pisano, 1995). Similar conclusions by Hayes and Wheelwright (1994), Taguchi and Clausing (1990) indicate that high quality is much more dependent on policies and practices embedded in a plant's infrastructure or in the methodology of product design. While these fundamentals are no less important in the business environment of the 1990s, quality is considered as "no longer a source of *unique* competitive advantage in many industries" (Carter, Melnyk et al., 1995).

Flexible Manufacturing (1980s)

In addition to TQM, one of the more powerful forerunners of Agility is flexible manufacturing. The "[Flexible Manufacturing Systems] (FMS) are the wave of the future, the new industrial revolution" (Merrifield, 1987). These systems call for the building of small, cohesive teams. The ideas include: managing process improvement not just output, broadening the role of engineering management to include manufacturing and treating manufacturing as a service (Jaikumar, 1986). Implementation generally addressed different characterizations of flexibility: process, product and volume (Skinner, 1985). These programs were almost exclusively manufacturing line focused. Technical solutions were often brought in at enormous costs to companies. More recent research has shown to highlight the idea that some types of flexibility are more valuable than others (a flexible product delivery system as opposed to a machine tool with six-axis rotation capabilities) and have been offered to assist trade-off decisions (Chambers, 1992) . Companies today are wary of expensive flexible manufacturing systems and have stated some disenchantment with the results. Krafcik (1988) found that the level of flexible technology in a plant has little effect on productivity performance. Furthermore, the use of robotics in manufacturing had virtually no correlation with productivity. Conclusions from other empirical studies by Jaikumar (1986) indicated that the problems were primarily in the way the new technology was managed. These flexible manufacturing systems were usually placed on top of a powerful, deeply embedded and unproductive logic of mass production. Companies have tried FMS and the miracles of technology as key "black box" solutions to cure their manufacturing woes (Jaikumar, 1986).

Time Based Competition (1980s)

Many mis-identify Agility as equivalent with Time Based Competition (TBC). Many ideas are similar, but TBC had an overwhelming myopic focus on speed. The ideas of time based competition were first conceptualized in 1988 by George Stalk. Stalk recognized a trend occurring within many industries. The goal for many companies was to get products designed, developed and delivered to customers and earning returns as soon as possible (Stalk, 1988; Merrills, 1989). The critical factor was to decrease cycle time for production of both standard products and special orders. Blackburn (1990) saw two different forms of this competition: fast to market and fast to product. Early introduction of these concepts of time based competition were heralded. Schmenner (1988) looked at just-in-time as the statistically significant technique for speeding up productivity, Eisenhardt and Westcott (1988) and Eisenhardt (1990, 1992) looked at speeding up decision making. Vesey (1990) saw speed on the manufacturing line as key, and Dumaine (1989) examined speed in managerial work. The common element is speed. Spanner, Nuno et al., (1993) defined four characteristics of time that were considered the key dimensions: flexibility, cost, quality, and customer service. Many theorists looked to broader solutions to cycle time reduction, but there was mostly focus on the product development process. While many companies were recognizing that there were some essential changes in the marketplace, firms were finding it very difficult to compete in this arena (Gupta, Hahn et al., 1991; Hum, 1992; Hum, 1995). Perhaps the difficulty was in the narrowness of the competition concept.

By 1993, TBC was becoming discredited by actual cases under investigation in Japan. There was a "reckless" focus on speed which led to a proliferation of product variety. TBC was successfully implemented, but these companies were producing new products with such speed that the variety could not be handled by the market (Lillrank, 1995). Stalk (1993) also studied some Japanese companies that had pushed these ideas to their extreme. He found that in many of these companies the dedication to the time strategy had become like a "death grip." The focus needed to be both within the company and across external suppliers and customers. The employees and customers also needed to be connected as closely as possible to maximize the benefits of both (Stalk, 1992). TBC primarily failed because it lacked a strategic focus on overall benefits of speed. Thought needed to be given to exactly how increased speed would improve competitiveness.

Lean Manufacturing (1980s-1990s)

According to Kidd (1994, p. 10) Lean manufacturing is a necessary yet not sufficient condition for agility. The question must be considered of what exactly is lean manufacturing and what success has it enjoyed in industry. Conventional wisdom in the 1970s and 1980s indicated that the only way to remain successful with increasing competition was to move production facilities to low-wage environments. Particularly in the auto industry, productivity and quality levels were considered determined by an assembly plant's location. Some investigators looked beyond this conventional wisdom and tried to identify why Japan, a relatively high wage country, could consistently maintain high quality and productivity. John Krafcik (1988) of the International Motor Vehicle Program at MIT termed the primary reason as Lean manufacturing.

Western production systems after World War II built behemoth factories that were buffered from nearly every external complication. There were high inventory levels in case there were shortages in supplies or problems in quality. Assembly lines were structured to keep moving even with equipment malfunctions. Excess labor was maintained to keep up productivity levels. Repair areas were exceedingly large to handle the problems that the non-stop assembly lines pumped out. This production methodology is historically an excellent method of production for steady returns, economies of scale and increased utilization rates. Unfortunately, competition in many industries dictated that these benefits were insufficient (Krafcik, 1988).

Lean competition in the auto industry, namely at Toyota, kept inventory levels at absolute minimums keeping costs down and quality problems detected early. Utility workers are replaced by teams who fill in for absent co-workers. Quality and in-process defect detection are central features of bufferless assembly lines making repair areas tiny. The idea is that this configuration brings greater risk to the manufacturer, since unforeseen 'hiccups' might stop the production line completely, but it also brings greater potential competitive gains (Krafcik, 1988).

The ideology of Lean enterprises really took off in the manufacturing community with the 1990 publication of *The Machine That Changed The World* (Womack, Jones et al., 1990). Unfortunately, this idea became misapplied and the definition that stuck in the popular mentality was that to be lean means to do everything with less, half the factory space, half the human effort, half the investment. Wasteful activities, unnecessary inventory and long lead times are eliminated by programs such as concurrent engineering, JIT, TQM, and cost reduction in overhead. Instead of applied across the entire manufacturing process, implementation programs in industry generally applied Lean techniques to discrete activities (Womack and Jones, 1994) or as solutions to specific problems (Hayes and Pisano, 1994). The effect of this paradigm in US industry was to downsize and eliminate any excess in resources and personnel without sufficient recognition that you can only do more with less by changing internal processes. This has led Steve Goldman of the Agility Forum to claim that for most companies, "lean is just one step away from anorexic" (Goldman, 1996). According to Hayes (1994) the lean manufacturing paradigm focused too much inwardly and did little to bolster and organization's overall strategic flexibility.

This is not entirely how lean was conceptualized. Jones (1992) held as the first essential characteristic of a lean production system that production is customer driven, not driven by the needs of manufacturing. Processes were not to be so optimized to destroy new product flexibility. Indeed early literature attests that plants with lean production policies would be able to manufacture a wide range of models with high degrees of quality and productivity (Krafcik, 1988). When reviewing the movement to Lean in the US and trying to identify why industry was having problems, Womack (1994) begins to use the same terminology that is seen in discussions of Agility. He states that "if individual breakthroughs can be linked up and down the value chain to form a continuous value stream that creates, sells, and services a family of products, the performance of the whole can be raised to a dramatically higher level. The notion of the value stream defines the lean enterprise—a group of individuals, functions, and legally separate but operational synchronized companies" (p. 94).

Overall however, lean is the extreme optimization of current processes that are still operating under the mass manufacturing paradigm. It can often leads to lower levels of flexibility which if hit by unanticipated changes are less capable than ever of meeting the new requirements. Even the early investigators in the MIT program used the term "fragile" instead of lean (Krafcik, 1988). The ideas in lean manufacturing are not useless, but for much of industry, they are not sufficiently broad in scope.

Reengineering (1990s)

This dissertation is certainly not the first study to look at methods to improve business performance and competitiveness. In a 1990 Harvard Business Review article, Hammer (1990) was looking to address some short comings of Time Based Competition. He believed that just speeding up processes (usually through automation) did not address fundamental performance deficiencies. The only way to achieve dramatic performance improvement was to break away from outdated rules and restrictive assumptions. The goal was to gut procedures that no longer made sense in the current environment and recreate them from scratch to produce some required outcome. Hammer and Champy (1993) put forth a set of seven ideas to help companies reach their high performance goals: organize around outcomes, not tasks; have end-users perform the process; put information processing into actually producing the information; utilizing information systems to enable geographically dispersed resources to behave as though they were centralized; abandoning serial processes in favor of parallel activities; moving decision points and control to where work is being performed; and, capturing information once and at the source.

Reengineering was one of the few business theories that was not primarily built upon Japanese management techniques (Lillrank, 1995). Even though the marketing techniques of Hammer and Champy's work *Reengineering the Corporation*, have been called into question (Sheridan, 1994), the ideas and case study example cited within are considered sound. Like TBC before it, reengineering took the business community by storm. It was applied to logistics systems (Richardson, 1995; Richardson and Trunick, 1995), cost management systems (Borthick and Roth, 1993), information system reconfiguration (Davenport, 1993; Grates, 1994), new product development (Miller, 1995) and supply chain systems (O'Sullivan and Geringer, 1993).

Unfortunately, after a few years of examining the results of reengineering it was found that it was successful in only 12% of the companies (Blonkvist and Goble, 1994; Sheridan, 1994; Kotter, 1995). Success was generally measured as reductions in costs and cycle time.

The problem was not in reengineering being a valuable concept, but of its mis-application in short-term projects and renewal of minor processes (Sheridan, 1994). The use of this concept in the field generally focused on outdated systems. The goal was to squeeze as much as possible out of a system that needs to be replaced. Thus, in most cases the fundamental premise of reengineering was not applied effectively, namely, destroying old processes and coming up with completely novel ways to solve problems. Many companies were overlooking cross functional issues and using poorly defined measurement and reward systems (Blonkvist and Goble, 1994). Davidson (1993) saw the need for the use of "macro reengineering" which needed to align multiple, discrete operating improvement projects with broader programs, plans and visions. Also, recognizing that the change effort takes numerous phases which all must be completed successfully is cited as a requirement to successfully implement reengineering programs that must be comprehensive in scope (Kotter, 1995). The real issue according to Henry Duignan of Ross Operating Valve company is for manufacturing firms to develop new forms of wealth creation. The challenge is to create subjective knowledge value as an integral part of the manufacturing process (qtd in Sheridan, 1994).

Mass Customization (1990s)

Coined by Stanley Davis (1987) in his book *Future Perfect*, mass customization was to make it possible for marketers to customize their offerings for individual buyers even while manufacturing for masses of customers. Kotler (1989) declared his belief that the "mass market" is dead its segmentation has created the era of mass customization. B. Joseph Pine II from the IBM Consulting group is yet another author declaring the end of the mass production paradigm. In *Mass Customization* he compiles evidence and builds the case that a new paradigm is emerging wherein variety and customization are achieved through flexibility and quick responsiveness (Pine and Davis, 1993).

These views are certainly different from the traditional mass production view which emphasizes tight control, vertical communication, and continuous improvement which provide incremental improvements in existing processes. According to Spira and Pine (1993), sustained advantage in mass customization derives from constant innovation and value creation. There is investment not just in technology, but in the people whose experience and flexibility form the backbone of the new competitive environment. Few companies have actually chosen a strategy of mass customization. Of these few, Lutron Electronics, has created one product that is so integrated and user-configurable that one model can be configured to reduce power consumption, react to external lighting changes, or be programmed to create different lighting environments throughout the day (Malone, 1995).

While the aspects of mass customization are critical to businesses in the future, the use of mass customization as a paradigm falls short. There is a danger of following the Japanese example of creating such product variety that the market cannot handle the diversity (Stalk and Webber, 1993). Also, simply because a company can create highly customized products does not mean it is ready to completely change its product line and enter a new business. It does not mean that a company can partner or collaborate quickly in new ventures. It also says little about how the human factors impact such businesses. These problems have been at least partially recognized. In 1993, Boynton, Victor and Pine (1993) defined two new organizational designs: mass customization suited for dynamic product change with stable processes, and continuous improvement suited for stable product change with dynamic processes. The authors predict that it is the synergy between mass customization and continuous improvement that will define the basis of competition for the next century.

Just-In-Time (1970s, 1980s, 1990s)

Businesses have always seen advantages to having close responsive relationships with suppliers. Components delivered quickly, with high quality and at a low price are important and yet sometimes difficult attributes to achieve simultaneously. In fact even in the 1910s, Ford believed the most efficient way to produce a vehicle was to minimize the time that elapsed between beginning and completing production. The solution for Ford was vertical integration that allowed huge-volumes of standardized products. There were explicit to maintain continuous flow and low in house inventory. Just-In-Time would be an apt description of the inventory systems that was used in most parts of the ford complex until the late 1920s (Hounshell, 1984). As companies were forced to become increasingly decentralized after WW II the great barrier system was established that put significant physical and especially psychological separation between companies and their suppliers. Unfortunately, it was not long before the idea that "companies could not minimize lead time and minimize inventory at the same time" became accepted as fact (Skinner, 1969).

Ford's early vision notwithstanding, Taiichi Ohno former Vice President of Toyota is credited as the father of the Just-In-Time (JIT) system (Shapiro, 1987). As defined by O'Grady (1988), JIT is a philosophy that defines the manner in which a manufacturing system should be managed. At first observation, JIT is a system to received goods exactly at the time that they are required. The essential objectives of JIT are to attack fundamental problems of production, eliminate waste, strive for simplicity, and devise a system to identify problems (O'Grady, 1988, p. 14). Effective JIT programs must be based upon collaboration with established high levels of trust and cooperation with suppliers (Spekman, 1988). JIT benefits are to include: improved quality, more visible finished products, easier detection of defects, less labor hours for rework, less material wasted, smother output rates, and shortened lead times (Shapiro, 1987).

There have been some attempts to create descriptive models of JIT. The environment of JIT manufacturers and the threats and opportunities created for their small suppliers is proposed in work from Caron St. John and Kirk Heriot (1993). Karmarker (1989) provides a framework for tailoring JIT systems to the relevant manufacturing and market environment. Many look at JIT as simply a method to improve logistics operations (Braithwaite, 1992; Udo, 1993; Udo and Grant, 1993) or as a fundamental component of making time the critical basis of competition (Hall and Jackson, 1992).

Since the 1970s many companies have tried JIT programs with different levels of success. Shapiro (1987) presents a number of JIT cases including Omark Industries, Xerox, GE, Whirlpool. The main problem in industry is the attempted use of JIT as a panacea (Karmarkar, 1989; Fisher, Hammond et al., 1994). While closer relationships with suppliers may provide some of the proposed benefits, they cannot be obtained by JIT alone without some overarching framework for implementation (Pine, Victor et al., 1993; Hayes, 1994;

Goldman, 1994). Fisher (1994) tells managers to think beyond JIT and quick response and focus on "accurate" response. Overall, JIT programs "offer an approach to better forecasting and production scheduling that is designed to ensure a better match between demand and production for products with relatively short lives" (Pisano, 1994). In review of the successes and failures of JIT the conclusion appears that manufacturing must be viewed in terms of information flows (Pisano, 1994). Since the goal of JIT is really to smooth out the bottlenecks and gluts of materials in the production process, the heart of any technical implementation of JIT is the use of information technology.

Information Technology (1950s-1990s)

Arguably the greatest force economic and marketplace drivers is the accessibility and ease of transmission of information. This include simple telephone communication with cellular phones to the transmission of complex data files containing information on how to build nuclear devices. A few visionary forward thinker recognized some implications of this change in the early 1950s. Herald Leavitt and Thomas Whistler (1958) coined the term "information technology" declaring that it will spread rapidly, making centralization much easier, and provide more useful information to top management.

Leavitt and Whistler (1958) defined information technology as composed of several related parts 1) rapidly processing information, 2) application of models to decision making problems, 3) simulation of higher order thinking in computer programs. This definition is still valid today. In 1958 they predicted correctly that IT would move the boundary between planning and performance upward allowing large industrial organizations to recentralize forcing a radical reorganization of middle-management levels with some moving down some moving up. These predictions were loudly criticized at the time. While the reversal of decentralization occurred some 25 years later than they anticipated, the trends are now obvious to all (Applegate, Cash et al., 1988). The authors also predicted that the line separating top and middle would become more distinct which has only become more blurred (Leavitt, 1958; Applegate, 1988). In 1957, William Skinner, another great forward thinker in manufacturing, predicted that the computer specialist would replace industrial engineers as the key personnel with "top management view." However, by 1969, Skinner (1969) was concluding that both sides were plagued with parochial viewpoints which did not allow them to see the complete business entity. Forrester (1958) advanced that idea that completely new management concepts would rest on advances in the data processing industry.

Information technology has immeasurably altered the way business is conducted. No longer are there hundreds of clerks calculating our bank accounts like in the late 1800s. Now we can call over the telephone and borrow money from a bank and apply it towards some purchase made over the internet. Information technology is changing the way businesses create strategy (Henderson, 1990; Boynton, Victor et al., 1993; Haeckel and Nolan, 1993; Henderson and Venkatraman, 1993; Ives, Jarvenpaa et al., 1993; Luftman, Lewis et al., 1993). Information technology plays a critical role in extending the enterprise well beyond the traditional organizational boundaries permitting shared applications across legal enterprise boundaries (Konsynski, 1993). The use of information technology quickly becomes intertwined in business process redesign (Short and Venkatraman, 1992; Pollalis, 1994; Knuth, 1995). Davenport (1994) recognizes that both top-level and broad support for change is critical in IT driven redesign. Information systems create the option to organize structure along process lines abandoning other structural dimensions such as function product or geography. Another area of information technology application is in interorganizational activities including partnerships, alliances and virtual ventures (Johnston and Vitale, 1988; Konsynski, 1993; Nagel and Allen, 1993).

Benchmarking (1980s, 1990s)

Yet another tool of the corporate tool box that was developed during the 1980s was Benchmarking (Kinni, 1994). Benchmarking is the process of identifying, understanding and adapting outstanding practices from organizations anywhere in the world to help an organization improve performance (Pozos, 1995). The International Benchmarking Clearinghouse (IBC), a non-profit organization in Houston, Texas, lists four steps that are critical to benchmarking: plan, collect, analyze, and improve. The planning step requires that the function or process to be studied, as well as the key data and information needed to measure it, be identified and the best benchmarking partners be located. During the collection step, information is gathered and analyzed. This analysis phase reveals performance gaps between "what is" and "what could be." This step also identifies best-practice enablers, which are defined by the IBC as a "broad set of activities that helps enhance the implementation of a best practice." In the improvement step the practices uncovered in the benchmarking study are implemented and monitored (Kinni, 1994).

Unfortunately, benchmarking is generally expensive and it is often difficult to transfer and implement the knowledge obtained. The difficulty of studying these knowledge transfer problems has been the sources of significant research by many authors (Kozmetsky, 1988; Gibson and Smilor, 1991; Lillrank, 1995). However, benchmarking has been credited by many companies (IBM, EDS, Hewlett-Packard, Price Waterhouse) as being particularly useful in coming up to ISO and other industry specific standards (American Productivity & Quality Center, 1993; Rabbitt and Bergh, 1993).

Supply Chain Management (1990s)

"Managing suppliers is no longer a task for old-style purchasing managers," claims David Burt (1989). Supplier Chain Management is becoming a common technique employed by manufacturers and is fast becoming a requirement for competition. *Closeness to supplier and customer are fundamental to developing manufacturing excellence* (Roth, Giffi et al., 1992, p. 154). Strategic manufacturing is becoming a partnership between the large corporations that preside over design, assembly, and marketing of finished goods and fewer, smaller, and smarter suppliers. Initiating this partnership and keeping it competitive are not easy. Firms are engaging in careful research and mutually beneficial relations with suppliers. In some cases companies are finding that when capacity permits, firms are better off with a single-source supplier. Burt (1989) identifies five key issues that will determine whether a firm will achieve dramatic results when linking more closely with their supply chain: 1. whether the firm is sensibly organized to select suppliers, 2. whether the design process team includes suppliers, 3. whether the suppliers are addressing quality standards, 4. whether the suppliers are earning a fair profit, and 5. whether supplier relationships are managed to ensure long-term growth in suppliers' skills.

Closeness to some key suppliers has always been considered important in manufacturing; however, the traditional adversarial approach exhibited in most relationships is giving way to collaboration based on ability to establish high levels of trust and cooperation with suppliers. Spekman (1988) lists the dimensions of collaboration as: communication and conflict resolution, coordination of work, and planning. O'Sullivan (1993) who uses the label "value chain" when discussing this issue, reports that natural interrelationships play a crucial role in allowing the enterprise to respond quickly and accurately to new demands.

The expected benefits from supply-chain excellence include: 1. improved organizational agility to respond to demand pattern shifts, 2. improved integration of suppliers and customers to better service customer needs, and 3. flexible "true demand-based" manufacturing and distribution processes to support unique customer requirements (Thomas, 1994). The area of supply chain management has received considerable industry attention in the past few years. A methodology was created, piloted and tested in the automotive aftermarket in the UK and Spain (Harland, Williams et al., 1993). The results of the work have generated a user guide, supported by a case study book containing work examples. Similarly, General Electric Wiring Devices' (GEWD) experience in developing a total cost supplier selection methodology is the subject of the work by Smytka (1993).

Other Proposed Solutions

There are any number of other solutions for improving business performance that are offered to manufacturers including: Excellence in Manufacturing, Zero-based budgeting, Customer Driven, Interactive Planning, Learning Environment, Peak Performance, Decentralization, Recentralization, Downsizing and Right-Sizing. Whether these individual concepts are presented as programs, techniques or strategies, they all try to enable the desirable results of growth, improved production methods, greater competitiveness or simply increased profitability. Ideas often overlap and conflict. Some of the more effective recent programs have been characterized as Japanese. Shapiro (1987) examined over 900 companies looking at the success of implementation of systems that were typically characterized as Japanese: JIT, specialized quality control process, management by teamwork, and widespread employee involvement in decision making. He concluded that there were no unique factors in these Japanese philosophies that could not be adapted by any culture including the US. However, these ideas must be adapted to a comprehensive framework for manufacturing.

The movement to a new paradigm rarely has a clear demarcation in time (Kuhn, 1985). That is evident in the early historical presentation of the various stages of manufacturing. New paradigms cannibalize and transform outdated techniques into visions of the future. Solutions presented in this section are considered as pieces or components of the emerging new paradigm. Too often these ideas have been used as singular solutions; "inevitably, some ideas were discarded quickly; then simply could not be implemented, proved ineffective, or were useful only in special circumstances" (Pisano and Hayes, 1995, p. xiii). Each concept has been debunked as comprehensive solutions by many various studies including Skinner, Jaikumar, Markides, Stalk, among others (Pisano, 1995). The following chapter presents many of the encompassing frameworks that are providing the latest visions of this new manufacturing era.

NOTE

1. The principle characteristics of Sloan's model included: substantial vertical integration of the production of goods and services within the multinational enterprise, replacement of market transactions by internal coordination and deployment of resources, heavy reliance on central control and ownership, expansion of size and role of corporate head office function, and the development of large, specialized staffs in areas such as human resources, training and information technology (D'Cruz and Rugman, 1993).

CHAPTER 3

Manufacturing in the 21st Century

Pisano (1995) recognizes the need for "substantial changes in a company's control systems and fundamental manufacturing philosophies . . . if it is to implement successfully most of the new manufacturing approaches." There is a wide array of opinions calling for change. Some notice that the internal management accounting systems need renovation (Kaplan, 1984), others claim the role of the employees needs to be reconsidered (Klein, 1989), and many call for a broader approach, "revamping and re-envisioning the corporation" (Pisano, 1995).

Having developed a clear foundation of manufacturing and the fact that change is occurring and calls for change are widespread, this chapter will first focus on what features will be critical to continuing manufacturing excellence. The remainder of the chapter will relate many paradigms from the literature that attempt to describe the new environment.

CRITICAL FACTORS FOR FUTURE SUCCESS

Most would agree that the principle criteria for success under the next form of manufacturing is the ability to handle change proactively rather than simply reacting to changes. Change has always been with us as is emphasized by this quote from 1958.

> The problems of change have always been of concern to management, but until recent years they have been handled at a rather leisurely pace and in a routing fashion, according to standard organizational practice. Today changes are coming on the

management scene in so many forms and from so many directions
that we hardly become accustomed to one before another is on us. . . .
Shrugging off change as difficult or waiting to follow in the leader's
footsteps are no longer satisfactory practices (Moore, 1958).

The new aspect today is that a firm's ability to actively excel in an
environment of change will be a critical factor to success (Goldman,
1993; Dove, 1994).

In addition to the ability for proactive change, there is the
following general consensus in the literature limiting the effectiveness
of specialization, that is "being good at only one element [in
manufacturing] will not lead to success" (National Center for
Manufacturing Sciences, 1991, p. 5). Roth, Giffi and Seal (1992) add
that there will "not [be a] single 'correct' organizational structure."
Keichel (1993) expands and declares there will "not [be] just one type
of organization in future, but a variety of them interconnected more like
a spider's web." Most businesses today grudgingly accept the idea that
perhaps there is no silver bullet for 'improving' their operations.
Comprehensive or *systemic solutions* must be found to solve
encroaching problems. "Success in the new manufacturing era will be
achieved by dealing with the enterprise as a whole. It cannot be
achieved by dealing only with manufacturing as narrowly viewed
today" (Preiss and Goldman, 1991). This encompassing viewpoint of
manufacturing can be seen as an emerging trend. "Research into
manufacturing needs to focus on manufacturing as a whole not
individual parts" (Kidd, 1994, p. 366). Pisano (1995) reinforces that
improving manufacturing and competitive performance will require
restructuring several levels in the organization as well as across the
whole production system. As seen in Figure 3.1, this restructuring must
be viewed as a fundamental rejuvenation throughout the company
involving the critical variables of culture, coordination, people,
information, technology (Vollman, Collins et al., 1992, p. 58).

Paradox is a concept that frequently arises when looking at success
factors for future manufacturing. Ken Kresa CEO of Northrop
Grumman proclaims the idea of "integrated decentralization." The
concept is that strategic management and assets will remain centralized
while value chain management becomes completely decentralized. The
disassembling of companies into an array of independent parts without

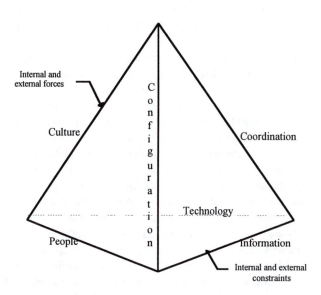

Figure 3.1 Framework for Manufacturing Restructuring

Source: Vollmann et al., 1992, p. 59.

an overriding structure will not be possible in the future. It will be a decentralized yet centralized structure that will look quite different from companies now. Another paradox is seen in Joseph Schumpeter's ideas of Creative Destruction recently modified by Nolan and Croson (1995). He envisions an environment of internal entrepreneurship, disorganization while simultaneously working to re-invent all aspects of the corporation and then re-connect those aspects back into the clear goals of the corporation (Peters, 1994).

The ability of continuous innovation has been a widely recognized success factor for many years (Hamel and Prahalad, 1994; Utterback, 1994). In 1958, Leavitt (1958) stated that future competition between firms should center more and more around "capacities to innovate." The ability to innovate really means nothing if new learning and innovations are not converted into sources for competitive advantage, "the key to success is to excel in both learning and converting that learning into commercial products and processes" (Bowen, Clark et al., 1994). Kozmetsky (1987) ties the abilities of innovators with the requirements of future educational systems. He asserts that the US "must link centers of innovation and manufacturing . . . with public/private infrastructure institutions." This will cause a need for new types of educational institutions. The manufacturers themselves may have a key role in these new institutions.

Other authors point to people as critical to future success. Companies must have the agility "to unleash a powerful team of people supported by the right technology" (Skinner, 1986). Leonard-Barton (1994) emphasizes that people must constantly build and refresh their individual areas of expertise and that companies must look to get a mix of disciplines looking at and working together on pertinent problems. An environment must be created where workers use their intelligence with staff helping to facilitate these workers. Hayes and Wheelwright (1984) see the need to build the skills and capabilities of the workforce and build technical competence throughout management and develop real worker participation in the learned-art of "running the business."

Other items often cited as future success factors include the use of systems to control the flow of materials through the production chain, from suppliers all the way to end customers (Pisano, 1995). Many believe that simultaneous engineering will be a differentiating characteristic (National Center for Manufacturing Sciences, 1991; Roth, Giffi et al., 1992, p147). Future success will ultimately rely upon most existing success criterion including: quality, reliable delivery, short lead times, customer service, rapid production introduction, flexible capacity and efficient capital deployment (Skinner, 1986). These control systems as well as other improvement systems are often technology based. In the early 1980s GM invested billions in "high tech" production equipment in items such as robots, CAD, CAM systems, and CNC machine tools. There was virtually no productivity improvement (Preiss and Goldman, 1994). At NUMMI where Toyota contributed their management expertise, productivity nearly doubled with little investment in advanced technology (Appendix B, mini-case: NUMMI).

New accounting practices are seen more as basic element of survival than a success factor. Hayes and Ramchandran (1988) focus on how traditional performance measurement and capital budgeting processes bias organizations away from investment in new production technologies. The current form of capital budgeting fails to take adequate account of organizational learning, skill creation, and how functional isolation prevents the full potential of programmable automation. The methods also tend to distort the growth of manufacturing overhead (Miller and Vollman, 1985). New accounting practices must allow production to be based more firmly on actual costs and revenues rather than masked by averages and variances against expected outcomes (Drucker, 1995). These new practices must have more relevant meaning to operations and will not be developed by accountants alone (Miller and Vollman, 1985). Non-financial measures must be included to present a more holistic picture. These measures might include skills and morale of workforce, innovation, and learning experience (Kaplan, 1984). There have been some moves to generate these new accounting systems where time based accounting is merged with activity based accounting (O'Connor and Bilby, 1991; Lee, Jacob et al., 1994; Drucker, 1995; Booth, 1996). Flanagan and Bilby (1991) developed software that assists simultaneous engineering through life cycle cost analyses where costs are captured in real time and reverberate throughout accounting systems.

Some authors attempt to link success factors with implementation approaches. Buzacott (1995) defines two specific methodologies: integrated manufacturing and cooperative manufacturing. In an integrated manufacturing environment the company tries to automate as much as possible using flexible manufacturing concepts. This style of manufacturing is capital and information intensive. The other methodology is cooperative manufacturing. Companies take this approach particularly when it is difficult to anticipate disturbances. In response companies organize such that the organization is closely linked to its environment, people within the organization are inherently flexible, the people are also closely linked with other people in other organizations, and there is extensive use of flexible manufacturing facilities where the machines easily adopt to a variety of production tasks.

The question arises as how to coordinate each of these "plans" or factors for improving and better insuring manufacturing success. There is remarkable little research across researchers showing which techniques are actually more or less effective. Table 3.1 charts four well

Table 3.1. Criterion for Organizational Success from Different Authors

White House Conference on Productivity, 1983[1] Seven Factors for Success	Walt Rostow (Rostow, 1993) 5 Criterion for Success	Bowen (1994) 7 Holistic Elements	Peter Drucker (1990) 4 Key Items of Future
1) Less authoritarian and more interactive management	1) Train young potential executives in history	1) Focus on core capabilities	1) Change social organization of plant
2) Labor accepts greater responsibility in firm competitiveness	2) Management reconciles innovation with the efficient management	2) Establish a guiding vision	2) Create "new" manufacturing accounting systems
3) Government moderates impact of competitive process	3) Small, innovative units at every stage in the R&D spectrum	3) Strong leadership	3) Flexible yet standardized modular "flotilla" organization
4) Comprehensive quality awareness	4) R&D Inventors governed by two rules: —willing to share the development, helping translate an idea into a viable operation —be prepared to let operator get the bulk of credit	4) Ownership and commitment	4) Systems design of the factory where the factory adds economic value.

Table 3.1 (continued)

5) New reward systems	5) Managers maintain close, regular relations with leader of R&D team	5) Push the envelope	
6) Strong programs of education and training		6) Prototypes	
7) Changes in government procurement practices to share risk in new technology implementation		7) Integration	

respected authors who have each developed a list of criterion for success in organizations. The next section will look at work that has been done to formulate a stage on which manufacturers can enact these multiple criteria.

VISIONS FOR FUTURE

Few theorists have suggested methods for transforming existing manufacturers into those that will posses and excel in this long listing of success criterion. Those few have attempted to present frameworks which tie the success factors together into an integrated vision for the future. This section will first present authors' depiction of the workplace of the new paradigm; the next section will present some of the latest developments in manufacturing strategy; then, a number of frameworks for manufacturing is presented that have been developed by well-known visionaries. The last of the proposed frameworks is Agility which will be the subject of the remainder of this dissertation.

THE FUTURE WORKPLACE

The way in which people interact in businesses changes significantly in the new paradigm. Many have looked at describing the differences between the future workplace and the accepted workplace which was created as a result of the mass manufacturing paradigm. The control and specialization system was developed only because it best suited the traditional manufacturing paradigm. It has become apparent in many industries that the role of the employee is undergoing transformation. The end result will be a manufacturing system that best competes in the new era.

Keichel (1993) predicts a number of changes in the workplace in the next century. These trends include: 1) the average company will become smaller, employing fewer people; 2) the traditional hierarchical organization will give way to a variety of organizational forms, the network of specialists will be foremost among these; 3) technicians will replace manufacturing operatives as the worker elite; 4) the vertical division of labor will be replaced by a horizontal division; 5) the paradigm of doing business will shift from making a product to providing a service; and 6) work itself will be redefined to include constant learning, more high-order thinking, and less 9-to-5 responsibility.

As strengthened in other research (Amos, Gibson et al., 1996), the line organization has been and will continue to lead the major changes in the workplace. "[The line organization is] out in front shifting the division of labor" (Kiechel, 1993). Forrester (1958) predicted this move of the line' organization and the merging of many line and staff functions long before it became apparent across industry.

"Workers" are reinventing themselves and are typically better educated, often indifferent to unions, willing to forgo job security, and want and expect more challenging / interesting work (Shapiro, 1987). Work is less task oriented and more project focused. In project work, employees must re-invent themselves every few years, and according to Apple Computer, individuals should "passionately support the vision while on board"—even though that may or may not last a long time (Peters, 1994).

Employees will be rated on multiple performance criteria and have expanded boundaries of control (Buzacott, 1995). Peters(1994) foresees organizations built around the idea of curiosity with a "curiosity quotient" as one performance criteria measurement. Nomura Securities issued a report discussing the "creation intensification" factor wherein they saw manufacturers becoming dependent on human imagination. Companies will be placing extreme emphasis on work force development because under the successful paradigm of the future companies will be "selling a product of intellect" (Kubinski, 1995).

MANUFACTURING STRATEGY

Harvard scholar Wickham Skinner (1969) defined strategy as a set of plans and policies by which a company aims to gain advantages over its competitors. It is also something that other plans can build upon. Later, Skinner (1986) defines manufacturing strategy as that which "defines the competitive leverage required of(and made possible by(the production function." The strategy allows the entire *structure* to be managed in the whole over the long term. A strategy is considered the most fundamental aspect of business planning and operations. Companies develop strategies that they determine will provide them the best competitive advantage.

A principle contributor to the area of manufacturing strategy is Terry Hill. His framework of manufacturing strategy is well accepted in the literature and is frequently cited. The key aspects of Hill's model (Hill, 1992) include:

- define corporate objectives,

- determine marketing strategies,

- access how products win orders,

- establish the correct manufacturing mode—the process choice, and

- provide manufacturing infrastructure to support production.

Hill also provides reasons for manufacturing's typically reactive role in corporate strategy. He cites a separation either physically (remotely located manufacturing facilities) or perceptually (cultural separation— status problems) between production management and corporate management (Hill, 1989).

At the turn of the century when manufacturing was first studied as a science, most researchers were looking for one elusive generic strategy for manufacturing. John McLean, a Harvard professor in the 1930s and 40s, developed the "Contingency theory." This theory argued that different approaches to manufacturing would be required based upon the competitive contexts. This argument has been traded off and on again through the years, but evidence show that there is some differentiation between strategies. Recently, De Meyer (1992) completed a significant empirical study of 176 European firms. In his analysis he found that manufacturers were pursuing different strategies as exhibited by clusters in the data. While admitting that the labeling was somewhat arbitrary, he combines his analysis with other empirical studies of US firms and divides strategies into four areas: 1) low cost manufacturing, 2) high quality manufacturing, 3) highly flexible manufacturing, and 4) highly dependable manufacturing. Roth and Miller (1991) with similar techniques in the US found a set of somewhat different strategy clusters which were labeled: 1) high performance products, 2) manufacturing, and 3) marketing-oriented group where manufacturing does not seem to be key to the firm's competitive strategy. While clusters were found in each study of the type, they did not lead to a generic strategy that was applicable for both Europe and North America.

Voss (1992) gives an important comparison of the existing literature concerning manufacturing strategy. He notes that there is increased interest in this topic due to the recognition of its importance to national economies. The question remains of whether there exists a uniform strategy or framework under which global manufacturers can operate. From Skinner (1969) to Hayes and Wheelwright (1984) authors have determined that it was not possible for firms to pursue multiple strategies effectively and that there was a need to focus on the most appropriate course of action. The quest remains to help companies determine that appropriate course.

PARADIGM PROPOSALS

It is a much easier task to identify paradigms when reviewing history. It is certainly more difficult to identify a paradigm in the midst of a transition. In the transition from entrepreneurial craft to the American Factory System and then again from the American Factory System to the System of Mass Manufacturing, nearly 20 years passed before businessmen and academics could recognize that they had entered a new era. Certainly Ford, Carnegie, Rockefeller and other entrepreneurs of the late 1800s and early 1900s benefited from recognizing and acting early in the new system.

As evidenced in Chapter 1, the United States and in fact the entire world is entering a new era of manufacturing. Today we can benefit from the wealth of available information. Researchers, politicians, theorists, and manufacturers, have been looking at the changes occurring and the anticipated success factors for the future. They have been carefully observing the most recent activities of industry trying to recognize identifiable trends. Many solutions have been offered with varying degrees of success (as summarized in Chapter 2, Table 2.1). A few researchers have postulated and described this new paradigm that is occurring. They hope that manufacturers take advantage of early recognition of the new paradigm and use the opportunity to propel their companies to the forefront of the new era. This research focuses on Agility as one of these new frameworks or paradigm developments.

While Agility will be the focus of this dissertation, seven other industrial models offered in the literature are discussed in the following sections: Federalism, Service Factory, Focused Factory, Collaborating Organization, Four Stages, World Class Manufacturing, and Learning Organization. These models overlap; no one completely describes the manufacturing and business paradigm of the future. Each framework describes a view of the coming world of manufacturing and only through careful review of each proposed theory along with clear evidence from industry can a comprehensive framework emerge. Some may accurately argue that these are not all of the models of approaching paradigms offered, yet they provide sufficient overview of manufacturing and organizational future thinking. Notably, each depiction holds the common opinion that *the most reliable future competitive weapon of manufacturing will not be cost reduction.*

Presented first is Shapiro's (1987) "new industrial model" which is a listing of important criteria. According to Shapiro (1987) the new industrial model should:

- satisfy and be compatible with individual, group, cultural and environmental needs,

- be flexible enough to accommodate the best and most useful elements of our traditional manufacturing model as well as new elements,

- not guarantee lifetime employment, but increased importance of training,

- blend specialists with generalists,

- support formation of teams where appropriate,

- encourage outside of work activities (informal communication),

- adopt programs that have proven efficient, and

- enable manufacturing to produce high quality, competitively priced products and services.

Federalism

Charles Handy (1992) applies the political concepts of federalism to manufacturing. He embraces the belief that autonomy releases energy. His framework is based upon independently acting people who do things their own way while working towards the common interest. This common interest is the key that requires that people be kept well informed, well intentioned, and well-educated. Handy sees his framework as a way of life to be enacted in the very soul of the business. The framework is built upon five principles of federalism: subsidiarity, interdependence, uniform way of doing business, separation of powers, and a twin citizenship to maintain strong federal presence while simultaneously encouraging regional independence. These factors rely heavily on trust, empathy along with formal power and explicit control which is used to maintain governance.

Service Factory

As depicted by USC professor Richard Chase and Harvard professor David Garvin, the service factory places manufacturing squarely at the "cortex" of the business where the factory has a four pronged role (Chase and Garvin, 1989). First, the factory serves as a laboratory which does more than perform experiments, but also supplies supporting data based upon rigorous testing. Second, the factory serves as a consultant by conducting problem solving in the field. Third, the factory of the future will be a showroom. It will serve as a working demonstration of the systems processes and products which it manufactures. Finally, the factory will serve the role of the dispatcher. It will be the linchpin of the aftersale support which requires flexibility, responsiveness, ever-tightening customer/supplier linkages. Each of these four components will require manufacturing and marketing to work especially closely together and understand customer expectations. Managers must be an intimate part of the effectively-laid out shop floor and be well trained in communication and presentation. This factory will not be directed by technology. Instead it will be directed through a clear coordinated strategy that recognizes and maximizes the competitive advantage of working collaboratively.

Focused Factory

Based upon years of research data, Wickham Skinner observed that contrary to accepted industrial practice, bigger factories with huge production capabilities are not necessarily better than smaller factories (Skinner, 1974; Skinner, 1974). In his development of future manufacturing he suggests that most companies would benefit from smaller, more focused factories. These factories would actually focus exclusively on their relative competitive abilities. This in more recent business terminology corresponds to core competencies.[2] The focused factory consists of five key characteristics: process technologies, market demands, product volumes, quality levels, and manufacturing tools. In his article "Productivity Paradox" (Skinner, 1986), the author updates and expands on his call for fundamental changes in "manufacturing structure and technology." Skinner infers that the greatest impediment to the new manufacturing framework is the continued focus on conventional productivity and cost-cutting approaches.

Collaborating Organization—The 5 Partners Model

University of Toronto professors Joseph D'Cruz and Alan Rugman (1993) formalize a model that redefines the competitive environment. In their view, manufacturers are no longer primarily concerned with traditional single entity rivals. The critical factor is to out perform the business system or network of competitors. The framework of this model is competition based upon five interconnected partners: the "flagship firm," key suppliers, key customers, competitors, and non-business infrastructure. The concept is that companies who build upon this model will create an effective business network. International boarders and nation states become secondary in importance to the alliance network. Under this depiction, the flagship firms lead the national industrial strategy process cooperating closely with government replacing less effectual politicians and bureaucrats. The flagship firms provide the strategy for the network assuming leadership in its execution. The other four network partners have limited strategic autonomy yet provide effective and efficient operationalization of that the overall strategy. Employees are more interchangeable between the partner entities, yet maintain a strong sense of loyalty to the overall network.

The Four Stages

It is clear that not all manufacturers are at the same "level." That is, some simply produce products and change only when forced to by market circumstances. Others are continuously seeking to be on the competitive edge. A limited few are continuously scanning the horizons to identify new manufacturing practices, technologies and markets. A systematic effort to identify and classify these different "levels" was completed by Stephen Wheelwright and Robert Hayes. They analyzed a number of companies and attributed to them various roles and functions that they portrayed. They called the roles or levels, "stages of development along a continuum" (Wheelwright and Hayes, 1985). These stages range from reactive in stage 1 to proactive in stage 4.

- **Stage 1** (internally neutral) describes companies who get the job done without creating problems for other functions.

- **Stage 2** (externally neutral) companies must improve manufacturing competence to at least match the level of their competition. Shift from stage 1 to stage 2 generally occurs when companies are faced with increasing competition.

- **Stage 3** (internally supportive) companies recognize the value of a systematic strategy. These companies begin to effectively coordinate the "manufacturing choices: capacity, facilities, technology, work force practices, human resources, performance measurement, quality, and systems (Skinner, 1986) as important to their competitive strategy. The most progressive stage of manufacturers appears in companies who rest their strategy on a company's manufacturing caspability.

- **Stage 4** (externally supportive) companies integrate the entire chain of product delivery. Major marketing and engineering decisions always involve manufacturing. Skinner (1992) lists the critical elements of stage 4 as learning, management of attention, problem-solving information, indirect (systems and values) control, process evolution / worker dependence.

Several questions arise from this 4 stage framework for manufacturing. Must companies move along each stage chronologically? How do companies transition themselves to move between stages? Skinner (1992) lists four variables to identify if a company has reached stage 4: in-house innovation, exploitation of internal manufacturing capabilities, attention to manufacturing infrastructure, clear link between product design and manufacturing process design.

World Class Manufacturing

World Class Manufacturing is a nebulous term which reflects different shades of meaning to different individuals. Using data from a cluster study, De Meyer (1992) equated world class manufacturing with what he termed to be 'manufacturing innovation.' According to Roth, Giffi and Seal (1990), the concepts now attributed to 'world class' prior to 1986 were termed 'manufacturing excellence' (p. 7). This early definition was stated as:

> a dynamic process that provides unique value, competitive advantage and delight to customers suppliers through the development of internal operations capabilities that foster continuous improvements in human assets, technology, materials, and information flows that are synergistic with the total business, and that provide sustainable competitive opposition to the firm's target markets (Roth, Giffi, Seal, 1992, p. 137).

The phrase "world class manufacturing" was first publicized in 1986 by Richard Schonberger who coined the term because it captured the "fundamental changes taking place in industrial enterprises" (Maskell, 1991, p. 3). The popularity of this ideology has grown and in 1988 Hayes, Wheelwright and Clark listed seven critical attributes of world-class manufacturers. They included (Voss, 1992): becoming the best competitor, growing more rapidly and being more profitable than competitors, hiring and retaining the best people, developing a top-notch engineering staff, being able to respond quickly and decisively to changing market conditions, adopting a product and process engineering approach which maximizes the performance of both, and continually improving. The National Center for Manufacturing Sciences (NCMS) in Michigan has worked diligently to provide some structure for this paradigm viewpoint. Figure 3.2 shows the framework for world class manufacturing that Giffi, Roth and Seal developed in 1990.

Learning Organization

Learning from experience has always been important to manufacturers. Companies generally expected knowledge transfer to occur through interpersonal contact from one experienced individual to a lesser experienced individual. Traditionally, formalized plans for learning have been rare and usually focused on management (Barrington, 1986; Rios, 1993). Most companies now recognize the importance of learning as an active process that should be incorporated into project planning and overall business strategy (Glick, Huber et al., 1990; Howard, 1993; Bowen, Clark et al., 1994; Pisano, 1994; Bonfeld, 1995). According to such sources, learning should be the primary goal of every organization (Bowen, Clark et al., 1994). As Drucker puts it, knowledge and learning are "the primary resources for individuals and for the economy overall" (Drucker, 1992).

While not the first to promote idea of "The Learning Organization," the term stuck in the business psyche after the publication of *The Fifth Discipline* by MIT author Peter Senge (1990). Senge argues that the only way organizations of the future will cope with change in a new world of work is if they internalize the notion that learning is for everyone in the organization. Successful organizations of the future will be those that thrive on constant change, manage chaos, and have an ongoing desire to invent new ways to view the world for individuals within—and without—the organization (Sullivan, 1991). Organization learning occurs through shared insights, knowledge, and mental models and builds on past knowledge and experience, relying on institutional mechanisms such as policies and explicit models. Properly managed, learning occurs as a function of time, independent of cumulative volume.

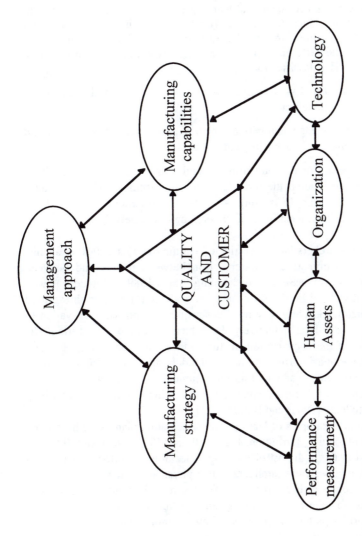

Figure 3.2. World-class manufacturing framework
Source: *Manufacturing Strategy*, (Giffi, Roth et al., 1990, p. 9)

Many companies have attempted to address this critical factor of learning, but have been trying to apply the relatively new but now familiar techniques of corporate communication—focus groups, surveys, management-by-walking around. These have been found to actually block organizational learning even as they help solve certain kinds of problems (Argyris, 1994). Clouding the issue is that different *types* of learning are not clearly understood. Edgar Schein (1993) outlines the different types of learning occurring over various time horizens. His classifications are:

1. habit and skill learning which requires often time consuming repetitive practice,

2. knowledge acquisition which requires motivation, insight and changes in behavior, and

3. emotional conditioning and learned anxiety which is considered the most "potent" of learning activities because learning lasts long after the original causes have been discontinued(making "unlearning" extremely difficult.

Many researchers have investigated learning and its critical elements. Open and objective communication between people and between organizations is essential for learning (Stata, 1989). Attitudes, as well as knowledge and skills, are very important. For integrated organizational learning, employees require an intrinsic motivation to think constantly and creatively about the needs of the organization. The leaders of the organization, in turn, make conscious efforts to map, challenge and improve the mental models operating within the firm. Even consumers add to this environment of learning and become learners when they use smart products, which both oblige and help them to learn (Davis and Botkin, 1994).

Many examples of learning implementation plans have been cited in the literature (Barrington, 1986; Lillrank, 1995). Nevison (1994) has looked at the high cost of learning especially in white-collar projects which involve more intellectual than physical effort and whose costs are largely staffing costs. He offers a model of integrated lessons indicate that the cost of learning can be estimated and incorporated into the correct pattern of progress allowing more realistic and accurate baseline cost plans.

Marquardt (1996) has put together an excellent framework based upon the important dimensions and characteristics of a learning organization. These characteristics include such features as learning is continuous, creative, agile, flexible, adaptive, and renewable. The characteristics are part of the systems-linked learning organization model which is made up of five closely interrelated subsystems that interface and support one another (Figure 3.3).

Figure 3.3. Systems Learning Organization Model
Source: *Building the Learning Organization* (Marquardt, 1996, p. 21).

MOVING FROM VISION TO REALITY

Manufacturing will continue its transition whether new forms are recognized or not. Despite evidence and frameworks such as those cited, there is a gap and time lag between research and application.

A great many business executives have much too slanted a view of what research (or the latest new techniques) can offer and either dismiss them out of hand or expect the impossible. A continuous and systematic use of research (especially that that requires deep cultural change) as an integral part of decision making is still a rarity in American business . . . deliberately ignored or never getting a chance to affect thinking of key people. New ideas are threatening to people, they always face administrative barriers, and there is a simple environment of resistance to change (Newman, 1978).

While industry does not require or depend on academic development of new paradigms, they have decided that manufacturing matters (Skinner, 1992). Still, manufacturing is managed pretty much the same as it has been for 50 years, in spite of the steady failing of manufacturing in global competition,. The rate of US productivity growth has been declining steadily since the 1960s (Voss, 1990; Pisano, 1995). It was noted in business journals by 1971 (Skinner, 1971). While some have blamed government, Hayes and Wheelwright (1984) put the blame squarely on management who were pursuing "modern management techniques" which had been developed during the 60s. These techniques separated the management from the line operations, focused primarily on short term results, and emphasized marketing and financial resources over manufacturing and technological resources.

Academics are realizing that the traditional operations research and industrial engineering taught to exploding market of MBAs in the 1980s disguised this mandate for change (Voss, 1992). Also slowing this acceptance of the importance of manufacturing is industry's inclination to purchase pieces of academic or consulting knowledge and apply it "willy-nilly off the shelf" (Skinner, 1992). Companies continue to look for "remedies" that are basically structural in nature which are "easier and quicker for a company to make . . . than changes in organizational policies and attitudes" (Hayes and Wheelwright, 1984). The pursuit of high productivity, low cost and high quality has been seen by managers in the 1990s as not enough. The very best competitors in the world in many industries are developing the ability to respond quickly to rapidly changing and unpredictable consumer demands (Pisano and Hayes, 1995).

NOTES

1. Report generated by 175 senior level leaders from business, labor, academia, government as quoted in Shapiro (1987)

2. Leonard-Barton (1994) defines core competencies as the essence of what makes an organization unique in its ability to provide value to customers over a long period of time. The building of core competence consists of four interacting elements: knowledge and skills, managerial systems, physical systems, and values.

CHAPTER 4

Methodology

As of early 1996, over 90% of existing literature on agility was from popular press articles (Figure 4.1 and Figure 4.2). In most cases little effort was made to substantiate or provide systematic empirical research.

At the outset of the current research, a prototype model was generated to describe the antecedents and results of Agility. Attempts were made to generate surveys which could provide statistical information on the relationships between proposed variables. Unfortunately, the question of which individuals would be most appropriate to respond to such surveys was unclear. Also, there were no companies that could be identified that could be classified as completely agile.

The nebulous state of the concept of Agility was such that exploratory research needed to be conducted before more systematic, traditional academic investigations could be meaningful. Therefore, this research utilizes qualitative methodologies including the application of case studies. Justification for the use of these techniques is provided in this chapter which draws heavily upon the dissertation work of Thomas Roach (1992) who used a similar approach when developing a systems development model in complex organizations. The study design is described in terms of the purpose of the research, the selection of research sites and subjects, and the research environment.

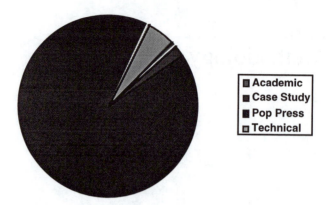

Figure 4.1. Breakdown of 300 articles directly related to Agility (1986-1996)

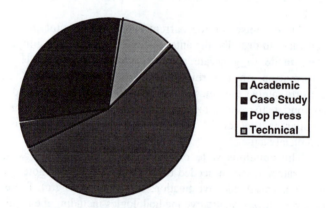

Figure 4.2. Breakdown of 200 articles in areas closely related to Agility (1986-1996)

QUALITATIVE RESEARCH METHODOLOGY: REVIEW OF THE LITERATURE

Complexities associated with the development of theory and its integration with research methodologies in the social science disciplines have been identified by Blalock (1980), who states that boundaries among and between groups and contexts have not been well defined. Standards, group norms and role expectations may also be imprecise. "Measurement that depends in some essential way upon these fuzzy boundaries or standards thereby becomes exceedingly difficult" (Blalock, 1980, p. 32).

Qualitative methods encompass a variety of non-quantitative techniques ranging from interviews to participant observation (Merton, Fiske et al., 1956; Scott, 1965; Forcese and Richer, 1970; Filstead, 1971). A common characteristic of qualitative methodologies is their quest for preserving the context within which certain phenomenon occur (Van Maanen, 1983; Lincoln and Guba, 1985; Eisenhardt, 1989). Van Maanen (1983) conceptually describes these processes as being "in vivo", a medical term meaning observed functioning within a living organism. The concept of collecting data "in vivo" retains the contextual essence of cause and effect relationships, an important aspect when concerned with organizational issues, participant behavior and the external environment which impacts on both. Mintzberg (1979) also strongly advocates the importance of on site data collection.

Increasingly in our research, we are impressed by the importance of phenomena that cannot be measured—by the impact of an organization's history and its ideology on its current strategy, by the role that personality and intuition play in decision making. To miss this in research is to miss the very lifeblood of the organization. And missed it is in research, that by its very design, "precludes the collection of anecdotal information" (Mintzberg, 1983, p. 113).

Qualitative methods are generally associated with exploratory and descriptive research studies which are a precursor to further quantitative research (Blalock, 1969; Forcese and Riches, 1970; (Glaser and Strauss, 1967; Glaser and Strauss, 1970). Glaser and Strauss further state that qualitative methodologies are useful not only as a precursor to further quantitative research, but as an appropriate and adequate methodology for the establishment of substantive theory.

Qualitative research is by its very characteristics an exercise in exploration. The researcher is often not sure of the structure of the results he will obtain until he has gone into the organization and "mucked around a bit" with the research issues at hand. Mintzberg (1983) is clearly in favor of obtaining "soft" data on site as a method of explaining what "hard data" means and as a basis for building theories.

More and more we feel the need to be on site, and to be there long enough to be able to understand what is going on. For while systematic data create the foundation for our theories, it is the anecdotal data that enable us to do the building. (Mintzberg, 1983, p. 113).

It appears that a goal of the qualitative researcher is to provide the explanatory and descriptive rationale which is often not provided by quantitative methods. This then provides the basis for theory grounded in practical application. Daft and Lewin (1990) state that:

> ... building theory on the basis of in depth understanding of a few cases is different from the traditional theory testing goal of statistical rigor, parsimony and generalizability. However, this type of research can provide the genesis for new theory that may spawn further research that uses traditional methods (Daft and Lewin, 1990, p. 6).

When, in the late 1970's and early 1980's, end user computing technology was first introduced, organizations had no clear guidelines on how to manage this new approach (Doll, 1981; Rockart and S., 1983). It required that researchers conduct descriptive studies in the field investigating how it was being applied before prescriptive guidelines could be formulated (Benbasat, Goldstein et al., 1987). Benbasat, Goldstein, and Mead (1987) state that, "We believe that the case research strategy is well suited to capturing the knowledge of practitioners and developing theories from it" (Benbasat, Goldstein, and Mead, 1987, p. 379).

Benbasat, Goldstein, and Mead (1987) offer three reasons for case study research as a viable information systems research strategy:

1. The researcher can study information systems in a natural setting, learn about the state of the art, and generate theories from practice.

2. It allows the researcher to answer 'how' and 'why' questions.

3. Research an area in which few studies have been carried out (Benbasat, Goldstein, and Mead, 1987, p. 370).

Cheng and McKenney (1983) offer three general criteria for accomplishing useful organizational research: (1) relevance to the concerns of the practitioners, (2) applicability to real world settings and (3) the ability of managers to relate the research findings to their specific concerns. Mintzberg (1983) offers a similar philosophy and advocates that the researcher interact with the organization directly in the gathering of data.

CASE STUDY METHODS

Scott (1965, p. 261) described the acquaintance with field methods as being "indispensable to the student of organizational behavior." He chooses to define field methods in a broad sense of the term to include the in-depth focus of Hughes (1960) and Katz and Kahn (1966) and a much more superficial focus which does not require the "intimate" observation of behavior as defined by these authors. Scott (1965, pp.261-304) differentiates methodological approaches as a function of the degree of intimacy that the investigator shares with the study population. This provides the basis for the two potential extremes on his continuum of approaches to field study. These extremes are identified as: (a)—sustained participation by the investigator and (b)— temporary investigation by the investigator. The techniques used throughout the breadth of this continuum include such methods as interviewing, observation, document and record collections and informant reports. Mintzberg (1983) has observed that in depth of analysis of small samples may be more appropriate for organizational theorists than larger samples with superficial analysis.

Eisenhardt's (1989) research investigates previous work on qualitative methods and "extends it in areas such as a priori specification of constructs, triangulation of multiple investigators, within case and cross case analysis, and the role of existing literature," (Eisenhardt, 1989, p. 533). She develops a framework for theory building based on case study research and views a priori specification of constructs as helping to shape the design of the research. She cautions, however, that the researcher must realize these constructs are tentative. One must allow for the possibility that the research question may change or shift, and that initial constructs are not guaranteed a place in the final theory.

Eisenhardt (1989) gives special emphasis to data analysis as the "heart" of the theory building process, but also views it as the most difficult part. She proposes within case analysis as a key step. "The importance of within case analysis is driven by one of the realities of case study research: a staggering volume of data," (Eisenhardt, 1989, p. 540). Within case analysis typically means detailed case study write-ups for each site. While the write-ups may be purely descriptive, they may be central to developing insight to crucial issues as they help the researcher to cope with the enormous volume of data. The goal of within case analysis is to allow the researcher to become "intimately familiar with each case as a stand-alone entity" (Eisenhardt, 1989, p. 540) thereby allowing the unique patterns of each case to become apparent before attempting to do cross case analysis.

The strategy for cross case analysis is to counter a researcher's tendency to draw conclusions based on limited data, be overly influenced by more elite respondents, or drop disconfirming evidence by looking at data in many divergent ways (Eisenhardt, 1989). Eisenhardt lists several ways that this may be accomplished:

1. Select categories or dimensions and then look for within group similarities coupled with intergroup differences. Dimensions can be suggested by the research problem, existing literature, or researcher's choice.

2. Select pairs of cases and then list the similarities and differences between each pair.

3. Divide the data by data source (Eisenhardt, 1989, pp. 540-541).

Use of these tactics should force the researcher to look beyond initial impressions, improving the likelihood of developing reliable theory and increase the chance of capturing new information which may be present in the data.

APPROPRIATENESS OF TECHNIQUES FOR CURRENT RESEARCH

Agility encompasses the disciplines of the quantitative sciences, computer science and the social sciences. It is this multi-disciplinary aspect of Agility which presents the researcher with the problematic issue of what methodology to use in the execution of related research (Hamilton and Ives, 1982; Baroudi and Orlikowski, 1989; Lee, 1989). The quantitative sciences and computer science field rely heavily on quantitative research methodologies. However, the social sciences rely on both quantitative and qualitative methodologies depending upon the focus of the research and which author's perspective you embrace. Blalock (1970, p. 88) stresses the importance of establishing accurate measurement of variables if causes of the social phenomenon are highly interrelated or it we are to "refine the analysis beyond the common sense level". Blalock (1970, p. 92) does allow, however, that measurement in the social sciences is highly indirect and that in itself is a significant problem to overcome for the researcher. Van Maanen (1983, p. 11) questions the direction which quantitative techniques are taking us in the area of organizational research. He states that:

> . . . the overwhelming role played by the survey instrument in organizational research has led some observers to suggest that the field is becoming simply the study of verbally expressed sentiments and beliefs rather than the study of conduct (Van Maanen, 1983, p. 12).

Becker (1970), Pettigrew (1973), and Mintzberg (1983) have all stressed the importance of accomplishing "social science research in a hands-on environment." These same authors question the appropriateness of quantitative analysis in many social settings on the basis that the relationships which provide much of the contextual structure are not preserved when using quantitative methodologies. Daft (1983) places considerable value on the organizational context of observing data. His statement regarding such an idea expresses both the favorable aspect of on site data collection and the shortcomings of the conventional paradigm. He believes that direct observation in organizations will produce enough information and questions to "last for a productive career," (Daft, 1983, p. 543). He expresses a great deal of difficulty with researchers who collect data, run correlation's and report statistics, but in publishing the data it becomes abundantly clear that they have never observed what it is they are describing. As a result, authors are often unable to draw conclusions about what the numbers truly represent and make research applications in the organizational context. Several researchers (Benbasat, 1984; Weick, 1984; Ginzberg and Schultz, 1987) maintain that the field of information -systems should also be considered an applied discipline as quantitative research alone will not give one the tools to apply the results to the organizational setting.

Peters and Waterman (Peters and Waterman, 1982) voice a similar concern on a much broader scale in their analysis of what makes up the characteristics of an "excellent company." They identified that the value placed on quantitative analysis as a basis for business decision making in the American society was inappropriately overemphasized and in many cases did not adequately describe all the important variables associated with a business decision environment.

If a parallel can be drawn between the development of concepts and theories to guide decision making in a social context and the development of concepts and theories as a result of research efforts— that parallel would also emphasize the need for theory development using methods other than the traditional quantitative methods which are dominant in research processes regardless of their focus (Weick, 1989; Whetten, 1989; Daft and Macinstosh, 1990).

The investigation of systems development processes in complex organizations requires that the context within which these processes take place be included in the research (Van Maanen, 1979; Emory, 1985). This context is the organizational environment and the dynamic interplay between various organizational participants associated with the development and operation of the information system. From this perspective, it can be seen that organizational issues constitute a significant portion of the total research effort. The research methodology must therefore be appropriate for the study of organizational issues and behavioral aspects of organizational participants. We must look to the Social Science disciplines such as Sociology and Organization Theory to find methodologies which are appropriate to this research.

The study of organizational issues such as power and political influences on the development, use and maintenance of information systems is appropriately pursued by application of qualitative research techniques. There have also been strong arguments proposed which support the use of qualitative methodologies as the preferred approach to the establishment of substantive and grounded theory (Glaser and Strauss, 1967; Glaser and Strauss, 1970; Glaser, 1978; Yin, 1981). The traditional paradigm of administering a survey questionnaire and performing statistical analysis on the results was considered inappropriate for the focus of this research. We are searching for cause and effect relationships within their normal environmental and organizational context. Cunningham (1983) has described this type of research as "action" research.

The concept of action research fits into the overall category of qualitative methodology which includes various techniques such as interviews, observation, document collection and other similar processes. Cunningham (1983, p. 405) further indicates that action research is based on the researchers ability to perceive correct causes and relationships in the dynamic environment.

Another key issue of the research questions stated in Chapter 1 is the perception of reality held by various hierarchical levels of organizational participants with regard to the effectiveness of an information system. The nature of these perceptions of reality are not easily quantified and as such do not lend themselves to rigorous statistical analysis. Ives et al (1980) provide a suitable framework for the conceptualization of these influences but the obtaining of empirical data to provide a measurement of the effect is yet an elusive goal of the information systems theorist. We must depend upon the qualitative methodologies of the social sciences to describe the magnitude and interaction of these forces. These methodologies focus on case studies, field methods, exploratory and descriptive studies. It seems appropriate to utilize these methodologies when studying the impact of intangible forces on the sufficiency of an information system functioning within an organizational context.

RESEARCH METHODS FOR CURRENT STUDY

The methods used in the present research study derive from Glaser and Strauss (1967,1970), Mintzberg (1983), Lincoln and Guba (1985), Kirk and Miller (1986), and Eisenhardt (1989). Mintzberg (1983) describes an emerging research strategy which he calls "direct research". This "direct research" strategy represents his composite formulation of research themes and patterns which have proved most useful to him since he began his doctoral dissertation in 1966. Mintzberg (1983) specifies a total of seven themes. These themes are summarized as follows:

1. The research is as purely descriptive as the researcher is able to make it.

2. The research relies on simple—in a sense elegant—methodologies.

3. The research is as purely inductive as possible.

4. The research is, nevertheless, systematic in nature.

5. The research is measured in real organizational terms.

6. The research, in its intensive nature, has ensured that systematic data are supported by anecdotal data.

7. The research seeks to synthesize, to integrate diverse elements into configurations of ideal or pure types. (Mintzberg, 1983, p. 106-114).

Mintzberg's themes are in consonance with philosophies espoused by other qualitative based organizational theorists (Bacharach, 1989; Eisenhardt, 1989). Van Maanen (1983, p. 10) states the qualitative researcher seeks to describe reality by "moving closer to the territory they study in the physical sense as well as in the intellectual sense by minimizing the use of such artificial distancing mechanisms as analytic labels, abstract hypotheses, and preformulated research strategies".

Zelditch (1966, pp. 566-576) approaches the issue of qualitative vs. quantitative research strategies not from a dichotomous perspective but rather from the perspective of mutual respect for each type of strategy, suggesting that strategies be determined by their relevance to the study's purpose. Such philosophies allow, if not encourage, deviation from the "standard" quantitative research study designs when dealing with issues that have a high social science content.

Eisenhardt (1989) presented a framework she developed for theory building based on case study research. Her process includes a sequence of eight steps:

1. Getting started—Definition of research questions. Possibly a priori constructs.

2. Selecting cases—Specified population. Theoretical, not random, sampling.

3. Crafting Instruments and Protocols—Multiple Data collection methods. Qualitative and quantitative data combined. Multiple investigators.

4. Entering the Field—Overlap data collection and analysis, including field notes. Flexible and opportunistic data collection methods.

5. Analyzing Data—Within case analysis. Cross case pattern search using divergent techniques.

6. Shaping Hypotheses—iterative tabulation of evidence for each construct. Replication, not sampling, logic across cases.

7. Enfolding Literature—Comparison with conflicting literature. Comparison with similar literature.

8. Reaching Closure—Theoretical saturation when possible (Eisenhardt, 1989, p. 533).

CHAPTER 5

Development of a Theory of Agility

Agility was first conceptualized as a focus of business in the U.S. in 1991. As described in earlier chapters, the precepts were built from industry first hand through active efforts of trying to survive within turbulent environments. This chapter reviews the development of the topic of Agility towards building a new paradigm for business operations. To date, literature on Agility falls into four areas: description, case study, concept development, and implementation tools. The bulk of this literature is description and largely based upon press articles. While, academic articles abound on many topics considered critical to agility; they only rarely use or cite the term, Agile. In short, the academic acceptance of the concept of agility has been tenuous. Although the topic is receiving increased attention and concept development more case study research is being called for and consulting groups are attempting to develop diagnostic and implementation tools for agile concepts.

21st MANUFACTURING ENTERPRISE STRATEGY: AN INDUSTRY-LED VIEW (PREISS, 1991)

The recognition of economic problems and upheavals caused by the explosion of technology and changing market forces did not go unnoticed in Washington D.C. In a 1986 speech, Senator Robb was on of the first to apply the term agility to an economic context:

... Both business and labor must make some changes if the US is to recover its economic agility. Adaptability is needed, and productivity must be linked to pay. Government has a role to play in the pursuit of a sound and healthy economy (Robb, 1986).

President Bush and members of Congress agreed with the Senator and commissioned a study on the new emerging business paradigm. The study was a six month effort with a 13 member industry inner core (Figure 5.1). The government and academic sponsors included the Secretary Program Office, the Navy MANTECH Program Office, and Lehigh University (Preiss and Goldman, 1991; Preiss and Goldman, 1991). The participating companies were interested in formalizing their developing ideas and learning how to best operate in their explosively dynamic markets.

13 INDUSTRY PARTICIPANTS WHO CO-DEVELOPED:
21st Century Manufacturing Enterprise Strategy
Air Products
AT&T
Boeing Helicopter
Chrysler
Ford Motor Company
General Electric
General Motors
IBM
Kingsbury
Motorola
Texas Instruments
TRW
Westinghouse

Figure 5.1. Initial Industry Participation in Development of Agile Concepts

The resultant report, *21st Century Manufacturing Enterprise: Vol. 1 & 2* (Preiss and Goldman, 1991), detailed a key competitive enabler of this new paradigm. That enabler was described as a national industrial network—a comprehensive industrial database—combined with services that allow groups of companies to create and operate proprietary virtual entities. This type of network would only function effectively if there existed a standardized legal framework for the creation of consortia with collaborative intellectual property rights and responsibilities built into easily implemented contracts.

The authors of this study developed this visionary plan based upon their experience and expectations as well as theories and academic cited in this dissertation. The team created an infrastructure overview that contained elements critical to support the development of this new paradigm. In their work they defined the infrastructure as that which was needed to support the nation-wide *and* corporation-wide levels of agile manufacturing systems (Figure 5.2).

Two clear fundamental thrusts of this two volume document was that the manufacturing needed to be revitalized in America and government had a key role to play in working with industry to make it a reality. This 1991 study was heavily influenced by that year's concepts of time based competition and defense conversion (Kuhn and Nozette, 1987; Stalk and Hout, 1990; Stalk and Hout, 1990; Stalk and Hout, 1990; Governor's Task Force on Economic Transition, 1993). Though these two ideas have lost much of their luster by 1996, the report stands as the first attempt to put together all of the related emerging ideas into a comprehensive new framework for manufacturing. It effectively applied the name of "Agile Manufacturing" to an emerging paradigm in manufacturing that has been heralded since at least 1966 with Skinner's proclamation that mass manufacturing was an "outdated mode of production" (qtd in Pisano, 1995, p. xv).

The investigators identified a few key factors as being critical to their vision of "Agility." These factors include: the ability to introduce completely new products quickly, the development of evolutionary product lines, and the development of strategic relationships with suppliers and customers in ways not attempted in the past. These factors describe "agile" abilities that industry would accomplish through the effective integration of three resources: technology, management, and work force.

Figure 5.2. Envisioned Agile Manufacturing Infrastructure

COMPETITIVE FOUNDATION & CHARACTERISTICS	MANUFACTURING ENTERPRISE ELEMENTS	IMPLIED ENABLING SUB-SYSTEMS
COMPETITIVE FOUNDATION		
Continuous Change	Business Environment	- Continuous Education / - Modular Reconfigurable Process Hardware
Rapid Response	Communication & Information	- Customer Interactive Systems / - Organizational Practices
Evolving Quality Journey		- Distributed Databases / - Performance Metrics & Benchmarks
Environmental Responsibility	Cooperation & Teaming Factors	- Empowered Individuals & Teams / - Pre-Qualified Partnering
ENTERPRISE CHARACTERISTICS		
Concurrency	Enterprise Flexibility	- Energy Conservation / - Rapid Cooperation Mechanisms
Continuous Education		- Enterprise Integration / - Representation Methods
Customer Responsive	Enterprise-Wide Concurrency	- Evolving Standards / - Simulation & Modeling
Dynamic Multi-Venturing		- Factory America Net / - Software Prototyping & Productivity
Employees Valued		
Empowered Individuals in Teams	Environmental Enhancement	- Global Broadband Network
Environmentally Benign		- Groupware / - Streamlined Legal Role
Flexible (Re-)Configuration		
Information Accessible & Used		
Knowledgeable Employees	Human Elements	- Human-Technology Interface / - Supportive Accounting Metrics
Open Architecture		- Integration Methodology
Optimum First-Time Design		
Quality Over Product Life		
Short Cycle Time	Subcontractor & Supplier Support	- Intelligent Control / - Technology Adaption & Transfer
Technology Leadership		
Technology Sensitive	Technology Deployment	- Intelligent Sensors / - Waste management
Total Enterprise Integration		
Vision-Based Management		- Knowledge-Based Systems / - Zero-Accident Methods

Figure 5.2. Envisioned Agile Manufacturing Infrastructure

Adopted from Source: "21st Century Manufacturing Enterprise: Vol. 1", p. 53, 1991

A BRIEF VISION OF AGILITY

In the depiction of the "agile enterprise," integration of resources would be accomplished in ways not possible in traditional mass manufacturing structures. In such enterprises information flows seamlessly, passing through manufacturing, engineering, marketing, purchasing, finance, inventory, sales, research and extends on to suppliers and customers. Concurrent or simultaneous engineering is considered standard. Every stage of a product's lifecycle is represented by product design teams. Collaborative working becomes common both within a physically dispersed company as well as across different organizational entities. Software and communication equipment that facilitate sharing information and working together are effectively utilized and allow for large scale software/hardware changes quickly without disruptions. Trust and mutual responsibility weigh heavily in such organizations and require a capacity for localized enterprises to make and implement many decisions at the point of information. The ability exists to allow the organizational synthesis of resources from multiple companies resulting in a virtual company which can behave as a single entity dedicated to one project. Companies are designed to be modular.

Agile companies emphasize speed, flexibility, and collaboration, and they focus on core competencies. Agile companies are characterized by the seamless flow of information both internally and externally between suppliers and customers. All company resources—technological and human, internal and external (including partnerships and alliances with customers and suppliers)—are to be used in a coordinated, interdependent if not synergistic system with the ability to achieve short product development cycle times and to recognize and respond immediately to sudden market opportunities (Agility Forum, 1994). Clearly, even approaching such an ideal type leads to challenging tasks for managers, technicians, and employees.

Agility puts a premium on cooperation and collaboration between suppliers and customers. To clarify, "cooperate" means to act or work together with others for a common purpose; to combine in producing an effect. "Collaborate" means to cooperate with an enemy. Collaboration in the sense that it is described in the literature is the process of working together with competitors for a common purpose while maintaining separate identities (Gibson, Preuss et al., 1990; Gibson and Rogers, 1994).

In future relationships between agile customers and suppliers, there will be a larger range of pre-sale and post-sale product support services (Agility Forum, 1994). In this arena, the fastest route to marketing new products will often be to identify the functional resources that are currently available and synthesize these resources electronically into new business relationships. Company infra-structures will need to develop to allow quick and direct linkage along the customer-supplier chain.

Physical products will not be the only items transferred between and within companies. Products will meet the marketplace's "multi-needs . . . [delivering] a bundle of services rather than just satisfying a single need" (Kozmetsky, 1993). The products will be constructed from multiple technologies/processes which will include: pre-sale special design services, pre-sale service of Just-In-Time supply or order consolidation, joint product design, system integration services, post-sale maintenance, post-sale upgrade components, post-sale decommissioning and recycling, joint marketing to other potential users of the product or service (Sheridan, 1993).

Manufacturing will be held accountable for the maintenance of respect for the environment, health and energy concerns. The impact of manufacturing processes and products upon communities as well as on regional and global environments will be seriously considered (Kozmetsky, 1993).

The anticipated role of agile manufacturing will incorporate current technology and business principles into a new "necessary" condition for manufacturing survival (Preiss and Goldman, 1991; Agility Forum, 1994). Agile manufacturing will return to the high variety of products offered by the craft era of manufacturing, but will allow the low unit costs which characterized the industrial mass manufacturing era (Figure 5.3). There will be no single mass market, but a collection of market segments without any pronounced economies of scale. Consumer goods as well as capital goods will become multidimensional with each brand having their own market niche (Thore from Kozmetsky, 1993). The divisions and boundaries between job functions will tend toward unclear, vague, virtual.

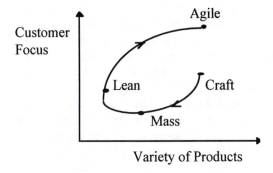

Figure 5.3. Movement of Manufacturing

Adopted from a presentation by Smith (1994)

TWO POTENTIAL MODELS FOR AGILITY

The 1991 report hit the business world with somewhat less than a bang. There were the standard business press articles on the subject from Business Week to Time (Quigley, 1990; Port and Carey, 1991; Schine, 1991; Byrne, 1992; Ettlie, 1992). However, the general business public is quite wary of "new panaceas." Academia, who had virtually ignored the work of Skinner (1956, 1958, 1966, 1971), Wheelwright (1966, 1972, 1978) and others who were constantly sounding the battle cry that focus on manufacturing was critical to long term competitive success, seemed to view the concept with suspicion (Ettlie, 1992). Traditional academic researchers are especially wary of accepting a "lumped together conceptualization" that did not have the standardized functional divisions of Management, Production, Marketing, Accounting, etc. At an Operations Research conference in 1994, one prominent professor dismissed any framework of agile manufacturing that did not have a major component labeled "Marketing." On another occasion an engineering department chairman from a prominent university dismissed the idea of engineers being trained to understand concepts of Management and Marketing since "it is businessmen who are responsible for the current declining state of manufacturing."

The concept of agility has spread nonetheless and has been particularly well received among manufacturers. However, the understanding of the issues remained vague (and do still) to many. Still, industry, government and academia representatives thought that the umbrella concepts of agile manufacturing had merit and warranted further development. Paul T. Kidd, CEO of Nextgen, a small boutique consulting firm in the United Kingdom, has been working on the growing perception of a paradigm shift in manufacturing since 1983. In 1991, he wrote a book about the fundamental nature of the paradigm shift in manufacturing. In 1994 he authored *Agile Manufacturing: Forging New Frontiers* as part of his work with Manufacturing Knowledge, Inc. (Kidd, 1994). His goals were to deepen understanding and define implications to business concerning the changing state of manufacturing, develop new concepts in agility which could be transferred to industry; and build user friendly methods and tools which exploited agility.

Building upon the work of the 21st Century Manufacturing 1991 report, Kidd recognized the need for a definition of a conceptual framework (Kidd, 1994). He warned against the possibility of the infrastructure model (Figure 5.1) being taken as a prescription for success. In 1993, he presented his copyrighted conceptual framework for agile manufacturing (Figure 5.4). His additions and adjustments included changing "Environmental Responsibility" to "Social Responsibility" as well as adding "Total Customer Focus" to the competitive foundations component.

At the heart of the conceptual framework espoused by Kidd were four core concepts:

1. a strategy to become an agile manufacturing enterprise,

2. a strategy to exploit agility to achieve competitive advantage,

3. integration of organization, people and technology into a coordinated, interdependent system which is the competitive weapon, and

4. an interdisciplinary design methodology to achieve the integration of organization, people and technology (Kidd, 1993).

GENERIC FEATURES MODEL

- Integrated enterprises
- Human networking organization
- Enterprises based on natural groups
- Increased competencies of all people
- Focus on core competencies
- Virtual Corporations
- An environment supportive of experimentation, learning and innovation
- Multi-skilled and flexible people
- Team working
- Empowerment of all the people in the enterprise
- Knowledge management
- Skill and knowledge enhancing technologies
- Continuous improvement
- Change and risk management

Core concepts
- Strategy to achieve agility
- Strategy to exploit agility
- Integration of organization, people and technology
- Interdisciplinary design methodology

Competitive foundations
- Continuous change
- Rapid response
- Quality improvement
- Social responsibility
- Total customer focus

Figure 5.4. A Conceptual Framework For Agile Manufacturing

Source: Manufacturing Knowledge, Inc. (1993; Agile Manufacturing: *Forging New Frontiers. p. 24.*

Kidd continues to develop the field of Agility in Europe and calls for research on the dynamic relationship between simultaneously developing and exploiting agile capabilities leading to the creation of new opportunities (Kidd, 1995).

DEVELOPMENT OF IMPLEMENTATION TOOLS

After the completion of the 1991 Iococca report, the industry/academic team developed a self audit that companies could review to try to assess their performance along agile criteria which were based upon the four dimensions of agile competition. They warn against the question of "Is my company agile?" as opposed to "Is my company making progress in the right direction, how fast are we progressing, and how are we relative to the competition?" The detailed questions for the "agility audit" are not meant to be academically or statistically rigorous, but rather to be seen as a starting point for developing a more organized approach.

In 1992 the original Lehigh academic team developed an early version of a survey of Agility in an attempt see where companies stood on these concepts which they proposed as the future of manufacturing. Their study did support the authors' claims on the future of manufacturing particularly in new product development processes. In fact, four core enablers were found to be jointly deployed in support of this process: concurrent engineering, man-machine interface technologies, inter-company collaboration, and information sharing within and among companies (Goldman, 1995). A preliminary study demonstrated that when the enablers were implemented in a *coordinated* deployment, the following improvements were found: 53% reduction in cycle time, 58% in quality improvement, 28% in product development cost reductions. These measures certainly do not reflect the complete impact that agility might have on business, but they do lend credence to the idea of implementing these core agile enablers jointly. Finally, the study concluded that technology chosen to support business practices played a more important role the technology alone in reducing cycle time and lowering cost within the product development process (Goldman, 1995). Unfortunately, the study was extremely limited in scope as it included data from only 11 companies. No regression analysis was possible to relate the proposed dimensions of agility to the pseudo-benchmarking study. Also, the detailed design of the analysis made it impossible to obtain quantitative data without hundreds of hours with each company.

The primary academic experts involved in the original study, Steven L. Goldman, Roger N. Nagel, and Kenneth Preiss, reconsidered and improved their research stated in 1991 and authored, *Agile Competitors and Virtual Organizations* (1995) where they define four dimensions of agile competition: 1) enriching the customer, 2) cooperating to enhance competitiveness, 3) organizing to master change and uncertainty, and 4) leveraging the impact of people and information. The early infrastructure for agility shown in Figure 5.1 was updated in the book as shown in Figure 5.2. Similar to revisions made by Kidd (1994) the *competitive challenges* items were altered to include the customer and wording was changed in an attempt to make the infrastructure more appropriate to business.

In the 1995 book *Agile Competitors and Virtual Organizations*, the team presented the results of two years of study upon their theoretical development of the concepts of agility. They were able to more elaborately explain the concepts of agility as they have been observed in recent manufacturing trends. An important shift in thinking was that the concept of "agility" was not purely a manufacturing concept. It could be applied to any business in any market whether that business produced hard products or offered special services. In the tradition of Skinner (1969, 1971), Wheelwright (1982), Hayes (1978; 1988), etc. manufacturing was seen as an integrated, central, and vital component of a businesses operations. Thus, whether the company focus was on providing high quality tractors to mid-west farmers or if the company was providing hamburgers to teenagers, the four dimensions of agility offered a vision of the future.

Also included in *Agile Competitors* was a revised form of the survey. The team presented a list of measurements that are projected to be useful in assessing progress that a company is making towards agility. Some measurement items are similar to Baldridge Quality measures and some measurements are based upon the activities of "leading companies;" however, the determination of leading companies is not fully explained. The critical issue that is highlighted by the suggested list of measurements is that many of the areas considered important to manufacturing(agile or otherwise(do not have any particular measures, such as customized product opportunities, percentage of company wide disciplines in each project team, percentage of total executive time spent with other companies, new team assignments per person per year, and what happens to those who fail or succeed in terms of salary and promotion. However, little emphasis has been placed within industry to determine a value of some of these items which, if considered, might lead to the pursuit of particular agile attributes.

An important premise in agile manufacturing or world-class manufacturing is that companies cannot afford to be followers. They must be actively involved in the ongoing search by academics, industry, and government of what to measure, how to measure and how to evaluate the results. As noted when referring to the move to take advantage of mass manufacturing, "entrepreneurs did not wait until measures were developed before making progress" (Preiss and Goldman, 1994).

Other theoretical development has been accomplished by associated consultants and staff members of the Agility Forum as well as a large number of participating volunteers from industry. In an effort to compile and push the frontier in thinking on agility, the Agility Forum has sponsored 5 conferences on Agile Manufacturing. Starting out very small in 1992 in Bethlehem, the conferences have been growing in reputation and participation. The conferences to date: 1993 in Orlando, 1994 in Austin with over 200 participants, 1995 in Atlanta with over 500 participants, and 1996 in Boston with over 900 participants. The first three conferences consisted primarily of slide presentations and discussions by experts in related and enabling concepts such as TQM, Lean, and Learning Organization. Conferences have progressed in scope to more workshop oriented where industry participants exchange their ideas and experiences. The 1997 conference in San Diego was considered a hands on industry conference.

To supplement the various on-going conferences, workshops and research, the Agility Forum has developed a "knowledge base" which develops agile concepts within a "system model of agility"[1]. The four key areas of the system model are: Market Forces Driving Business Change, Enterprise-Level Agility Attributes, Agility Attribute Enablers, Generic Business Processes (Figure 5.5). This model is envisioned to link with a new emerging technology that may prove crucial to agility, sentient technology.[2]

Market Forces Driving Business Change	Intensifying Competition
	Fragmentation of Mass Markets
	Cooperative Business Relationships
	Evolving Customer Expectations
	Increasing Societal Values Pressure
Enterprise Level Agility Attributes	Solutions Provider
	Collaborative Operations
	Adaptive Organization
	Knowledge Driven Enterprise
Agility Attribute Enablers	Integration
	Reconfigurability
	Cooperation
	Flexibility
Generic Business Processes	Enterprise Management
	Demand Identification / Creation
	Product Realization
	Demand Fulfillment
	Metrics

Figure 5.5. Agility Forum's System Model of Agility

Source: Knowledge Base, The Agility Forum, Lehigh Institute

This technology offers great promise in moving towards the "knowledge" needs of virtual enterprises which might be separated by vast geographic, cultural, technological and linguistic differences. According to Noyes (1995) in sentient technology's current state of development, a half dozen good engineers could design a new petrochemical plant in six months instead of the typical time of several years with two hundred engineers using conventional technology. Of central importance here are warnings of solely a technical focus in implementing agility without due considerations of improving upon the skills of individuals (Kidd, 1995; Kozmetsky, 1993).

AGILITY: THE DEFINITION REFINED

While agility has been defined in a variety of ways, a common theme is that it is a concept separate and unique from mass manufacturing.

Agility implies breaking out of the mass-production mold and producing much more highly customized product—when and where the customer wants them (Sheridan, 1993).

Still, many definitions of agility are most concerned with demonstrating that this concept builds on existing and innovative manufacturing directives:

Agility is the ability to build on and integrate the principles of quality, empowerment, and the industrial engineering principles of lean manufacturing, but to go beyond a production emphasis to focus on throughput and to align performance measures to support this emphasis with the net result a gain in market share (Carol Shaw), as quoted in Vasilash (1993).

The above definition, many could argue, leaves out important aspects of change, responsiveness, and dynamism which are also often associated with agility. Webster's New Universal Unabridged Dictionary (1983) defines agility as: the nimbleness of an entity to move quickly. Practitioners and entrepreneurs often emphasizes that agility is the ability to thrive in a time of uncertain, unpredictable, and continuous change (Dove, 1994a; Dove, 1994b; Dove, 1995a; Dove, 1995b; Dove, 1995c; Dove, 1995d; Dove, 1995e; Dove, 1995f; Dove, 1995g; Dove, 1995h; Dove, 1995i).

A widely quoted definition of agility comes from Steven Goldman of the Iacocca Institute:

Agility refers to the ability of a company to thrive {and prosper (Smith, 1994)} in a competitive environment of continuous and unanticipated market change—to respond quickly to rapidly changing, fragmenting, global markets (Preiss and Goldman, 1991) that are served by computer-networked competitors with routine access to a worldwide production system, markets that are driven by demand for high quality, high performance, low cost, customer-configured products and services (Goldman, 1994).

The above definition was first introduced in the Iacocca Report entitled *21st Century Manufacturing Enterprise Strategy: An Industry-Led View, 1991* with the supplemental components added as attributed.

The present research argues in favor of the importance of the ideas of quickness and changing market environments. In fact, without the increasing level of uncertainty in the environment, the "agility" level or nimbleness of a company would hardly be critical as exemplified in the past 100 years of mass manufacturing. Central to the definition of agility is nimbleness. Only nimbleness in conjunction with other items such as product quality and/or reliability will lead a company to "thrive and prosper" in the age of chaos (Peters, 1994).

Drawing on the above formulations, the present research has proposed the following definition of agility:

> Agility refers to the nimbleness of a company to quickly assemble its technology, employees, and management via a communication and information infrastructure in a deliberate, effective, and coordinated response to changing customer demands in a market environment of continuous and unanticipated change (Amos and Gibson, 1995).

This definition answers the who, what, why, when, and how questions. *Who* is defined as the company: its technology, employees, and management. *What* refers to agility. The *why* is due to the atmosphere of continuous and unanticipated market change. *When* is specified by quickly. Finally, the *how* is by means of a communication infrastructure; it is the enabler or catalyst to accomplish nimbleness.

THE EXPLORATORY MODEL IN AN AGILE BUSINESS

The conceptualizations and models of Agility created to this point have allowed researchers to understand and begin to develop more fully the precepts of Agility. However, clear linkage between variables which lead to different levels of Agility remain absent. There is depiction of what Agility is, yet remarkably little on what business might alter in order to achieve Agility. Also, there has been little longitudinal case study analysis. The remainder of the chapter will introduce the antecedent model for Agility that was evaluated in the case study analyses.

Before introducing the proposed model, the clarification between operating strategies and core requirements must be emphasized. Agility is not a *strategy* that businesses must implement to become more competitive in the environment. Agile business practices are proposed to be a core requirement for conducting business in the future (Dove, 1994a). The much studied concepts of Lean/Flexible manufacturing (Bahrami, 1992; Parthasarthy and Sethi, 1992), mass customization (Pine and Davis, 1993; Tedlow and Jones, 1993), networking (Nohria and Eccles, 1994), Just-In-Time (Manoochehri, 1984; Raia, 1986; Dion, Banting et al., 1990; McDaniel, Ormsby et al., 1990), are all operating strategies that an agile firm can implement if that firm so chooses. Concepts such as reengineering, total quality management, SPC, etc. are transformation strategies that are intended to *transform* a company into a more "competitive" organization.

The proposed model of agility (Figure 5.6) defines five key variables which contribute directly to increasing a firm's agility: communication connectedness, interorganizational participation, management involvement, production flexibility, and employee empowerment. The model suggests agility will most likely occur when: the level of communication "points of contact" both external and internal is high, the level of collaboration between firms in the form of alliances or partnerships is high, management involvement in participatory business infrastructure changes is high, the production flexibility of the manufacturing capabilities of the firm is high, and the level of employee empowerment is high.

Outcomes of agility focus on shortened cycle times for product development as well as business processes which lead to quicker response to customer demands for high customization with customers often integrally involved in product specifications and design. These outcomes of agility in conjunction with high quality and reliability will lead to the desired aspects of improved competitive position, high market share, and profitability.

ANTECEDENT AND INTERVENING VARIABLES TO AGILITY

1. Communication Connectedness. The level of communication connectedness within the firm refers to (1) the technical aspects of Smultiple linkages, and (2) the behavioral aspects of communication. Both of these aspects of connectedness refer to external coordination with customer-supplier computer systems as well as the internal dissemination of information. In short, communication connectedness refers to communication which crosses organizational boundaries as

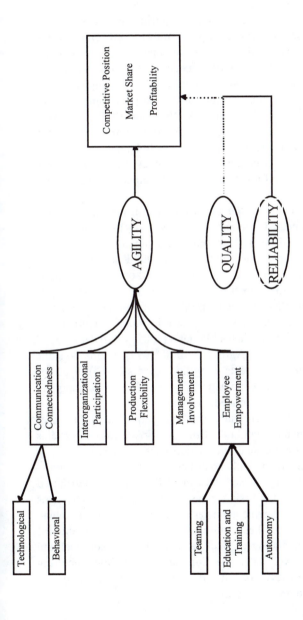

Figure 5.6. Proposed Antecedent Model of Agility

well as communication across teams within the firm and across boundaries to other firms.

The critical aspect for business is acquiring, assimilating, and utilizing information on how to best perform their core competencies. Many experts have suggested that the conventional flow of information must be broken (Leonard-Barton, Bowen et al., 1994). The changes are occurring in the telecommunications industry today to completely alter the standard communication structure. Information is being received from a multitude of points and sources. As Newman (1978) pointed out when anticipating the changes technology will have upon communications, "gathering information is one thing, determining what to do about the findings is another" Effective focus must be on ways to communicate the good information to the right people at the right time via the right medium.

Many sources have cited the advanced capability of the computer controlled, interconnected communication system as the essential tool that businesses will utilize in their fight to remain competitive in the fast-paced technological marketplace (Cash and Konsynski, 1985; Kotler, 1989; Kotha, 1994). Ives (1984) presents how the information system can be used as a competitive weapon through building barriers against new entrants, changing the basis of competition, generating new products, and changing the balance of power in supplier relationships all of which are elements in Michael Porter's (1985; 1990) depiction of competitive forces. Asava (Agility Forum, 1994) emphasizes the cultural and management aspects of agility. Rogers (1986) discusses how the "human" aspect of communication technology is as important as the technologically advanced media systems.

Many companies are currently employing distributed databases which handle information within the firm. Interorganizational systems (IOS) are defined as automated information systems shared by two or more companies that significantly contribute to enhanced productivity, flexibility, and competitiveness (Cash, 1986). Both distributed databases and IOSs are the basis for the anticipated systems. Systems must be developed that can maintain verbal communication within and between organizations, these systems must also be capable of transmitting data (including product designs) in the theoretical and graphical stages as well as in the Computer Aided Manufacturing (CAM) mode to send CNC code directly to machines that actually tool particular parts or complete products.

There are a few key areas for such systems: product data exchange standards, tools for efficient searches of product databases, and information models that simulate the processing capabilities of manufacturing plants (Candadai, Champati et al., 1993). The information system will also assist in the preliminary qualification of potential partners. Qualification information such as finances, access to transportation models, quality programs, education programs for employees, and overall plant performance records must be readily accessible for quick linkages between companies.

The technical resources and human needs are distributed via elaborate information systems, predetermined standard business processes (which allow for customization), and distributed databases into highly coordinated, interdependent systems capable of delivering required information instantaneously. Information must flow seamlessly among all internal functions as well as between external suppliers and customers.

One potential measure of agility could be the ease with which information is transmitted and disseminated within the company. This information must be absorbed and acted upon appropriately in all particular cases. Many information systems today transmit data, but the information is not acted upon because it is in a form that cannot be readily assimilated by the appropriate personnel (Fisher and Raman, 1992). The information glut or overload needs to be eliminated within the agile firm. This will require significant front-end investments in time and money to install distributed databases and information systems that are object-oriented and based upon open systems. That is, the standards for the information need to be maintained at a modular level that facilitates and encourages the creation of new processes. Once the communication of information standards are in place and the agile method of business become de facto, little additional costs will result from a large scale change in business processes. If fact, it will be expected that agile businesses will be "re-engineering" themselves on a continual basis (Youssef, 1992).

An important aspect of communication connectedness is that national and international networks can link companies with their suppliers and customers which provide the capability to access distributed databases disbursed along a wide geographic area. The EINet from MCC ("MCC To Develop National Agile Manufacturing Network.", 1994) and the (yet to be completed) Factory America Net

(Preiss and Goldman, 1991; Earls, 1995) are targeted to provide companies with standardized information services that will provide information on topics ranging from purchase order forms used by particular suppliers to the specific courses taught at companies. The networks will even maintain information concerning the resources that companies dedicate to education and training programs. Such systems will have the ability to upgrade standards in products as well as communication protocols.

Even in the face of new technologies, research has revealed that the most effective technology transfer mechanism is a person to person process (Kozmetsky, 1987). The technology utilized to increase the communication connectedness of a firm must keep this fact in mind. Thus, there is a need to develop a broader approach to technology deployment and technology development criterion (Kidd, 1994, p. 366). An effective model of collaborative communication that was utilized in this research is provided in Appendix C.

P1. The level of communication connectedness in the firm and the ease and timeliness associated with its use is positively associated with agility.

2. Interorganization Participation. This antecedent variable refers to the level of business activities that cross company boundaries. Agile companies employ multiple strategies involving agreements between companies. There are three main types of participation each of which involves different aspects of commitment: commodity, alliance, and virtual partnership (Preiss and Goldman, 1991; Agility Forum, 1994). The difference between the types of interorganizational participation is essentially intensity. Ideally, agile firms will have a mix of these relationships where no priority is placed on any one aspect.

Commodity Relationship

Commodity relationships are based on long-term contracts and logistic systems for delivery. In this type of relationship the supplier will choose its customers as well and will base the decision on price and long-term stability of the prospective client (Agility Forum, 1994). Suppliers are chosen based on price, quality, timely response, and reliability.

Commodity relationships are easily dissolved making the modularity aspect of agility apparent. Agile modularity means that companies are easily plugged into one another and can scale up or down as required by the circumstances.[3] Communication links between companies for purchase orders, invoicing, etc. are established within agile firms to the degree that transferring from one supplier to another is easy and inexpensive. Attempts to apply high switching cost barriers will be ineffectual in this environment due the ease of communication interconnections and modularity of company agreements. However, unlike today's commodity arrangements, tight linkages between the companies will be commonplace (Agility Forum, 1994). Business processes and daily work routines will involve members from each party. Commodity relationship partners will also be involved in product design even if they are not included in the final product production. Their inclusion in the design process will enhance the robustness of the design and add knowledge to the suppliers which can in turn be used in other commodity agreements (without legal liability) (Agility Forum, 1994).

Alliance To Virtual Relationship

The alliance and virtual type of agile relationship transforms the traditional functions of purchasing agents and sales representatives (Preiss and Goldman, 1991; Agility Forum, 1994). Ostensibly, computer network systems obsolete the necessary inquiries on price quotations, delivery time, and product quality, as well as eliminating source selection problems, negotiations based upon price, receiving inspection and warehousing, reconciling receipts and invoices, payment, and after sales warranty service. Purchasing processes will be quick and sourcing and sales decisions will involve personnel from product development, quality, and manufacturing functions. Logistics systems will be interconnected and shipping will become an integral part of the purchasing system (Agility Forum, 1994; Pandiarajan and Patun, 1994; Vastag, Kasarda et al., 1994).

Agile Relationship

In the ideal type of agile enterprise, products at all relationship levels will become more customized (Agility Forum, 1994). The more customized the products the higher the intensity of the relationship and the higher the value added from the supplier. Transactions will be more of a varying mix of products, information, and value-adding services focused on the customer's needs. The more specialized the product the more valued is the knowledge and expertise of the supplier in the development of the completed product.

Much has been written about virtual relationships and the advantages and disadvantages of this form of interorganizational participation (Flaig, 1992; Teece, 1992; Pollalis, 1994; Preiss and Goldman, 1994). Ideally in the virtual enterprise, sourcing decisions based upon established relationships will lead to the formation of more cooperative relationships in which a supplier is treated as provider of solutions. Companies will seek expertise and facilities from suppliers because of low costs and quick response. In these interconnected relationships suppliers and the company will share both rewards and risks. People assigned to this collaboration work closely together in fully integrated operational processes while remaining with their respective companies (Agility Forum, 1994). In such cases the supplier pool is often limited to one single supplier company and the modularity gives way to integrated mutual dependence.

The nearest form of interorganization participation that is under widespread use in the current paradigm is multi-business collaboration. This area has been studied extensively and is directly related to interorganizational aspect of Agility (Figure 5.7). Many projects require collaboration, where no one company has the necessary skill, resources and risk tolerance to go it alone (Merrifield, 1987). It must be noted that there is a "distinction between collaborative efforts for creative purposes (new ideas, directions, concepts, methods etc.) and those for innovative purposes (implementing or moving in new directions—cross licensing, join bidding activities, venture capital, incubators, intellectual property licensing, etc.)" (Kozmetsky, 1987). Some legal structure has been applied to collaboration for innovative purposes; however little legal precedent has been established for creative work. There remain many collusion issues and violations of fair-bidding processes associated with alliances and virtual types of relationships, especially in government contracts. The legal issues must be solved before this level of participation intensity can be fully realized, particularly within the defense industry (Howes, 1994).

Trust and Dependence

From the integrated yet modular partnership between companies at the commodity level to the synthesis of physical and human resources in the "virtual company" relationship, companies can adjust and scale their relationships easily. A relationship of trust based on mutual dependency between supplier and customer must exist to motivate the flow of information. The highest level of trust is demanded with the virtual relationship. The agile company should have high levels of interorganizational participation in a mix of relationships that span commodity to virtual.

Interorganizational trust and dependence are vital components of interorganizational participation for they relate the success of customer-supplier partnerships. In an agile competitive environment, it is not necessary to own resources necessary to create, make, sell, and support goods and services. In fact, it could be a competitive burden. Companies must rely on partners at all levels in all required roles.

This would include dependence on employees of other firms, dependence on manufacturing or computer equipment owned or operated by partners, instances of dependence on R&D performed by outside firms, etc. Just-In-Time supplier relationships are also included as well as straight to factory floor supplier product delivery where quality is determined and certified by the supplier company without redundant and unnecessarily expensive checks upon product receipt (Gibson and Rogers, 1994). Arrowplane Aircraft has enabled one such system in a current project underway with one of their suppliers, Composit Materials, Inc..

As there are no backup or redundant systems to protect the company against particular alliance or partnership linkage failures, this concept of interorganizational dependence cannot exist without high levels of trust. In the aspect of interorganizational dependence, risk is reduced through the usage and success of integrated resources, demonstrating the inter-dependent nature of the defined agile antecedents.

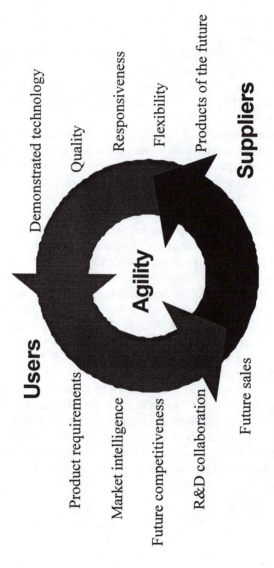

Demonstrated technology

Quality

Responsiveness

Flexibility

Products of the future

Suppliers

Users

Agility

Product requirements

Market intelligence

Future competitiveness

R&D collaboration

Future sales

Figure 5.7. The Agile Collaborative Process

Adapted from Richter, 1993, p. 37

P2. The level of interorganizational participation and the distribution of relationships between commodity, alliance, and partnership is positively associated with the agility level of the corporation.

3. Production Flexibility. This antecedent variable to agility refers to the technical aspects of manufacturing capability and the ease and timeliness with which a product line or entire factory can be re-configured to produce a new product or process. It also relates the automation of the processes of a firm and their reconfigurability.

It has been recognized that the nature of flexibility is hard to capture (Gupta, 1989; Evans, 1991; Gupta, 1993) and different types of flexibility sometimes overlap and conflict. A flexible manufacturing system can be a single machine or complex combination of machines, robots, material handling and storage devices, control and monitoring devices, and human operators. Desirable attributes include the ability to process different part types, facilitate quick changeovers, enable multiple part routing, and to control variety (Gupta and Buzacott, 1994). These flexible manufacturing systems must be continuously evolving manufacturing systems, not just machines that can produce "Part A" today and "Part B" tomorrow.

Classifications of flexibility range from machine level, cell or plant level to corporate level. An agile company has built upon each classification and is considered flexible at the corporate level. It is assumed that in these agile companies there are significant uncertain elements in the manufacturing system's environments. The links between the communication and the information systems allow the full capability of the flexible systems to be realized (Parthasarthy and Sethi, 1992).

Many firms attempt to employ "flexible manufacturing systems" in order to achieve agility. However, they often ignore some of the other antecedents of agility that are presented in the proposed model such as employee empowerment and communication connectedness. As a consequence, they do not obtain their objective. It is only after flexible production and flexible management are installed within a company that an empowered workforce is enabled to implement the innovations that they generate (Goldman and Nagel, 1993). Presley (1994) states that automation is not simply an act of automating the processes a company currently performs. It must be realized that new manufacturing technologies fundamentally change the nature of the firm.

These warnings aside, the production flexibility variable as defined in the present research is specifically technically oriented and requires machine and equipment investments as well as significant programming to automate production tasks.

P3. The level of flexibility within production manufacturing systems is positively associated with agility only if the other components of the model are present.

4. Management Involvement. This antecedent variable refers to the level of active participation management takes to alter the infrastructure to enable the implementation of agile practices. This variable assesses the "buy in" by the firm's leaders to become agile by fostering activities which institutionalize agility within the firm.

"Over and over again as we tried to determine what differentiated the world-class companies from their competitors we returned to a single word 'management' " (Roth, 1992, p.141). The role of management within agile organizations is different from typical mass manufacturing organizations (Nagel, 1992; Voss, 1994). With agility, managerial duties are focused on providing physical and organizational resources in support of the creativity and initiative of the workforce. Organizational walls need to be routinely reconfigurable. Executives need to set strong specific goals with vague means of achieving them. Management will be actively involved in continuous workforce education and the aggressive pursuit of expanding the quality and capability of the workforce. Management will not only institutionalize processes but will also "recognize the need to institutionalize learning" (Bowen, Clark et al., 1994). In some ways management involvement means "hands off" employees, i.e. give them autonomy. The primary objective of management will be to create an organization capable of quickly configuring subsets of its resources in response to the particular requirements of individual customers (Goldman, 1993).

Management involvement is a critical element in increasing the level of agility in a firm. It is management's role to implement business processes that lead to reconfigurability and flexibility. Management protects workers and encourages boundary spanning. Studies have identified that the track record for the implementation of information technology (Benjamin and Levinson, 1993; Voss, 1994), and flexible production systems have often times not led to improved performance. The reason for such failures was determined to be because investments were heavily biased toward technology rather than toward managing changes in process and organization structure and culture (Evans, 1991; Bahrami, 1992; Parthasarthy, 1992). Managers of agile firms must avoid excessive emphasis on technology. Behavioral and cultural change must also be institutionalized within the firm. This can be accomplished in two ways. The first emphasizes turning managers into coaches. The terms for this management idea has been varying in the literature including: facilitator, coach, mentor, and more recently coordinator (Kiechel, 1993). This was directly predicted in by Leavitt (1958) who stated that "the notion that managers ought to be coordinators should flower in the 1980s." Under this management formulation, instead of maintaining layers of supervisors, managers set up procedures to empower their employees but still maintain a clear and focused set of overall company objectives that are effectively conveyed across the company. Changes in the infrastructure must be so complete within the organization that it becomes impossible for companies to return to the hierarchical form of management (Howes, 1994).

If, for example, employee empowerment processes (discussed more in a following section) have not been sufficiently institutionalized in the company, a new manager who maintains a mass manufacturing-style personality can create havoc and recentralize decision making (Howes, 1994). The critical reason that centralized decision making can no longer work is the great volumes of decisions that must be made quickly given an external environment of continuous and unanticipated change (Nagel, 1994). This institutionalization implies a critical success factor of consistency of top management (Sheridan, 1993). It has long been recognized that "support from top is vital to success of ventures which faced obstacles as formidable as changing peoples attitudes, habits, viewpoints" (Newman, 1978).

While it is important not to over employ solutions based solely on technology, it is equally important to maximize the benefits of breaking changes particularly in the communications arena. Company leaders must watch out for managers who suffer from "technology aversion" and must ensure that the understanding of the technology is not too narrow or mechanistic (Hayes and Wheelwright, 1984).

External Management Involvement:
The Role of Unions

The discussion of labor unions has an important place when considering the organizational paradigm for the future. The labor movement grew from the deplorable practices of unscrupulous business owners who held little to no value for their "human assets." However, today Labor is often seen as a great impediment to reaching the new vision of Agility. A primary reason of this is the inherent institutional nature of the Labor union. It is difficult to change the union which was built upon the best practices of mass manufacturing. Yet, if changes were accomplished to the benefit of its members it could greatly enhance the effectiveness and strengthen the chances for success of new business practices. These changes often call for a closer collaboration between Labor and Management.

From 1910 to end of 1930s companies tried to have "Employee Representation Plans" which were seen as competitive and counterproductive to traditional labor unions. They were outlawed by the Supreme court in 1938 as violations of the National Labor Relations Act since they tended to be dominated by management (Shapiro, 1987).

Unfortunately, this has encouraged an even wider separation between labor and management. It became acceptable for management to blame Labor for production and competitive difficulties. It also became acceptable for Labor to try to milk companies for all their worth. Management has believed a standard way of thinking since the manufacturing crises became very apparent in the face of foreign competition especially in the late 70s and early 80s was that the cheap labor sources in Mexico and southeast Asia were the answer to ailing manufacturing in the US (Pisano and Hayes, 1995).

Markides and Berg (1988) challenge this idea and cite studies that reveal that manufacturing offshore is bad business. The true costs and risks of moving production offshore are usually badly underestimated. Managers are making decisions based upon minimizing the cost of manufacturing as the primary principle of "good manufacturing." Markides and Berg (1988) point out that labor costs account for less than 15% for the typical company and not more than 10% in most industries (Skinner, 1986). In cases where the reason for offshore production is to get closer to a local market or for better access to raw materials offshore manufacturing is more justifiable, but many companies would be better off in the long run in redirecting their efforts toward improving their domestic operations. This has led some to claim that "controlling variable labor costs will become a lower priority [in new manufacturing environments]" (Kaplan, 1984).

At the *Factory of the Future*, AT&T Power Systems, Dallas, Texas, management works with unions to redefine the roles of the line workers and create labor contracts with greater flexibility than previously available. Empowered teams are formed with facilitators that replace traditional supervisors. On each team is at least one union representative. This representative monitors group decisions and identifies contractual issues. If a contractual issues is identified, the representative presents it before another team of union representatives who are physically located at the facility (Underwood, 1994).

In one case, receiving teams at this Dallas location were able to decide that they did not require overlapping shift hours. The change to "butt to butt" shifts would traditionally reach the union's national levels before resolution. Months would pass before action would be taken. Since the ability to alter these contractual issues had been localized, the teams were able to decide and implement the plan within one week (Underwood, 1994).

Clearly, with such authority and flexibility for the employees placed within these new forms of union contracts, the management of a firm could not arbitrarily re-institute hierarchical procedures. Therefore, union contractual participation is considered a key method for management to implement and institutionalize agile practices.

P4. The level of management involvement in implementing activities towards the goal of agility is positively associated with the level of agility within the firm.

5. Employee Empowerment. The level of employee empowerment refers to (1) the ability of individual employees to make decisions that could impact either their work area or the entire firm, and, (2) the level of employee responsibility for defining their own duties based on company goals where the means to meet those goals have not been explicitly defined. Empowerment has been termed employee participation or involvement (Wandmacher, 1994) and is considered an important aspect of improving the competitiveness of any business. As used in this research "empowerment" is greatly influenced by organizational culture and unfortunately, little work has been done on the linkage between manufacturing strategy and organizational culture (Misterek, 1992).

Within agile organizations employees become the most valuable and sought after "assets" of companies (Likert, 1958; Preiss and Goldman, 1991; Nagel, 1992; Agility Forum, 1994; Goldman, 1994). As early as the 1920s, the ideas of participative management sought to take advantage of the "potential capacities of its human resources" (Likert, 1958). Participative management was defined as permitting a portion of management to be managed, granting a share of management to the managed, and creating a rapport between the management and managed (Moore, 1958). The famous business researcher, Likert (1958) studied the effects of participative management and determined that it succeeded better in employees attitudes, relationships with superiors, employee satisfaction than the traditional hierarchical methods.

These early ideas of participative management which were becoming better known in the 1950s were merged with that era's obsession with statistics. It was believed that specific measures could be taken to "adequately and accurately reflect the qualities of the human organization in terms of loyalty, skills, motivations, capacity for effective interaction, communication and decision making" (Likert, 1958). The objective of these measures was to allow managers at lower levels to take on more operating responsibility. Forrester (1958) warned at the time that the over application of qualitative measures to the human aspects of organizations could lead to a "micro-management mentality . . . where every permutation [has] to be considered by management." This indeed happened and fueled the explosion of middle management to the point where it could not be maintained.

Once again some of the tenants of participative management are cited when depicting the agile organization. The critical factors about people within organizations are once again being viewed with an eye to their impact on competitiveness. People and not technology solve problems encountered in the business environment. The change inherent in the Agile world make it imperative for management to have the "enthusiastic cooperation of its work force where all are linked to the success of its plant" (Shapiro, 1987). If change is an inherent characteristic of Agility, then Employee empowerment must allow employees to better control this environment. It has been noted that "people do not resist change or criticism, but they do resist being changed and do resent being criticized (Moore, 1958).

Employee empowerment is an essential element of agility that cannot be easily manipulated (Kidd, 1994). Therefore, three sub-elements have been identified that contribute to empowered employees. These elements are teaming, education, and autonomy.

Teaming is central to depicting firms that are considered agile. Teaming refers to the ability of a firm to formulate groups that are able to immediately attack problems. "Groupthink" was greatly feared in the 1950s (Leavitt, 1958), but such 'group' teams require little time to work and interact together effectively.

It is argued that teams must be cross-functional and self-directing. Team structures are to include not only factory floor personnel but also managerial and technical teams. Some companies will form teams focused around products and some on technology. Teams will cross company boundaries and reward systems will be established to motivate members to be independent of traditional line management.

Companies will encourage entrepreneurial traits within teams. Advantages of such traits have been noted for some time (Hirschman, 1958; Shapero, 1971). A critical factor that companies will consider will be that sparks of creativity more often occur in those with a varied mix of previous occupational experience including marketing, finance, production, management and research and development. This highlights the need for the cross functionality within teams.

Education refers to the overall training program that the firm employs for both technical and interpersonal skills. The education factor measures the commitment of the company to redefine the role of each employee as required, rather than wholesale replacement of employees with others who come "to the table" with the needed skills. As Keichel (1993) simply states it, "work will be learning." Job duties will be continuously redefined and will require continuous education on the part of the company and the employee to maintain relevance and usefulness as products and processes are developed and replaced. In the Agile world, education has little resemblance to the institutions of the past, "the great frontier of education is going to start at 22 instead of stopping" (Merrifield, 1987).

In many cases, the education that one employee receives may make that person more useful to a partner company particularly those companies that maintain virtual partnerships with the company. With less definition of organizational boundaries, that employee will be allowed and encouraged to move to the partner firm. These cases of continued education will greatly impact local industry directly affecting the small manufacturers. These "modular" employees will serve not only other related business, but also as much needed links between community, state and nation (Kozmetsky, 1987).

Autonomy refers to how power is used to resolve differences. In agile firms, management will be required to be more participatory and teams will be given more authority on deciding many issues. Particular employee decisions will not be easily overridden. This represents a great challenge to managers who are accustomed to controlling people through corporate hierarchies or through information control, but agile firms will allow autonomous individuals to work together in collaborative efforts (Limerick and Cunnington, 1993).

Organizations will encourage and be characterized by entrepreneurial, mission-oriented teams. Flat organizations will redefine the role of team supervisors into the "coach" concept. Agile firms establish procedures which empower employees to make decision regarding the formation of partnerships and alliances. Once problems are identified and defined, teams have the ability to make decisions.

Ideally, interfirm agile partnerships will be structured so that power is not used opportunistically. In many cases, firms will be of different sizes and have different levels of involvement in particular projects. More powerful partners may seek to take advantage of weaker partner. This will not occur within an ideal agile partnership.

P5. The level of employee empowerment within a firm is positively associated with the level of agility within an organization.

P5a. The level of employee teaming within a firm is positively associated with the empowerment level of the firm.

P5b. The level of continuous employee education within a firm is positively associated with the empowerment level of the firm.

P5c. The level of employee autonomy a firm is positively associated with the empowerment level of the firm.

Supporting Case Evidence

Many US companies, such as Hughes, GM, Sikorsky Helicopters, and Texas Instruments are working on different aspects of agility and are at vastly different levels of understanding and implementation. Therefore, this following case study research effort attempts to narrow the focus on an agile issue that most companies consider vital whether pursuing "agility" or not. This central issue is improved supplier management. Many companies are wanting to strengthen their relationships with their suppliers in order to decrease cycle time, improve quality, and increase overall efficiency. That is, they are pursuing attributes that are considered agile in nature even though many involved may never use the term "agile" to describe their work. See Table 5.1 for a listing of agile attributes as defined by the Agility Forum.

The first project investigated was between Arrowplane Aircraft Company (4,500 employees, 6 Bil sales -1995) of Key City, USA, and one of its key suppliers, Composit Materials, Inc. (72,000 employees, $ 12.5 Bil sales -1995). Arrowplane was seeking to achieve a number of the agile attributes including: rapidly bringing products to its customers, extending its customer relationships by continuously adding value, forming new cooperative relationships with its suppliers, allowing production decisions to be decentralized, and, in some ways, in altering its organizational structure to better fit diverse production activities.

The other company investigated was Thompson Enterprises (250 employees, $12 million in sales), also of Key City, USA, and one of its suppliers, Bilmo Systems Inc. (<25 employees, $1-2 million sales). Thompson's primary concerns are to bring products to market more rapidly to increase customer's perceived value, and to cooperate in new ways with its suppliers.

The selection of these two primary companies for investigation (Arrowplane and Thompson), who differ significantly on management techniques, sizes, and production processes, provides interesting comparisons and contrasts in the ways in which they chose to pursue agility.

Table 5.1. Twelve Attributes of an Agile Organization

1	Rapidly Bring Products to Market
2	Customer-Chosen Options: Reconfigurable and Upgradeable
3	Individualized Goods and Services
4	Ever Changing Models, Longer Lived Product Families
5	From Mass Markets to Niche Markets
6	Customer-Perceived Value
7	Extending Customer Relationships by Continually Adding Value
8	Leveraging Skills and Knowledge of Workforce
9	Cooperating Internally / Externally (Including with Competitors)
10	Organizational Structure that Fits Diverse Production Activities
11	From Centralized to Decentralized Decision-Making
12	Incorporating Societal Values into Decision Making Process.

Source: The Agility Forum, as part of its Course: "Introduction to Agility—
  Agile 101"

NOTES

1. The knowledge base may prove to be an effective resource and perhaps a future tool for industry in the continued search to fully understand agility. It is not entirely clear why the four dimensions of agile competition defined in the *21st Century Report* were replaced in the knowledge base with the four parameters of the System model, but the concepts are integral to both conceptualizations.

2. There are three progressing levels that help to explain the sentient technology theory: data, information and knowledge. Data is viewed as a collection of unrelated islands of facts, ideas and concepts. Information elevates the format of data to an arrangement that is useful to human understanding. This text document could be considered information, it is readable and conveys information to people. Knowledge, however, is the vast and intricate collection of concepts that are intrinsically, logically and dynamically linked in a complex

network. The human brain interprets data and knowledge and formulates these dynamic links. The sentient technology attempts to recreate this dynamic linking process on the computer. For a basic example created from the engineering environment from which sentient technology comes, a project might consist of any number of schedules, procurement requirements, costs projects, environmental regulations, CAD designs, etc. An engineer on this project would understand the fundamental association between all of these information items. The computer with sentient technology creates a "knowledge network" which "learns" these interrelations by "reading" all of the documents and items within its network. It creates nodes, relationships and linkages which have been patterned after the human thinking process (Noyes, 1995).

3. A potential method to chart such modularity was used back in the 1950s in the Integrated Helicopter Avionics System by Teledyne. This novel project conceptualization experimented with operational and activity based costing. Also, the system charted potential suppliers who were rated by value-added contribution. The project was operated along component helicopter parts in an overall process format as opposed to the typical functional break-outs. Designs took place concurrently at a time when the industry was perfecting sequential operation (Teledyne Systems Corporation, 1955). The project itself was successful; however, for various reasons the methodology was not frequently employed, perhaps the informational requirements and management of such a system were too great for the computers of the time. In any case, with these concepts being considered today as imperative to future competitiveness, they may reach their full potential.

CHAPTER 6

Case 1: Arrowplane Aircraft Company and Composit Materials, Inc.[1]

COMPANY HISTORY

The aerostructure manufacturing facility under investigation in this research has a long and complicated history. Today, it is one of the leaders with its specialty, a key process within the larger construction of an overall commercial aircraft. In order to disguise the particular company under discussion, several background and other details have been omitted; however, the supply chain project itself lends well to the continued development of an agile framework.

Serving as a critical backdrop to the operations of "Key" Facility was the changing environment of the aerospace industry. US defense budget cuts following the end of the cold war coupled with the recessionary forces of the 1980s and its impact on commercial airlines' profitability adversely affected the growth of the aerospace industry. Aerospace firms were basically unprepared to respond to these significant challenges. It is estimated that over 150,000 jobs were lost in the US as a direct result of these industry changes (Tankha and Amos, 1995). According to most estimates, the industry as a whole suffered a 30% over-capacity in the early 1990s (Hayward, 1994).

The revenue figures shown in Figure 6.1 track the financial downturn for Arrowplane and, like the rest of the industry, downsizing was the company's primary response. Nearly half of its workforce was eliminated within four years, Figure 6.2. This created a dilemma that the company's obligations to its retirees loomed as large the business itself. The company was forced to reevaluate all of its procedural operations. It needed to do more with less, eliminate all non-value added activities and redirect the company on a course for future success. This case study is about one of these programs instituted by the company's executives that was to meet the challenge facing the aerospace business.

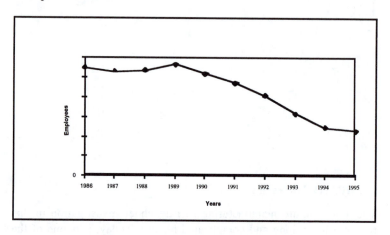

Figure 6.1. Employment at the Key City Facility

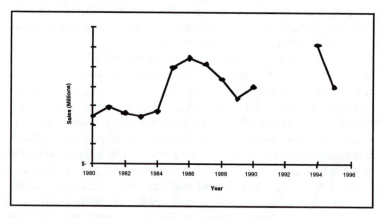

Figure 6.2. Sales Revenue at the Key City Facility[2]

CHANGING BUSINESS OPERATIONS TO MEET NEW CHALLENGES

Aerospace executives were slow to respond to the changing economic circumstances in the late 80s because most in the industry believed that defense business would pick up as it always had in the past. The early 90s saw Arrowplane trying to recoup its dwindling market share and make its huge operations more efficient. Table 6.1 shows the key motivating factors that pushed Arrowplane to implement new initiatives. Management spread the word through the company that the objectives that Arrowplane would seek and considered central to its future success included: more rapidly bringing products to customers, extending and enhancing customer relationships by continuously adding value, forming new cooperative relationships with suppliers, allowing production decisions to be decentralized, and, altering the organizational structure to better fit diverse production activities. One project that resulted from these executive directives was meant to increase the company's agility (although at the time this concept was not well understood).

Table 6.1. Critical Motivating Factors for Moving to Agility

• Customers Demanding Shorter Cycle Times	• Eliminate Overcapacity
• Decreasing Defense Contracts and Budgets	• Eliminate Non-Value Added Activities
• Increase Customer Satisfaction	• Fewer Military Clients, More Commercial Clients

WHAT TO WORK ON FIRST

Given the climate of the industry and the company's recent history, it is not surprising that when senior staff did respond to growing critical problems they looked for projects where improvements would have the most impact. In early 1994, senior executives determined some key areas that, if improved, would move the company in the desired direction.

One identified key area was inventory reduction. Arrowplane housed hundreds of millions of pounds of parts inventory in enormous warehouses. These inventories had to be accounted for, stored, and maintained. A significant amount of effort was required just to move inventory from one section of the facility to another as it was needed. This allowed multiple opportunities for materials damage in handling, receiving, transfer, and stocking. Additionally, Arrowplane paid suppliers for material up front. Often well over one year might pass before the material would be required in the manufacturing process. Sometimes up to two years would pass before Arrowplane received payment from its customers for its end products. Finally, materials, particularly from large mills, had to be purchased in large lot sizes. Extra material would have to be stored until it could be used on future projects. If design requirements for the particular material changed before it was actually used in construction, that material might simply be discounted as lost waste. By all accounts, the lost amount "was significant" and was conservatively estimated at 5%-10% of material costs.[3]

Another critical area targeted by Arrowplane management was to eliminate redundancy wherever possible. For example, the "dock to stock" system which was related to the inventory problems needed attention. Suppliers would bring products and material into the receiving area of Arrowplane at the Key facility where they were unloaded. The products and material were transferred to receiving and then inspected according to government standards, sent to the main stores receipt and maintained in inventory. Upon receipt of an issue order these products and material were transported to the carousel receipt area within the assembly building where they waited until they were issued into the stock bins. At the stock bins they were ready for immediate assembly. Even though this was a carefully organized process, it did not function efficiently. Management discovered when reviewing current practices, workers in the assembly area would often order many more parts and machine tools than they really needed in order to insure that these items would not be in short supply when they really needed them. Parts, materials, and machine tools would get bogged down at any one of the nine points to the assembly area which would create temporary shortages. When a worker would recognize a shortage, he or she would place a rush order for more of that item often resulting in a glut at some location within the process. There was no effective way for anyone to see what was in the entire system at any given time. Only after a review of all paperwork from each specific work-area could the "low and high" times be discovered. Even then, it was often difficult to precisely account for inventory and lost efficiencies.

Management at Arrowplane sought out pilot projects that might be implemented to improve these processes. Projects that would provide closer connections to the suppliers were analyzed based on their potential to eliminate steps that were not directly adding value. The goal was to have engineers design a part and send that design via computer directly to the supplier who would finish the part and deliver it to the assembly area within Arrowplane at the moment it was required for assembly. The critical elements to accomplish this just-in-time concept included closer ties with suppliers, an overhaul of the Arrowplane information systems, and significant changes in management and control procedures within Arrowplane.

In deciding which area to implement a pilot system, there were some important limitations. A negotiated contract would have to be achieved with a supplier that would be at least five years in duration. It was believed that requirements on the supplier to provide material in a timely manner would incur additional costs and potentially limit services to other customers. That is, the chosen supplier would need to depend on a steady stream of work from Arrowplane over an extended period of time. With such a contract valid over a period of years, a supplier could agree to significant discounts to Arrowplane that could be passed directly on to Arrowplane's primary customers.

No supplier could make such an agreement if Arrowplane went to the open bidding system to determine suppliers. Because of this constraint no military or government suppliers could be used.[4] Composit Material, Inc., a critical Arrowplane supplier, had recently approached management about the possibility of implementing a just-in-time procedure. Composit had completed one such project successfully with another similarly sized aerospace manufacturer to Arrowplane and the company was eager to expand to their other customers (Exhibit 6.1 on Composit Materials).

Composit would be an excellent partner, but Arrowplane needed to develop in-house expertise in how to run this unprecedented integrated supplier partnership. "Dan Jones," of production operations and material information technology support at Arrowplane, had been involved with the standards settings of Electronic Data Interchange

EXHIBIT 6.1 AGILE SUPPLIERS: COMPOSIT MATERIALS, INC.

Composit Materials, Inc. has long been the primary provider for the aluminum sheeting that is needed in the construction of many types of aircraft. The Composit milling facility located in Northern America, takes raw materials and forms a multitude of alloys and composites. Material ordered from the milling facility is rough and sold in bulk orders. The minimum amount that can be ordered is around two tons.

In the late eighties and early nineties, Composit acknowledged that all of its customers were facing some critical problems. Customers were conveying to Composit their critical needs:

- reduce inventory and improve cash flow,
- reduce labor, equipment and handling costs,
- meet end customer quality requirements,
- reduce scrap costs, and
- improve part quality.

Primary contractors such as McDonnell Douglas, Martin Marietta, Northrop, and General Dynamics as well as secondary contractors such as LTV and Grumman were feeling the pressure of military downsizing. Each company was pressuring for substantial cost cutting measures.

In 1992, one of the above companies (here referred to as Company 2) reached an agreement with Composit Materials, Inc. to build a facility that would deliver materials using the just-in-time concept. The new Composit facility would be built from scratch and would not suffer from any potential Composit internal bureaucracy. Composit agreed to build this facility close to its new partner/customer which happened to be close to many of its other major customers. Company 2 agreed to long term contracts with Composit at fixed prices and would outsource many of its early manufacturing steps to the small unit, receiving goods directly to its assembly areas ready for immediate use.

The newly formed Composit Labs (CL), as it was named, was completed in late 1992. It currently functions as a profit center and as an independent business unit within Composit Materials, Inc. The facility has around 25 employees and handles about 400,000 lb. of material per year and growing. Over 50% of that is polished aluminum used throughout the aircraft industry.

Exhibit 6.1 (continued)

The small facility gets its material directly from the headquarters milling plant and provides a number of options to their customers:

- just-in-time delivery,
- exact quantity shipments,
- no mill minimums,
- cut-to-size product, and
- application of protective film maskants.

Composit's construction of this facility for aerospace contracts has paid off handsomely. The company has added well over 50-60 customers that only require very small quantities of material. These companies could not order directly from the mill as the minimum purchase quantity was much too expensive. Some other customers included several key US manufacturers and many small Asian companies.

Composit Labs is able to get raw material from the mill at near cost prices. They can store the material until it is required at no cost to them. They can cut and polish material to the exact specifications of their customers. They can combine multiple cuts on each sheet of material that may be used for two or three different customers, so that almost no material is wasted. They have a recycling center where all unused scrap material can be sent back to Composit's headquarters where it can be reused. The non-union employees at CL are specialists in packaging and shipping the fragile material. They are also certified in the inspections and quality checks that are required by government regulations as well by the companies themselves. They tag the material while on site at CL as quality inspected material and it is not reexamined by Arrowplane employees until it is used in the assembly area of the customer company.

Composit has increased its level of agility, at least at this facility, and is able to supply a number of customers with highly customized products in shorter time periods than previously possible. Their increased agility can in turn lead to the increased agility of their customer.

(EDI) for years. EDI had been developed primarily for general military / government requirements. The concept was easily extended to include the very specific and rigid requirements needed by the aerospace industry. Recognizing that this medium would eventually be critical for his company, Jones saw that key "aerospace specific" variables were included in the various codes of the EDI transaction sheets. Those additions were now complete and ready for commercial tests.

The decision on the new pilot project was made by Arrowplane to start with a high-grade polished aluminum sheeting, one of the components that Composit currently supplied to Arrowplane. This project would take advantage of the new capabilities offered by the Composit Labs. The plan was to implement a completely new procedure of designing, supplying, delivering, billing and accounting for over 130 parts of polished aluminum sheeting. A team was formed within Arrowplane that would see this project through implementation. The leader of the team was Jim Smith from the information / technology (IT) department with Dan Jones, the EDI expert, as assistant project manager. The IT department at Arrowplane had traditionally served as internal consultants within the company across functional boundaries and were most accustomed to working on reengineering new processes.

Team members were selected from each of the departments that were considered directly or even indirectly involved. Members included representatives of the manufacturing and industrial engineers as well as representatives from warehousing and inspecting. Some members of the team simply passed along the plans and designs to individuals in their respective departments. Others played active roles not only in implementing the project but in coming up with solutions that could significantly transform their own work areas and responsibilities. Two key areas were the Quality and Procurement Departments (where a critical change in culture was required) and Information Technology (where the initial project set-up was critical to long term success). This cross-functional teaming approach was novel, at this time, within Arrowplane.

THE AGILE PROJECT

Team members understood that efficiencies at Arrowplane must get better if the company was to remain competitive. The project was envisioned to be much more than a just-in-time program. The goal was to implement a reconfigurable system, easy to maintain and easy to revise when needed. In short, an agile system (Figure 6.3).

Highly polished aluminum sheeting was critical in the construction of the wing sections that were part of Arrowplane's responsibility in its subcontract agreement with a customer. The material had historically been sold directly to Arrowplane from the Composit mill, located in North America, to be stored and used at Arrowplane's facility in Key City when called for by a particular design requirement. As needed, the material would be drawn from the warehouse stacks and physically transported to the building where it would received its "first cut." Then it would be heated and formed slightly into the correct shape as specified by the design requirements. End pieces and other small pieces would often be considered scrap. The formed material would then undergo a super-high polish so precise that a fingerprint or a hairline scratch might make the entire piece worthless. Arrowplane personnel would carefully wrap the polished material to avoid damage. Since the material was usually being prepared for use in the future, it had to be transported back to a warehouse, stored and later withdrawn, and finally moved to the assembly area and re-inspected to insure that there was no damage from each of the "non-value added steps." The Arrowplane procedures were precise and most material would arrive ready for assembly. However, some would inevitably be damaged and sent off as scrap.

These procedures were highly regimented with built in safeguards. Duplicate forms tracked the material at every step of the process which allowed for a complete record of the various materials from placing orders with suppliers to moving finished products off the manufacturing floor. Manufacturing systems had to be linked with separate systems that handled purchase orders and invoicing. All of these steps, which had to be tracked, significantly added to the non-value added activities, slowed up the entire process, introduced multiple error points, and increased costs.

Over the years, this vertical integration had allowed Arrowplane to be virtually independent from its suppliers. However, by 1992/1993 the disadvantages of this system became clear. Arrowplane found these disadvantages by examining the inventory management and identifying all of the non-value added activities.

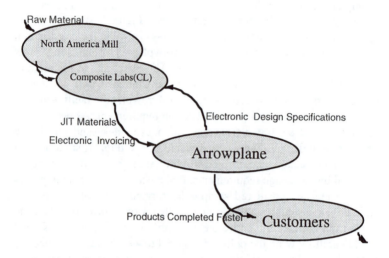

Figure 6.3. The Arrowplane-Composit Agile Supply Chain

The "agile" plan was to take full advantage of the JIT capabilities of Composit Labs (CL) and add the additional features of EDI specifically for the aerospace industry. Engineers were to complete designs at Arrowplane and send them directly to Composit via EDI transmissions. All transactions such as work orders, purchase orders, and invoicing would be electronically transmitted. Composit would complete the work and ship it to the needed production location at Arrowplane just-in-time. Composit inventory would appear in the Arrowplane computer system along with other material that was warehoused at Arrowplane. The partnership would be very close, making Arrowplane much more dependent on Composit for the timely receipt of goods as Composit would be dependent on Arrowplane for long-term materials purchases.

With this plan in mind, Arrowplane relayed their interest in the JIT capability of the new Composit facility and proposed an even closer link with this small Composit outfit located in Capital City. They discussed outsourcing each key step (draw, first cut, inspect, and package) as well as all quality and certification inspections. They convinced Composit of the advantages of using Arrowplane's EDI system. The Composit team in was eager to work with Arrowplane to try these new solutions. Negotiations began in the Spring of 1994 to implement this new project. Two members from Composit were added to the team within Arrowplane to work with them to accomplish this project.

IMPLEMENTATION

The technical work of the Arrowplane-Composit project was fully underway by March 1994. Smith and Jones planned a schedule that effectively completed the Arrowplane technical side by May 1994. The EDI system was implemented on IBM mainframe computers within Arrowplane. The most difficult problem encountered was interfacing with the various information systems that consisted of thousands of lines of code developed through 20 years of use at Arrowplane. However, Smith and his information team knew the system well and were able to make the required adjustments.

While this technical work was underway within Arrowplane, so was systems design at Composit; however, this program was more involved than the previous JIT programs. CL had to implement a new computer system which could handle the EDI data that would match the forms and values that Composit had traditionally evaluated as well as include items tracked by Arrowplane. This relatively small outfit in Capital City (less than 25 employees) is run essentially as a small business without access to large mainframes. However, a PC and a commercially available EDI translation package was all that was required at CL. The cost was less than $ 2,500 for the needed hardware and software. A computer programmer was hired part time to set up the system and customize it to meet all of Arrowplane's requirements. It took the programmer about six months working part time to complete the project.

Problems were encountered during the implementation of the pilot project requiring teams in Key City and Capital City to be flexible and responsive. For example, such a novel project required that all details be carefully specified such as 50 raw material codes and 132 finished parts that were to be delivered by Composit. Arrowplane had large amounts of legacy parts and unpolished materials left over from its old process worth over $ 1.5 million currently in its inventory. Arrowplane initially wanted Composit to purchase its material and then sell it back to Arrowplane as needed. Unfortunately, Composit Labs, which was run as an independent business unit, did not have the needed cash on hand to be able to purchase the material. An alternative solution had to be reached.

A compromise agreement was reached where Arrowplane would ship its inventoried material (only the skin quality parts relevant to the pilot) to Composit Labs, where it would be stored and used as needed. Arrowplane would still own the material, but eventually it would be used and Composit Labs could deliver new material.

A second early obstacle centered on personnel issues. The proposed JIT concept that reduced the 9 in-house Arrowplane steps down to 1 was fine in theory but it did not consider union issues. Over 50% of Arrowplane's employees were members of the Aerospace Workers Union and because of earlier downsizing the union members currently employed were older and senior workers.

Historically, unions in the U.S. aerospace industry unions built labor agreements based upon protecting the skills of its members. The unions helped insure that workers performing certain skills would be paid at certain negotiated amounts (almost always higher than their non-unionized peers). These amounts would increase based upon the development of an individual's skill as well as cost of living adjustments based upon time with the firm. In an environment where job duties were relatively stable, union contracts effectively insured workers of equity.

At Arrowplane each hourly job is narrowly defined and union members are categorized by skill which in turn specifies pay. These categories include skilled machinists who spend years learning how to do their jobs effectively and safely. Categories also include many lesser skilled jobs such as custodians, dock workers, and transport workers. Not surprisingly as salaries for the higher skilled laborers increased, the salaries for those lesser skilled laborers were successfully negotiated upwards as well. Today, individuals in these job classifications are often paid double and even triple the non-unionized wages for the same jobs.

Most critical to the implementation of the new Arrowplane process, Union job descriptions could not be adjusted much less eliminated without contract negotiations with union representatives. Therefore, the Arrowplane design team had no choice but to maintain many of the supply ordering and inventory steps of the old process, particularly the dock-to-stock jobs which were not up for renegotiations for three more years. The union contracts would under no circumstances allow outside suppliers to deliver items directly to the assembly area within Arrowplane sidestepping its internal transportation people.

The final process was amended such that items from Composit Labs would be sent to Arrowplane's receiving dock. There, they would be transported by Arrowplane personnel to the carousel receipt area. Upon carousel-issue orders they would be delivered to the stock bins. Incoming items from Composit would not be opened until needed in assembly. In this way paperwork would be virtually eliminated as the items would be maintained within a database at every step of the process. Anyone could check on the location and status of an item from the time the work order was electronically issued until it was in the stocking bins. Cycle times from material receipt to shearing (an assembly operation) would be reduced from 257 days to 37 days and work order time flow would be reduced from 15 days to 5.

PROBLEMS DURING IMPLEMENTATION

The technical issues with the Arrowplane-Composit project were completed in May 1994 on schedule and the Arrowplane design team began looking for optimum ways to measure progress and cost savings. There was the elimination of many redundant steps, despite the limitations imposed by the union, the elimination of inventory, and the elimination of the "cost of money."

Since the accounting systems at Arrowplane had not previously accounted for material or parts that were damaged or lost either in the warehouse or in any of the multiple steps along the process before the part was used, there could be no value assigned to such cost savings. In addition, the decrease in on-hand inventory due to the elimination of parts now supplied by Composit could not be measured. The pilot project affected only a minuscule portion of Arrowplane's inventory. No multiplier could be generated to demonstrate the effects on inventory costs if the pilot were expanded across additional suppliers. Finally, the cost of cash could not be effectively calculated. No accounting mechanisms had previously existed to track the value of a particular piece of inventory and calculated on interest paid on that inventory before it could be used and charged to the customer. This cost was assumed to be significant, but it could not be measured. So, early on the team knew that they might have difficulty demonstrating the dollar value success of the pilot project. But reductions in cycle time could be measured.

Another key delay for the pilot project was the negotiations between Arrowplane and Composit. The Arrowplane team had only anticipated two months to complete the process and it stretched to six months. However, Composit Lab's experience was that six months was consistent with their other large customers in JIT programs that did not even include the EDI implementations. The automatic invoicing and payment procedures required great attention to contract details. Arrowplane's procedures also required the approval of a long chain of senior management which added significant time to each step in the negotiations.

A key factor in the Arrowplane-Composit negotiations hang up was determining what to do with Arrowplane's on-hand inventory. As noted, it took some time for Arrowplane to concede that CL did not have sufficient cash to purchase its on-hand inventory. Later when the project got underway, accounting problems would add many unwelcome annoyances when pricing Arrowplane-owned and Composit-owned material at different levels as well as accounting for Arrowplane-owned material which was physically in another state. This seemingly insignificant problem added special code requirements and accounting procedures. But, a resolution was anticipated within one to two years when all of the Arrowplane-owned material would be used.

A key advantage of the new system would be Composit's ability to "look ahead" and see Arrowplane's production schedule and orders as they came through the system. This required Arrowplane to substantially update its forecasting capabilities. However, this feature would eventually be of great benefit to all suppliers as each could see items that relate to purchasing and scheduling of their own products. Both Arrowplane and Composit would be able to analyze accurate forecasts, a powerful and useful tool.

FIRST SHIPMENT AND OPERATIONS

The first work order was sent electronically to Composit Labs on September 29, 1994. There was a kick-off ceremony to congratulate the team on accomplishing their job. The first parts arrived as scheduled on October 6, 1994. A period of about six months was allotted to work out any bugs that developed. Dan Jones and Floyd Leeth, who was appointed as Arrowplane's JIT manager, handled monitoring of the ongoing project.

Since the electronic transmission of the first work order, the project has gone smoothly. However, there were a few significant problems which are important to discuss in order to understand lessons learned. One early problem occurred in December, 1994 when some parts of the highly polished skin material were ordered with a special protective maskant (a blue drag tape applied to specific edges of the metal. When workers "cut the bands," which were to signify a completed and inspected order from Composit, they discovered that the tape was missing. Arrowplane had been doing their own masking for years and still maintained that capability since it was needed for many projects. The parts were taken to the taping area, taped and sent back to the assembly area within a day. However, the implication was that if Arrowplane had completely outsourced this capability, they would have had to hold up production until the corrected order was received.

Fortunately, agreements had been reached during the set-up of this project on how to handle unforeseen glitches and problems. If a critical error was detected on the production line after delivery had been made, personnel from Arrowplane were to call Composit directly and inform them of the specific problem. Composit would then redo and re-submit the order within 24 hours. To be as responsive as possible, Composit would stop all other work orders to correct their mistake. The corrected order would be placed on a truck to Arrowplane before receiving the defective material back from Arrowplane. This would occur even before the source of the error had been identified. That is, whether the error was due to poor inspection from Composit or from inaccurate part numbers or design specifications from Arrowplane, the order would be corrected with highest priority. Of course, every effort is made to avoid such critical errors; but, such procedures demonstrates Composit's level of commitment in satisfying Arrowplane's requirements and concerns and in recognizing their own essential role in Arrowplane's manufacturing process.

A critical problem currently facing the Arrowplane-Composit collaboration reflects the level of agility within the supplier. While CL is quite agile and able to respond quickly to the changing needs of

Arrowplane while offering highly customized services, the center remains dependent on the larger Composit Materials only major milling facility. This facility is over 50 years old and has many processes that are slow and "out-of-date." Forecasters at the facility predicted a downturn in orders in 1995; however, the global market for the required materials has boomed beyond expectations. The entire aerospace industry is feeling the crunch of this increased demand in aluminum products.

Even the CL, a business unit of Composit Materials, has experienced difficulty in receiving shipments from headquarters. They have had to increase lead order times to six or more months as a result. Schedules are not being met throughout the aero industry. Accentuating this problem was the fall 1995 strike by some aerospace workers which may cause the Arrowplane facility to close certain portions of its manufacturing floor in early 1996. This example emphasizes that in the desire to move an industry toward agility, products can be delivered more quickly with specialized quality only if the entire supply chain meets equivalent levels of agility. In short, the level of agility that can be achieved in any industry depends on the ability of each partner in the collaborative process to meet its schedule and requirements. The agile chain is only as strong as its weakest component (Figure 6.3).

Other problems encountered in the pilot project are mostly associated with working the "bugs" out of the system. Arrowplane's Leeth spent significant time double checking work orders and seeing that flags pointed to possible errors such as mismatching part numbers, missing purchase orders, or incomplete dimension specifications. If a suspected problem was encountered, Leeth would call someone in the IT department at Arrowplane who would immediately add required code changes. Jones had monitored the progress of the project and posted transactions by hand for months after first shipment. This was the first "real-world" test of an EDI system in the aerospace industry. Early in project implementation, Jones spent significant time insuring the accuracy of each item. From six months through the end of year 1, he spent no more than a few minutes a day double checking all components.

Neither Leeth nor Jones expect that a future project implementation would require such close scrutiny. Both agreed that their efforts to double check the computer was more for their piece of

Exhibit 6.2. Daily Activities in the Arrowplane-Composit Skin Quality Project

"Floyd Leeth" was the first Arrowplane employee in charge of daily operations with the new EDI system. He had been with Arrowplane over 27 years and had worked for most of his career on the Manufacturing Floor as well as Planning and Procurement. He has maintained good working relationships in each of these areas. It was determined that this pilot project needed someone with Leeth's level of experience to quell fears within Arrowplane. He had the knowledge necessary to see the entire process.

Early on in the project, Leeth worked with Jones to help define variables required by the Arrowplane side of the process. He still is the primary contact concerning any questions over the 143 part numbers that are being delivered from Composit. If there are order changes, order mistakes, pricing changes, or any other issues that might arise, Leeth is the first point of contact. He has been trained and knows how to access any part of the JIT information system. In Leeth's case, it was especially important for him to feel comfortable with the EDI system and the special runs required for the pilot which were maintained on Arrowplane's manufacturing database.

—Case Specifics—

Items from 137 part numbers were selected for the initial pilot of the JIT skin quality project with a few added later. All information can be found on computer terminals which are linked to the mainframe computer in the Manufacturing Control System (MCS). The MCS is the company's database which tracks materials, schedules, and inventory. However, as most people at Arrowplane, including Floyd Leeth, report that they feel more comfortable with reports in a paper print-out, all open work orders may be printed in a summary sheet for review each morning. All of the information relating to skin quality material, which was used for the JIT pilot study, has the associated code *AJ*. Table E6-1 provides a sample of one of these daily reports.

Exhibit 6.2. (continued)

The first column designates the internal Arrowplane material code. If 80 appears as part of the first two digits then the item refers to the material that was first owned by Arrowplane and then transferred to the Composit Capital City site. A 77 in the first two digits identifies the item as being owned by Composit. Similar to many companies, Arrowplane works on a manufacturing day calendar, which consecutively numbers business working days and omits weekends and holidays. The Warehouse Unit Completion Date column shows the day that the work order was turned over to Composit defining their time allotted to work on the particular item. The end date (which is when the item is to be shipped out of Composit) is listed in the just-in-time column. The Unit Work Location column defines the current status of the work item. The 10381 means that the item has been shipped from Composit and invoiced, (there is generally a 2 day lag between the time the material is shipped from Composit until they send an invoice). The 10361 code means the work order has been received by CL but the invoice has not been sent. The 24612 code is a type of email indicator that means that the Arrowplane system has released the work order; however, the new computerized order has not been opened in Capital City.

In some cases at Arrowplane it is necessary for individuals in Planning to make a changes or for Production to release a new work order. Leeth must keep up with such changes, inform everyone involved, and insure that all changes are reflected in the schedules.

As can be seen in the report worksheet (Table E6-1), some of the JIT dates are after the current date. This problem occurs when Composit has a materials shortage and the mill is running behind. This forces Composit in Capital City to add 1 or 2 months lead time from the mill to get the material to the distant state where Composit Labs is located. This has created significant problems with attaining higher agility. Composit wanted to inventory items in yet another new regional facility; however, this facility was not ready. As a result, Composit and Arrowplane still have access to extra material at small (non-Composit) distributors to make up for any short term shortages from Composit's headquarters plant.

Table E6-1. Skin Quality Daily Report Summary

Material Code	Total Quantity	WHUCD[5]	JIT Date[6]	WorkOrder Serial #	Pric	Part #	U L[7]	Purchase Order #
775122265165	24.0	6637	6641	A03411	AJ	65B23607-017-018	10361	1480105
775122265223	30.0	6639	6631	Y92409	AJ	182T7112-001-002	10361	1480100
775122266551	12.0	6640	6628	Y88882	AJ	65B23610-001-002	10381	1480095
775171504936	12.0	6619	6589	Y51521	AJ	148N3113-005-500	10361	1480108
805122267265	12.0	6631	6623	Y85343	AJ	65B03293-003#02	10361	1480010
805174540957	12.0	6658	6650	A15871	AJ	186U1028-002-500	24612	1480020
805174540932	18.0	6643	6637	Y99490	AJ	186U1026-001-500	10381	1480036
805174663239	12.0	6655	6647	A09804	AJ	185N3004-001#02	10361	1480014
805174617524	25.0	6655	6648	A12132	AJ	65B02697-015-901	10361	1480024

mind that a real necessity. The new system did cause Leeth to learn additional computer skills and his discomfort with the system still had him printing out reports and checking paper instead of simply viewing the information on screen. These acquired skills have allowed him the option of moving into other areas in the company where his knowledge can be diffused to other functional areas and departments. Thus, the cost of training personnel for agility can be considered an investment that will pay off long after the initial project is implemented (Exhibit 6.2 on Daily Activities).

OBSERVATIONS

It is interesting to note how different individuals at Arrowplane reacted to the new EDI system with Composit. Initially, many employees, particularly those on the shop floor, did not believe that the program could work. They recognized the danger of having late shipments that could stop work at Arrowplane and prevent making production schedules. Also, if a part came in damaged a new part would have to be prepared and shipped and Arrowplane's production schedule would suffer.

As noted, in 1992, senior Composit management in Composit's headquarters made the decision to undertake a completely new approach and develop a new business unit. They isolated themselves and their associates from dealing with the day to day changes of this new JIT activity. The entire Composit Labs facility had been developed for JIT purposes. The innovation was the introduction of a new customer, Arrowplane, and its EDI system, which was readily accepted. No cultural shift or employee training was required. The small Composit Labs facility is unique within Composit. Most of the individuals were hired from the local area. There was no procedural history to overcome.

The Arrowplane Information group in Key City has worked diligently to accommodate the users of the JIT system, who range from managers to shop floor personnel. These users were generally unfamiliar with computers and are hesitant if not resistant to embrace them as part of their daily routines. One-on-one training was required to get these customers up to speed. The Arrowplane IT staff realized that the time required for technical training was minimal compared to the "hand holding" time required to make the users feel confident in themselves and with the new set of work tools. While the aerospace industry creates high tech products, their employees are often inexperienced in the latest technologies (Kivenko, 1995). In addition, most of the largest companies such as Arrowplane still maintain mainframe systems which are not user-friendly. In environments such as Arrowplane where layoffs were based upon seniority much of the familiarity with new technologies was lost with the most recently hired employees. In addition, the "older" and remaining workers were generally apprehensive concerning their often nebulous and undefined responsibilities with "computers."

Still, there was overall enthusiasm for the project from almost all involved. Downsizing at Arrowplane had created an environment where most felt overworked. Even though Arrowplane had fewer contracts, many employees were on overtime. Employees and managers realized that the current small workforce could not continue the same procedures that had been in place at the Key City site for 30 years. During this project's design and implementation few Arrowplane employees stated any fears of losing their jobs. Past layoffs had been based on seniority and all felt confident that sizable layoffs were a thing of the past. In an environment where few employees had less than 15 years with the company, one might expect the remaining individuals to be more resistant to change. However, the workforce felt a strong commitment to the continued success of the company and they wanted to affect changes that would benefit the company as a whole. Consequently, this project was easily sold to the individuals involved. They saw it as a way to help the company and, most importantly, it would alleviate some of their workload. Implementation of the project did not eliminate any jobs in quality, inspection, or procurement where the changes to procedures were most significant. However, it did have implications for these areas if the pilot project was successful and the basic concepts were expanded. The pilot EDI project was in this way ideal as a change agent: it was large enough to slightly reduce the work load, but small enough not to threaten existing jobs or immediately alter similar procedures with hundreds of other suppliers.

The enthusiasm in this project has been significant from all sources. Within Arrowplane and between Arrowplane and Composit, teamwork and cooperation are cited as most responsible for the project's initial success. The Information Team was especially recognized as critical to project implementation. Employees in manufacturing, procurement and quality felt that the Information Team was extremely responsive to their concerns and requirements. Most stated that their reservations about the EDI system were based on their fear of change, fear of using the new technology, or fear of leaving old "tried and true" procedures. Their overwhelming desire of Arrowplane employees was to recover and improve their overall production capabilities and to allow them to move ahead. Smith was able to effectively communicate the vision of how the new system could significantly improve the overall situation at Arrowplane while dispelling fears at the level of individual employees.

PROJECT RESULTS AND FUTURE

During 1995 there were celebrations and internal article write-ups within Arrowplane about the successful implementation of the pilot project and indeed some results were outstanding. The cycle time for this type of aluminum sheeting to move from the warehouse to its first cut was on average 257 days. This has been reduced to 20 days, of which only 1/4 of that time is the product on Arrowplane grounds. The 4-step process is paperless:

1. forecast,

2. work order,

3. status checks, and

4. product delivery and automatic invoicing.

Accounting difficulties have significantly impacted project results. Arrowplane's Accounting Department believes that the EDI project with Composit resulted in savings, but they cannot accurately determine Return on Investment.

In contrast, the substantial manpower hours and associated costs to implement the project are easily measured. It is believed that future projects will take less time and effort to implement and integrate. So, much of the front end cost of this project is transferable to other more comprehensive projects that are to follow. The implementation and system skills acquired and the programs developed by Arrowplane's Information Department can be used in other similar projects.

From the perspective of Arrowplane's implementation team, there is a feeling of a loss of momentum. The technical aspects were accomplished in only months, and they do not understand why the EDI project has not been expanded to other areas. They would like to see all machine tools supplied to the floor in a JIT manner. They believe that the only action required is the mandate of further action and the allocation of time and other resources to accomplish the task.

One primary reason for such delays is additional organizational changes during the pilot project. Arrowplane organizational charts have been altered significantly and people are concerned with coming up to speed on their newly assigned tasks.

Many strategic level decisions must be made before the future of the Arrowplane-Composit project is realized. For example, there is the question of whether Arrowplane will continue to store raw material. This task may be outsourced. Currently, 18% of material used within Arrowplane is in raw form. If these other raw materials were delivered JIT like the skin quality aluminum sheet, then Arrowplane could eliminate significant amounts of warehoused material. However, as discussed, union issues may render this option impractical.

Arrowplane has other JIT projects within its various facilities. In March 1995 Smith was transferred to another facility within the U.S. He noticed many projects that could be applied immediately to procedures at Arrowplane such as billing packages, further integration with suppliers, distribution of proposal information, and defining parts to be built.

CONCLUSIONS

In this Arrowplane-Composit case, it was difficult to specify numbers showing real and potential cost savings and of the EDI project. Nevertheless, the case descriptions demonstrate willingness on the part of both Arrowplane and Composit to try new solutions and find workable answers.

While no clear decision on the future of plant-wide implementation of agile initiatives may be apparent at Arrowplane; planning is underway to expand these concepts into the area of extrusions. Unlike the 140 isolated parts for the skin quality project, the conversion of extrusions to these agile concepts will require the manipulation and tracking of over 1500 parts which form the components in over 5000 separate part numbers. Consequently this problem, which is significantly more complex than the pilot EDI project, will require added dedication and enthusiasm.

Key Facilitators

Key facilitators to project success have also been identified in Table 6.2. The reason most cited for the success of the Arrowplane-Composit project was achieving "buy-in" by employees. Jim Smith invested significant time in discussing the project with key members as well as those that would play supporting roles in implementation of this new JIT-EDI system. He was also able to dispel fears. Mr. Smith and Mr. Jones actively sought suggestions from team members and those who would be related to or affected by the project. In this way he received a high degree of buy-in from individuals. An environment was created where no Arrowplane employee felt threatened by the new project, rather they envisioned the elimination of non-value added tasks and the simplification of the process as an effective way to improve business overall.

Table 6.2. Critical Facilitators to Midsized-Large Alliances To Apply to Other Agile Initiatives

• Obtain buy-in from employees within and outside the team
• Build cross-functional teams across departments
• Build high team enthusiasm
• Establish clear benefits to employees for project success: such as a better working environment and long term company success
• Start with a small, highly focused pilot
• Work for willingness to share information with key supplier
• Encourage supplier willingness to try new programs to improve customers operations

Critical Barriers

During the implementation of the Arrowplane-Composit project some critical barriers were identified which are generalizeable to the U.S.

aerospace industry, Table 6.3. Each barrier is considered an ongoing threat to the continued success of the project and future agile initiatives at Arrowplane.

Table 6.3. Critical Barriers to Midsized-Large Alliances To Apply to Other Agile Initiatives

• Inability to choose long-term partners due to government bidding requirements
• Inability to overcome Union concerns over job outsourcing
• Obstacles to updating existing and outdated information infrastructure
• Inability to overcome constraints of agility level of key suppliers

Lessons Learned

Logistically, Arrowplane's Primary Implementation Team believed that a disposition plan for existing inventory needed to be developed early in the design process. This became a stumbling block that held up the project. Consequently, the authority over all process decisions, including inventory, should be delegated to the team implementing the project. Delays due to time required to receive senior management approval were too extensive in the Arrowplane case. Also, a complete cost-benefit analysis should be conducted before system design and implementation. Because of difficulties in accounting for many of the costs at Arrowplane, the analysis question was avoided and the final review numbers looked less attractive than they might have been. It was learned that reviewers cannot avoid using and analyzing non-traditional accounting numbers. Numbers that were not significant or relevant to the strictly hierarchical, vertically integrated company, become of paramount importance to the agile company.

The Arrowplane IT team also soon recognized that quality requirements and responsibilities must be better defined earlier in the process. In the present case, these issues were dealt with over the course of the entire project because they were not fully appreciated in the front end as central issues. Quality requirements and responsibilities should be listed, carefully defined and then refined as the project unfolds. Finally, the process management team should design the "to be" process as fully as the existing processes are defined. The vague nature of the original Arrowplane process left many gaps to be filled in later. If future processes are better formulated and revisited at two week intervals throughout the implementation, it is believed that the project would flow more efficiently.

Finally, while no member of the Arrowplane team wished to eliminate unions, they all agreed that a new union-management partnership was needed. Indeed examples do exist of U.S. management working with unions to create an environment that can meet the challenges of agility. The adversarial nature between management and union must be reduced. Such concepts must transcend skill-level and seniority based authority and decision structures. Union members must be allowed to offer solutions that impact their own work environment. Such features are achieved through the careful definition of a central vision and mission for the company. To downsize by seniority was not the best solution to Arrowplane's situation; however, the nature and inflexibility of the union contracts made other alternatives extremely difficult.

Table 6.4 summarizes the key lessons learned in the pilot EDI project that will be essential to the successful completion of other such agile initiatives.

Table 6.4. Summary of Lessons Learned for Midsized-Large Alliances To Apply to Other Agile Initiatives

• Create disposition plan for inventoried items	• Complete cost-benefit analysis before initiation of project to better monitor success
• Allocate needed authority to implementation team, eliminate redundant approvals	• Completely define existing processes
• Define quality requirements	• Determine links to all other departments no matter how seemingly insignificant
• Define team members' responsibilities	• Include union members in team to insure best solutions and so that day-to-day problems can be planned early in the design process

NOTES

1. This case study was conducted with the approval of the organizations, yet the views presented are those of the author obtained through limited data collection sources (observation, interviews, 3rd party publicly available data) and should in no way be taken as representative of the entire organization. Therefore the names of the organizations have been altered.

2. Source: Public SEC Records. Data not available for 1992–1994.

3. Because of the vast amount of materials warehoused and accepted accounting procedures for inventory at that time, specific dollar amounts for damaged and lost material are not available, but estimated to be in the tens of millions of dollars.

4. The government bidding system which requires open bids each year would not allow suppliers sufficient time to recoup their investments in the new procedures or allow for such substantial discounts on their products. Ironically, Arrowplane was receiving mandates from the government to form closer ties with suppliers through just-in-time procedures and an overall conversion to Agile practices. Even though a key aspect of agility is the linkage with suppliers and the formation of "preferred supplier" lists, Arrowplane could only look to commercial suppliers as prospects in this agile experiment.

5. Warehouse Unit Completion Date: business day that item is to be ordered

6. Date that item is to be delivered from Composit to Arrowplane

7. Unit Location: Identifies where in the system the order currently resides

CHAPTER 7

Case 2: Thompson Enterprises and Bilmo Systems Incorporated[1]

COMPANY HISTORY

Thompson Enterprises is a privately held company located in the northeast corner of Key City, USA. Mr. Raymond Thompson founded the firm in 1973 which has 250 employees as of late 1995. The company produces thermoelectric A/C systems and assemblies. Approximately 60 employees have been added over the past 18 months as the company continues to expand. Revenue for 1994 was $12 million and was estimated at over $20 million for 1995.

CEO Thompson is continuously seeking to improve business. In the early 90s he pushed to have Thompson produce quality products which were comparable with any competitor regardless of size. His efforts led to Thompson winning the Baldridge Quality Award in 1992. Employees are encouraged to champion new ideas which will help the company meet its stated objectives. A key current objective is to decrease cycle time in the design and delivery of new products. This case study investigates Thompson's partnership with a local university consortium (UniSci) to design and implement such product.

CHANGING BUSINESS OPERATIONS TO MEET NEW CHALLENGES

For many years Thompson's key strategic product, a thermoelectric cooler, was primarily purchased by military customers. The cooler uses infrared detectors and is used to cool chips such as sensing devices on missiles like the Sidewinder. Recognizing the military market was shrinking, Thompson actively targeted commercial uses for its thermocooler. The component has been applied as cooling devices to such diverse products as motorcycles helmets and Igloo Picnic Boxes. With this dual-use strategy, Thompson was able to alter its dependence from 70% of company revenues in 1991 to less than 40% in 1994.

In addition to the shrinking military customer base, Thompson was also affected by rising expectations and demands of commercial customers to receive products in ever diminishing cycle times. The company did use a number of "standard" procedures, where employees worked within a specified design and production schedule. Thompson's commercial customers used the thermocooling devices as components in their own products which were in turn components for their customers' products. In short, the entire chain of suppliers had schedules that were driven by their most immediate customers as well as customers well down the supply chain. More and more the market is based upon last minute orders from large companies who demand nearly immediate response. Thompson recognized the need to restructure its product development procedures in order to make its delivery schedule as flexible and fast as possible while maintaining its high quality. Customers were now effectively setting delivery dates.

In Thompson (as in Arrowplane), there was no clear initiative for "agility." However, the company was motivated by many of the antecedents common to agility (Table 5.1). These attributes most important to Thompson were: bring products to market rapidly, produce individualized goods and services, develop ever changing models, raise customer-perceived value, extend customer relationships by adding value, and cooperate more with suppliers/customers, see Table 7.1. In short, the company was looking to become more agile.

DESCRIPTION OF THE PRODUCT

Thermocooler devices, the primary products of Thompson Enterprises, are semiconductor elements mounted on ceramic substrates. The complexity of each product varies with the number of semiconductor elements. Past product applications, particularly for military customers, called for up to 15 elements. Company designs and product development had been optimized for producing products of this complexity. Since 1993, the rapidly expanding sophisticated

Table 7.1. Critical Motivating Factors for Moving to Agility

• Decrease defense contracts and budgets	• Bringing products to market more quickly
• Fewer military clients, more commercial clients	• Increasing customer satisfaction
• Customers demanding shorter cycle times	• Increasing cooperation with suppliers / customers in order to provide customer higher valued products and services

commercial applications have required in some cases over 500 elements. This factor led Thompson to rethink techniques and procedures in every aspect of product development.

The importance of this company's quest for enhanced agility became more apparent to Thompson's leadership during various quality initiatives it undertook. Thompson committed a relatively large proportion of its resources to the development of these concepts.

The company is now producing as many as 12 new products a month. Customer requirements change so quickly that the company operates in a continual "rush" design schedule. As an added problem, the company experiences cyclical sales that are highly irregular and cannot be accurately predicted. The company needs to be capable of speeding and slowing production as each specific situation requires. Accordingly, a primary goal of Thompson has become cycle time reduction.

Thompson set the goal for reducing the overall cycle time from three months down to one week. Approximately 25%-50% of Thompson's product production processes can be automated and were targets for the first cycle reduction programs. The first step was to maximize automation performance by configuring and tooling machines. This process often took about three months. Thompson also worked on perfecting and customizing their in-house design of software. These two efforts reduced overall cycle time to 6 weeks. Additional changes in design tooling reduced design cycle time from 5 days to 4 hours.

These reductions were significant for the company, but overall cycle time reduction did not meet the one week goal. An analysis of operations revealed that the primary limiting factor was the speed in response from the suppliers. The process generally consisted of Thompson engineers creating designs on the CAD machines. These designs would be sent to draftsmen in the Layout department. There the photographic masks could be designed that define the diffusion patterns used to manufacture the specific chips. Some elements would require machine tooling which would be completed by specialty machine shops. Parts returning from these machine shops would be analyzed for errors. At least one error would be expected in the first pass. Typically errors are due to problems in design specifications or slight machining errors. The particular element would go through a redesign process eliminating the first round mistakes and a new part would return from the machine shop generally free from errors. If not, the redesign cycle would begin again.

Thompson's management believed that some of the changes successfully implemented internally now needed to be applied to its suppliers. This required the development of an agile design and implementation plan. Thompson looked to the local university/business consortium UniSci for technical assistance in this agile project. As result of this effort, many of Thompson's suppliers have changed significantly over the past two or three years. The company used a preferred supplier program that had been successful at Rockwell as a basis for creating a set of their own preferred suppliers. They began with a competitive supplier base of about 12 different shops which ultimately was reduced to three.

Given the highly industrialized nature of the Key City area there they are many local machine shops which can be utilized by Thompson Enterprises. However, since the company works in the aerospace and military electronics environment suppliers must meet high levels of tolerance, accuracy and reliability. Furthermore, Thompson needed suppliers willing to work with them on rapidly changing schedules and while meeting short turn-around times. They wanted suppliers with whom they could establish personal relationships and feel comfortable in placing a high level of dependence. One such company chosen was Bilmo Systems, Inc., located only a couple of miles from Thompson's manufacturing facility.

THE PREFERRED SUPPLIER

Bilmo was incorporated in February of 1983 as a machine shop capable of providing high quality, customized service to all of its many customers. The company was founded in true entrepreneurial spirit by two former engineers from a large electronics firm who currently serve as President and Vice President. They began making customized computer parts handling equipment for Apple Computer but soon understood that their true competitive advantage was in machining the customized parts themselves.

The company consists of less than 25 employees who are located in a small warehouse and who operate around 10 Computer Numerically Controlled (CNC) machines to produce customized products. Bilmo's primary customer is Thompson Enterprise who holds about 50 % of their contracts. Bilmo has been buoyed by Thompson's success and has seen sales double since 1992. Revenue from all projects has reached between one and two million dollars in 1995. Improvements, expansions, and reconfigurations are financed exclusively from profits. The founders feel strongly that they should avoid loans, fearing the increased financial risk. While the company does not have a formally written set of values, this core value is significant to Bilmo's mode of operations. The owners carefully scrutinize expenditures and are wary of purchasing new equipment or hiring new employees without clear and sufficient reasons. The owners remain fully aware of the estimations that there were many of the "1400 small machine tool shops that won't survive the next 5-10 years" (Merrifield, 1987, p. 28).

The company has made huge investments in the CNC machines which are not only expensive but relatively fragile (Exhibit 7.1). A poor machinist who makes a mistake during operations can irreparably damage a machine making it worthless. Other than the expensive tooling machines, the shop has a 386 type computer which is used in the front office primarily for tracking financial records. There is a second 386 on the shop floor that is used as a server for the CNC machines.

Bilmo's shop machinists have little computer experience or formalized drafting training. The shop machinists are non-union, but are highly skilled and experienced. The company has invested in the

EXHIBIT 7.1. NC MACHINING AND DESIGNING FOR SKILL ENHANCING TECHNOLOGY

Success of the small machine shop in the early 1900s used to depend primarily upon machinists' good planning and execution. Planning concerned the sequencing of machining operations and determining cutting parameters, such as depth of cut, feed and speed. The planning activity required some level of manual dexterity in setting up the machine tool and manipulating handwheels. With the introduction of automatic feeds and capstone lathes, planning became less important then execution and the two skills began to diverge. The development of Numerically Controlled (NC) machines first introduced in the late 1940s accelerated this trend towards separation of thinking and doing. Closed loop servo motors replaced handwheels as well as the autofeeds of the manual lathe. Professional programmers were required to determine the sequence of machining operations and cutting parameters. Thus, a physical separation occurred between the planners and the executors.

There is a critical fact in the machining process that makes this separation clearly impossible in some circumstances: "the machining process is not well defined or predictable" (Kidd, 1994, p. 312) It is up to the skill and experience of the machinist to cope with unforeseen problems and unpredicted disturbances. So, in practice NC machines had to have overrides and manual stop buttons that would allow a machining process to be halted. The strong belief by many managers, particularly in the 1950s that all problems could be overcome by "technology oriented" solutions contributed to an over dependence and then unwarranted disillusion with a promising technical solution.

Undaunted by what was seen as purely technical problems, new attempts were made to correct the situation. The problems with NC machines was that the machining information was in a form that only a machine could read. The proactive skill, knowledge, and experience of the expert had been designed out of the system. The introduction of the Computer Numerically Controlled (CNC) machines in the late 1970s allowed planning and execution to be recombined. In fact, Kidd (1994) cites a 1990 survey by 584 US manufacturing plants which found that programming costs of CNC machines are lower when people on the shop floor do the programming. They were designed to match the methods and

EXHIBIT 7.1 (continued)

thought process generally applied by machinists during actual machining operations. Now machinists could build upon their experience base but had to obtain the newly required skill of programming. Unfortunately, as reflected in the case at hand, if the programming requirements were excessively complex, few machine shops had machinists with the advanced programming skills. Special cases still went to programmers who generally did not have the experience base of the machinist.

The move to utilize the more recent CAD/CAM knowledge is reflected in the Thompson Case. New technologically derived advantages can be obtained from CAD/CAM integration. An effort was made in Europe in the 1980s to develop a skill and knowledge *enhancing* as opposed to *substituting* technology which facilitated the use of CAD/CAM. The workshop-oriented programs (WOP) provide a standardized programming environment for skilled people familiar with the machining process. However, in some cases the systems have been found too inflexible. The "user-friendly" interfaces have restricted freedom of action causing frustration and a bad image of the WOP system. This is part of the problem in the Thompson case. The system, in an effort to make it easy to use and generalizable, can be slow or tedious to program, particularly in complex or repetitive geometries.

Kidd (1994) claims that the problem can be overcome by designing to make skills and knowledge more productive rather than focusing on technical functionality and seeking to replace people's skills and knowledge. He offers three techniques that might help: 1) techniques developed should bear resemblance to people's existing skills, 2) system should not introduce artificial technical barriers to cooperation, communication and team working, and 3) the system should provide organizational flexibility so that the organization, working practices and job designs are not over constrained by the technology. Furthermore he supports the implementation of multiple methods where possible. This is the same conclusion UniSci scientists reached at Thompson with the NC Polaris program as well as the "souped-up" parametric type solution (an excel spreadsheet).

EXHIBIT 7.1 (continued)

This introduces the idea of designing for skill and knowledge enhancing technologies. Kidd (1994) offers three design oriented paradigms. The first is technology oriented design paradigm. It is the one most implemented in new technology situations, that is, primary concerns are with the technology itself and its functionality. This fundamentally the viewpoint held by Thompson personnel, implement the new technology, make it work, produce more parts. The second design approach is the human factors design paradigm. This strategy is based upon automating only those tasks that are not technically too difficult or expensive to automate. This is the approach taken by consulting scientists from a local university. Realizing that there were technical limitations that they could not quickly overcome, they focused on improving the ease of the system use and operation. A third design approach is the skill oriented design paradigm where the overall system is designed jointly using organization, psychological, technical and financial considerations together. This more agile concept promotes the development of technology that allows people skills to become more effective and productive. People's skill and knowledge can evolve with new tools that support them.

An interesting perspective on the changing effects of technology and progress in machine tools can be seen in Figure E7.1. Kidd claims that successful design must include the allowance for control and feedback. It would seem that the best design would be one that would still allow machinists to select the tools to use, depths of cut, feeds and speeds, etc. while operating the machine. It would allow them to use discretionary skills (Hazelhurst, Bradbury et al., 1969) to provide the opportunity to change actions in light of operating experience or results occurring within the process. A more advanced form of high level control and feedback is the open system concept. This term concerning manufacturing with system architecture was developed based on the International Standards Organization Open Systems Interconnection model (Kidd, 1994). Such a system is designed to be extremely responsive and adaptive. If applied to the machine tool case more options might be available that might provide a superior design. For example, a system could be designed to provide a type of interactive programming. The computer would allow for the machinist

EXHIBIT 7.1 (continued)

to enter parameters via the keyboard and have the computer estimate the consequences of these chosen parameters and make suggestions. In such systems machinists could do experimentation selecting some of the computers suggestions on perhaps feed and cut depth while choosing the speed independently. The consequences of this action would be seen immediately and changes could be affected if deemed necessary.

On all sides (Thompson, Bilmo, and the local university), it was hoped that once implemented the new process would allow the machinist to do other tasks and be more productive at their area of expertise. However, the effects of using the primarily technical design approach resulted in a de-skilling of the machinists, fragmentation of their previous work and additional loss of control over the process. The desirable "agile" attributes of individual skill, knowledge and judgment were designed out of the system without the possibility of alternatives. General principles that might propel movement to this design philosophy is to try to develop computer systems that are in some way related to people's existing skills or allow these skills to evolve; design systems as learning systems allowing room for individual work strategies and preferences; design systems that provide passive monitoring that can call attention to illegal or potentially damaging actions (Kidd, 1994).

These are difficult concepts to envision based upon years of the experiential knowledge in the Taylor methods. Separating decision-making and planning from the actual execution of the work as well as techniques of automating to eliminate skill is an engrained philosophy that is hard to see past. The potentially agile idea is to reject the concept of human-machine comparability (i.e. developing machine to perform the tasks of humans) and embrace the idea of human-machine complementarity (Jordan, 1963). Dozens of companies can attest to the fact that the pure technical solution created in the void of its impact upon the human factors will fail to live up to its ideal potential (many citations on technical failings.)

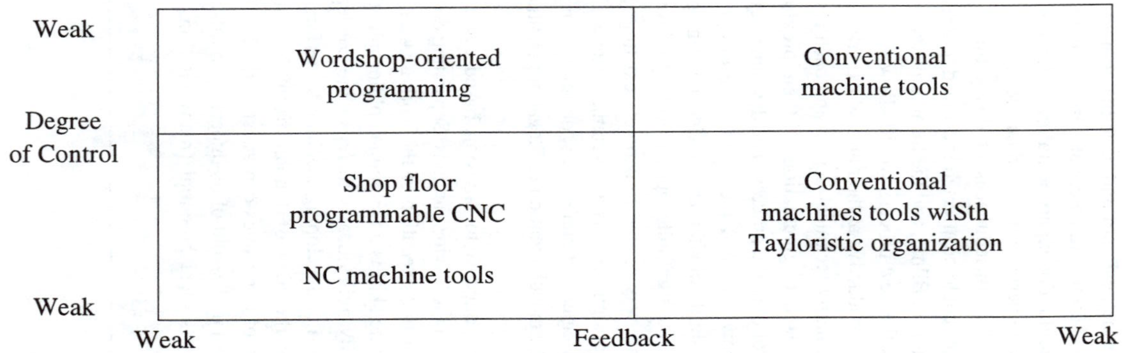

	Feedback	
Weak	Wordshop-oriented programming	Conventional machine tools
	Shop floor programmable CNC	
	NC machine tools	
Degree of Control		Conventional machines tools wiSth Tayloristic organization
Weak	Weak	Weak

Figure E7.1. Control/feedback matrix

Source: Agile Manufacturing: Forging New Frontiers, Kidd (1994), p. 320

Autocad Program, but it is rarely required for their operations. There are no funds dedicated for training machinists to work more with their computer systems as it has not been considered a necessity to date, nor have the machinists shown interest in developing these skills.

There is a high turnover rate of junior machinists which is consistent in this industry, but senior machinists are quite loyal to the company; however, only one machinist has been with the company since its inception. Employees are all expected to perform multiple tasks. Each employee can complete virtually any operation required in machining parts or operate any of the unique CNC machine. It is not infrequent that the two owners are on the shop floor along with the machinists working to insure the timely delivery of services.

The CNC machines which are the heart of the machine tooling shop can perform wide variety of operations such as cut, mill, drill, press, etc., but they require experienced people to operate them safely and effectively. Tolerances requested by customers are often specified to the millionth of an inch. The experienced machinists know that even with the proper setting on the machine a wide variety of deviations can occur when performing the operation. Some sources of error include: blade thickness, blade sharpness, machine vibrations at a multitude of operating speeds, and environmental conditions.

The machinists are experienced in reading the designs of the draftspeople and sufficiently compensating for these errors. Their experience tells them precisely when tolerances can be pushed to the limit and when they must rigidly comply. The quality of products a machine shop can produce is generally tied directly to the experience level of its machinists. Often the most critical aspect of high quality tooling is the order in which CNC functions are performed. The machinist determines the tooling sequence, whether to cut first, or to drill, or mill. Many feel that that the key knowledge and the true value added by the machine shop is often in this tooling sequence. The machine shop's ability to control these critical factors and produce high quality products are directly correlated to the experience of its machinists. The best machine shops can accurately tool blocks of metal in hours instead of days.

THE IDEAL SOLUTION

Thompson came up with ideas that would significantly reduce cycle time using a win-win strategy (Figure 7.1). Ideally, Thompson engineers would be able to complete computerized CAD drawings of new parts which would then be sent electronically to layout and then to Bilmo where machinists would receive the necessary design data on diskettes. Machinists would quickly use new programs, which were to be created by the UniSci experts, and which would greatly enhance and facilitate the NC code generation process. These programs would generate their own set of programs in the Autolisp format which runs under Autocad, the primary electronic drafting software package. The programs would be capable of automatically analyzing drawings and making complex geometric interpretations that generally required human programmers. With this process in place, more parts could be tooled in a shorter amount of time than had ever been possible. The increased efficiency at Bilmo would enable them to complete parts at lower costs while maintaining profitability and Thompson would be able to supply its customers with new products in record time.

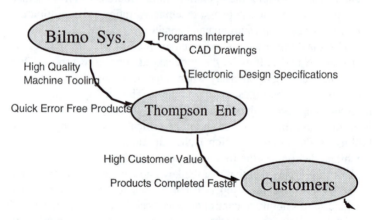

Figure 7.1. The Thompson-Bilmo Agile Supply Chain

Bilmo Systems had been sold on the concept based upon their continued desire to be a "team player" and a continued preferred supplier with Thompson. Also, they saw potential to apply the technology to other customers which could favorably impact their business. For Bilmo this was an opportunity to gain access to newer technology customized for their use. Quite applicable to this case, Roe (1993) asserts, "small manufacturer's rarely know what technology will create a flexible manufacturing environment, where or how to access [that] newer technology, or how to integrate automated systems with existing conventional processes." This was an opportunity for Bilmo to try these new concepts with virtually no up front expenditures.

Both sides were aware of the success Thompson engineers had achieved to date on the automation of their own processes, transferring drawings electronically through the key steps and onto the production floor. UniSci scientists were eager to apply these technology concepts within a small supplier which would have great implications for the thousands of small suppliers around the country.

However, in spite of the agreement, Bilmo management and machinists (and others within Thompson and UniSci) remained skeptical that such a system could actually function in a real machine shop environment. Bilmo was concerned about the integrity of its CNC machines. Potentially, code could be sent directly from Thompson to the machines within Bilmo. The machinists would have little to no interaction with the process. A key danger was that if coded NC instructions were sent directly to the CNC machines, then critical errors could damage the machines irreparably. For example, if the machine was loaded with a drill bit and a faulty instruction was received to mill or cut a piece, it would break the bit, ruin the part, and most likely damage the sensitive equipment which would be costly to repair or replace. Thompson reassured Bilmo personnel that this was an impossible event and that code would not be sent automatically into the machines. Only Bilmo personnel would load the software and could check it before application. This allayed immediate fears but skepticism remained.

IMPLEMENTATION

While the project was initiated in September of 1994, work began in earnest in early 1995. The university scientists looked into commercial packages that would help them in their task. They settled on NC Polaris, a program well known in the industry that had a well developed NC code generator which was key to the project. Autocad, Autolisp,

NC Polaris are all complex pieces of software which require extensive experience to operate effectively. They are far from intuitive. Since the machinists at Bilmo had virtually no computer skills, the university scientists added handy features to the program to customize it for Thompson and Bilmo users.

The university engineers continued to work diligently to make the programs as user friendly as possible. They added new routines for the Polaris program to access enabling it to interpret the drawings and geometries that were critical to Thompson's products. They added variable elements with the same names that the machinists and the owners had been accustomed to using. Also, realizing that the programs were to be executed on the 386 machine at Bilmo, care was taken to make the program as efficient as possible so that it would run quickly.

One central problem was identified early. There were some key difficulties encountered in manipulating Polaris to accomplish all of the tasks required. The problem was not that Polaris was a bad program, there were simply no software packages available on the market that addressed the unique needs of the small supplier shop. NC Polaris was targeted for customers who had to machine extremely complex parts with complex geometries and curvilinear shapes. The parts that Thompson designs are considered $2^1/2$ dimensional, Figure 7.2. That is, there are no surfaces which are not orthogonal. Many cuts and drill hole locations are very repetitive. One part might have 100 notches on one side and each notch has to be precisely placed; however no notches have slopes dependent on some complex exponential formula. Another similar problem was getting the program to leave some control in the tooling process in the hands of the machinists. For example, Polaris has standard milling operations for drilling pockets. This feature had to be customized so that the operator could maintain tool offset control. This meant that the operator needed to be able to turn a knob by hand in order to get the desired offset without shutting down the whole process by turning the machine off and on. See Exhibit 7.2 for the team's attempt to identify these problem areas and provide some solutions to the company that produces NC Polaris.

EXHIBIT 7.2. THE SUPPLIER'S SUPPLIER

The university scientists (UniSci) have been dedicated to supporting small manufacturing businesses in the Key City area for many years. One such project was to meet the challenges and difficulties of customizing the NC Polaris program to suit the needs and uses of small machine shops. During this customization they realized that they had learned valuable lessons that might improve the Polaris program overall. Polaris is a supplier and a potential supplier of software for thousands of small machine shops around the country. The program was written so that machine shops had to set up manufacturing procedures around the program instead of the program helping the way the machine shop actually operated. The team decided to approach the Polaris company, which was located in the Key City area. With such a potential market, it seemed likely that the company might be interested in the accomplishments of the university team.

However, Polaris was very clear on their intentions and interest. From a market standpoint they saw no advantage to having application specific code. The company explained to the university team that it makes profits not from the base software but rather on the post processors. For example, each CNC machine has its own programming environment. Codes and geometric movements are standard across machines for most basic motions, then each machine has its own separate syntax. Thus, the company's target market are machine shops and industrial plants that have many brands of CNC machines at the same location. The more the variety of brands like Bridgeport Mill, GMF, and Allan Bradley that the shop has internally, the more post processors the company sells. Best of all, Polaris only has to pay one time for the development costs of these post processors. They can then sell the same post processing translation software over and over for one to two thousand dollars apiece—an optimum business situation.

Even through the agile framework boasts of the benefits of closer supplier relationships, this is an exclusively commodity-based relationship. From Polaris' viewpoint there was no interest or perceived mutual benefit from establishing or maintaining closer relationships with customers. The company was not seeking to expand its potential customer base. *In short, it might be inferred that for companies to move toward the agile ideals of virtual partnerships, there must be a dependence or a clear incentive. for all stakeholders*

The principle hurdle of adding the programming requirements to accomplish the job with the Polaris software were essentially completed within six months. However, even with the added user-friendly items, the program still had the look of a tool that could only be operated by computer draftsmen experts with significant programming experience. Unfortunately, the programmer that worked for Bilmo left the company just as this new system was about to be implemented. The company, again hesitant to make unwise or hasty hiring decisions, decided that the vice president/owner could work the 386 computer for anything that was needed. He was a mechanical engineer by training and capable of learning the required interface.

However, the problem of the Polaris program being too complex for moderate to simple operations hindered the process. Before the university's assistance on the new program, data was calculated in a simple back of the envelope method that had been sufficient for years. The operators knew the parts very well and they knew which geometric design numbers were relevant to their requirements. The Polaris program had many variables still suited to generic tasks. This meant that it actually took minutes longer to enter the data in the new Polaris interface program than by the old method. In one anecdote on the situation, machinists and owners finding it difficult to express their anxieties or concerns with the course of the changes, would focus on problems with the word "process". UniSci technicians liked to use the term to explain how the new techniques would operate. Experts have long recognized the problems with well-intentioned attempts at exchange of views while innocently using unfamiliar "jargon." This has often been found to be not only unintelligible to the recipients, but brought to the surface hostile feelings (Newman, 1978). Adding this to the fact that the machinists did not particularly want to change the way things had been done and that they saw no clear benefit to them for using the new system, it became clear that the new system was failing.

Once the scientists at UniSci realized what was happening, they took it as a personal challenge to put something in place that the machinists and the owners would want to use. The back of the envelope calculations that Bilmo had been using had been automated slightly by the owners into a simple Excel spreadsheet. The spreadsheet crunched the numbers and the machinists wrote the relatively simple NC programs as input to the machines. The Excel formulas required were

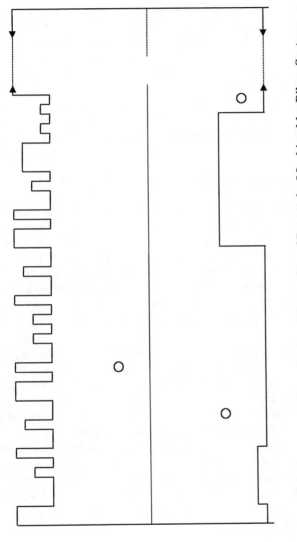

Figure 7.2. Simulated Cross Section Illustration of Part to be Machined by Bilmo Systems.
(Magnified Left Edge)

fairly basic and although the process was somewhat tedious, it was easy to do and familiar. The UniSci team decided to make this Excel spreadsheet more automated, a little more general and easy to use.

In relatively little time, they succeeded in accomplishing this parametric form of a solution. However, much of the functionality and the flexibility afforded by the more general purpose Polaris program was lost. New formulas would have to be added for any significant product changes which defeated the purpose of having a seamless flow of electrical data between software packages producing completed NC code. The work might help Bilmo in the short term (although complaints existed that it was still not intuitive enough for the machinists), but it did not effectively meet the objectives that were initially envisioned.

SUCCESS ON ONE KEY PRODUCT

The description of the Thompson-Bilmo alliance, to this point, might suggest that the project was a technical failure. Actually, the project succeeded technically. It could certainly be argued that work was needed to make the programs more user-friendly or more intuitive. Or, it could be argued that Bilmo needed to spend time to train its machinists with increased computer skills, or hire a "computer jockey" that could make the best use of the new system. However, it was other factors that had not been considered important up front that have been the major barriers to the project's success.

Once the NC Polaris code adjustments were made and the programming links between systems were accomplished, a full prototype test was required. The Bilmo owners worked with the UniSci team to make the prototype work. All of the necessary data—the "process knowledge"—was entered into the Polaris program concerning all details that were significant to that part (e.g. machine vibrations, optimal order of operations, and tolerance information). The prototype tests of this process worked flawlessly. There was great excitement by Thompson who saw that its goal of reducing cycle times to one week could become a reality lowering the cost of producing products. However, Bilmo saw a different set of results and they were not happy with the outcome.

IMPLICATIONS OF SUCCESS AND ATTENDANT PROBLEMS

The particular part used in the prototype had been designed by Thompson and tooled by Bilmo for some time. The Bilmo machinists involved knew the part's idiosyncrasies. Significant process knowledge was included in the automation programming process which entailed the human experience details concerning tool order, vibrations at certain machine RPMs, the optimum blade thickness, and other details that comprised the value-added information that Bilmo was able to provide through its services. It had taken months of tooling runs to gather this information and now it was neatly included in the Polaris program. On the positive side, once this process knowledge was entered into the program, there was little likelihood that errors could cause damage to the machines. But, despite these technical successes other behavioral issues have virtual stopped the process.

The completed code package was independent of any CNC machine and operator. Technically, there would be nothing stopping Thompson from deciding that another supplier could deliver the part more cheaply. Thompson could give that supplier the completed process program and that shop could produce the same quality parts that Bilmo had been providing. Even worse for Bilmo, Thompson could buy a couple of CNC machines and tool the needed products internally.

Thompson attempted to convince the shop that these fears were unfounded. They had no interest in entering the machine tooling business. They would allow Bilmo to keep the programs for their internal use only. The complete process knowledge codes would not leave the shop.

Not helping the situation was Thompson's reluctance to guarantee CNC machines against damage. There is an obvious danger that Bilmo could just say that the machines were damaged while running a Thompson part. It would be difficult to prove that the damage was caused by the program and not by an operator mistake while working on another part for another Bilmo customer. Also, Thompson was reluctant to say that it will only use Bilmo as a supplier. It could be an expensive and potentially disastrous business decision to lock its future in with a tiny supplier company.

In addition to these problems, there was the glossed over reality that the machinists were no longer as valuable once the programming process was completed. Once their expert knowledge was added to the program, they were finished with their traditional tasks. Thompson realized this up front and assured Bilmo machinists that they would still be needed, however, their duties would be changing. Admittedly, there are a multitude of parts that would have to be programmed in the same painstaking way as with the prototype. But, once these specifications were entered, the machinists' key roles would be diminished. It would also negatively impact any apprentice situations. Machinists would be needed to do more drafting tasks and more computer work. Yet, when new products came in that needed serious redesign, they would still require experienced machinists to gain the proper process knowledge in order to place that knowledge into another set of programs.

Ultimately, there is one central problem that has not been addressed with the Thompson-Bilmo alliance. There is an absence of a mandate for change from Bilmo's perspective. There is no clear benefit or penalty for Bilmo to completely change its method of operations. A complete cost analysis was not taken before the project began which would have provided metrics to determine if Bilmo could complete more parts in less time for less money. Also, it was hoped that Bilmo could use this system for customers other than Thompson. The impact of these factors has not been measured, nor is anyone clear on how to measure such factors. Now that the project is complete the true savings in time is somewhat disputed. Due to the technical difficulties, it seems unlikely that Bilmo could use the system for other customers. Other customer's products seem even less likely to be automated. Bilmo is a small shop that is not eager to spend resources tracking items of questionable usefulness, such as ratings, defects, output per hour, and time spent per part.

Bilmo is a small shop that finances itself from profits. If business profits are unwisely spent on business expenses, then there is a direct loss of personal income. There is already a narrow profit margin for the firm along with significant competition for fairly undifferentiated services. In such a small firm, the cost of change is a large percentage of operations. The case for that change must be very strong. The unwise hiring of one employee could cause severe financial stress. Likewise, eliminating experienced employees could have serious repercussions for the company's future health.

Overall, the Bilmo owners have a deep rooted business belief that the company should be trusted to do the job right in the allocated time period. There is unwillingness to forsake the "good 'ol boy network" of getting things done. This viewpoint is not necessarily negative. Change is disruptive and can be seriously detrimental to organizations and should not be undertaken lightly. Both sides must make a serious case for change so that the end result can clearly be envisioned and will improve everyone's situation. Benefits to one side are not just cause to force the other side to "fall in line."

BILMO OPTIONS

The Thompson-Bilmo alliance is currently at a standstill. Many issues must be resolved before effective solutions can be found. Some potential solutions to the problems will be suggested to demonstrate variety of options still available to Thompson and Bilmo.

Bilmo has serious reservations about automating any more parts which means imparting valuable process knowledge. Even if they were willing to input process knowledge into the programs, there are still the problems of the programs not being easy enough to use. Choices remain, however, each has drawbacks and negative implications.

Option #1

The machinists can be retrained for new duties. By all accounts the Polaris program is difficult even for design professionals. According to the UniSci technicians, training for engineers to truly understand the Polaris program would take at least two weeks of in depth training starting with a basic background in CAD systems. That would entail significant expense to a small company if the machinists were anywhere near that level of training, which they are not. As mentioned by one interviewee regarding the machinists, "they generally don't recognize drawings when they are just flipped." This is not their area of expertise nor is Bilmo prepared to significantly retrain their personnel. Regardless of these difficulties, UniSci technicians do believe that the Bilmo machinists can be retrained sufficiently with about 40-60 hours of intense training including using the packages in real work exercises.

Option #2

Fire the current machinists and hire back new individuals which have both skills. This could solve these problems, no training required and no resistance to the new programs. However, Bilmo is a very small family operated shop. It is certain that machinists with such multiple skills would cost more to employ than current employees, but fewer should be needed. At the personal level, senior machinists have been with the company for several years. One had been employed since Bilmo's founding. The owners feel a commitment to the machinists and are not willing to violate that trust. Furthermore, the owners are still not entirely convinced that the new programs will always function as promised. If things failed, they would be left with good computer whizzes who would not have sufficient experience in machining to understand the nuances of premium tooling. Understandable, Bilmo is reluctant to give up their premium asset, the know-how that the machinists have obtained over years of on the job training. Certainly, Bilmo's competitive advantage is its trained machinist. This loss of in-house expertise would seem to make this a poor option.

Option #3

Another alternative is to hire the "computer jockey" that would handle all of the computer related issues as they arose. This is probably the least disruptive solution. However, it is not clear that the person could increase efficiency sufficiently to completely justify the "low-tech" solution that the machinists now complete. This individual would certainly cut into some work of the machinists, but it might not be enough to justify a full time person.

THOMPSON OPTIONS

Thompson also has some options that it might utilize to resolve the situation. The company could take some action to help in areas of greatest complexity. In any event, Thompson must guarantee the integrity of the programs that contain process knowledge. Clearly, a company cannot relinquish its key core competency to a customer or supplier regardless of current mutual good spirit. A new component of Bilmo's service will become a software product. This can be guaranteed and perhaps licensed as needed by Bilmo who would maintain complete legal control.

Option #1

Thompson could guarantee the CNC machines. Some method might be found to insure Thompson that it was the automated program and not a machinist's error that created a critical failure. Since Thompson has confidence in the programs, Thompson might guarantee machine replacement costs with little fear that they would ever have to fulfill such an obligation. This might provide Bilmo some piece of mind and increase the level of trust between the companies.

Option #2

Thompson conducts training. Even if a computer person is hired that person would need training to become familiar with Thompson's systems. Thompson has successfully implemented many internal training programs. Currently employees receive 80-100 hours per years of technical training. This is high for any company; national averages range at around 40 hours (Amos, Gibson et al., 1996). Thompson might offer basic computer training to some of Bilmo's machinists. Or they might provide CAD training to help machinists better interpret computer drawings. Special arrangements might be required where Thompson assists Bilmo in obtaining better computer equipment; or a Thompson draftsman/programming expert might work part time at Bilmo completing the required computer tasks.

CONCLUSIONS

The funds for the pilot program were exhausted in the fall of 1995. Further work by all parties is required if the ultimate goal is to be reached. Perhaps, this is a case where it is not in the mutual benefit of both companies to maintain such a close knit partnership. Perhaps, Thompson needs a different supplier who is ready to meet the demands that they feel required to make. Or perhaps, to reach a the envisioned ideal of the "virtual partnership" which is touted for the agile environment, Thompson needs to clearly tie its success to Bilmo and Bilmo needs to ties its success to Thompson.

Key Facilitators

A few items were considered critical in facilitating the success of the project (Table 7.2). One key was the technical expertise that was provided to the project by the UniSci. Thompson did not have the time or resources to implement such a project within any supplier. Bilmo did not have the technical skill required. Both companies were impressed with the level of technical expertise and dedication that the UniSci technicians brought to the project. They were not only technically proficient, but they felt like this was an important project that might have implications on similar small machine shops around the country. They felt a strong personal stake in the success of the project and have stated disappointment and frustration at the final outcome. They believe that with a little more work the project could be a complete success.

The dedication to improvement by Thompson led to the trail of this energetic plan. Other larger company members of UniSci had from the outset strong suspicions that the project was impossible. But, Thompson wanted to push the limit of its boundaries. Internal draftsmen and computer programmers had completed successful projects with similar technical constraints. Their experience contributed greatly to the conviction within Thompson's management that the extension of these projects to suppliers was desirable and attainable a true test of Agility precepts. However, due to the project being managed as an outsourcing arrangement, perhaps these experienced personnel were not included enough to offer outside solutions to various technical problems.

One key issue facilitated early buy-in but actually became a barrier at the end of the project. At the outset all members felt confident that the project could work as touted. There was buy in from all sides. Unfortunately, Thompson was able to successfully sell the idea to Bilmo based upon assumptions that did not work out as anticipated. The Bilmo owners were at first eager when they believed that this new process would allow them to provide enhanced services to their other customers. When this became unlikely, their "buy in" was lost.

Critical Barriers

The Thompson-Bilmo project had a number of critical barriers that upon review could have been significantly diminished or even eliminated (Table 7.3). They can be generalized to other similar cases.

A central barrier was that no clear mandate for change was

Table 7.2. Summary of Thompson/Bilmo Project Facilitators

• Outside technical expertise from UniSci, a technical research consortium ($30K for all UniSci programs)
• Personal enthusiasm by UniSci technicians who were motivated by the greater implications of the project
• Thompson's own internal successful pilot projects
• Supplier willingness to try new programs to improve customers operations
• Moderate team enthusiasm, early buy in
• History of good relations, trust

established. Thompson had been working in an environment of continuous change for years and perhaps did not realize the dedicated effort that would be required to encourage change in an outside company. Bilmo had been successfully delivering quality parts to Thompson for years and did not see clear and sufficient reason for changing their methods of operations especially if that change might mean less power and profitability in the short run. Despite funding from UniSci, change would require additional expenses. Bilmo would be expected to produce more units for Thompson and the units were expected to cost less than before. It was not clear that revenues from the lower costing units would be made up in sales of higher quantities.

Linked to the problem of no change mandate was the lack of significant communication especially relative to behavioral and management concerns between the parties both before and during the project's implementation. While, the project was reviewed periodically in brief meetings in which technical status reports were presented, the underlying difficulties arising from the non-technical aspects were never uncovered and addressed sufficiently. This limited form of communication over time undermined established trust. Neither side wanted to be the first to take a risky position of placing an inordinate amount of dependence on the other. Each side remained unclear and wary of the motivations of the other.

Despite the hype, these were no clear measurable benefits of success in this project. Quantifiable measurements were extremely difficult for such trade off issues as whether to hire a computer "jockey" or extensively train in house machinists, whether Thompson or Bilmo should incur the risk of CNC machine loss, or how much did lack of communication of hidden motivations hinder project success. The desire to speed the project did not allow time for baseline measurements on time spent per part, defects per part and other potential measures. There was little willingness from either side to allocate resources in this way. Indeed, the measurements themselves might have had little meaning. For example, a cost-benefit analysis is hardly possible when there are so many unknowns and contingencies, such as how much faster can the parts be produced, how much will this save Thompson, and how much will this save Bilmo over time. These questions are important, but were not available for comparison to end results. This leads to a generalizable recommendation for obtaining some benchmarking positions at the start of any such project, even though the costs of these benchmarks might be significant.

In the Thompson-Bilmo case the central concerns were power in terms of control, personnel, and competitive competency. The larger partner with more power in the relationship could dominate the other. The actual desires and problems seen within the small firm might not be voiced. There is a danger of the smaller firm simply going along to please its powerful partner in hopes of maintaining a preferred supplier status. If Bilmo relinquished its competitive competency, there would likely be a power shift after system installation. Steps must be taken to consider and resolve each issue up front.

The technical as opposed to the behavioral difficulties also proved to be a significant factor in this project. While it was proven to the nay-sayers that the project could be technically successful, the level of technical sophistication required for general application was more than anticipated. Further advances need to be made in CAD to CNC machine communication. There are still networking difficulties and program glitches that require expert attention. Most importantly, the level of computer programming sophistication required by the programs involved is nearly out of reach for small suppliers.

In some cases such as this, problems arise that cannot be solved completely by the parties involved. As a potential source of the technical solutions, the Polaris software company was not interested in the particular situation as it was not directly relevant to their business. This vendor could potentially have significant impact on agile partnerships down the chain to Bilmo and then to Thompson. It might be inferred that when there is no relationship with a commodity supplier (Polaris) it could impact the agility and effectiveness of the entire agile supplier chain (Bilmo, Thompson, and Thompson's customers).

The economic realities of the small "mom and pop" supplier might be another unavoidable critical barrier to such a project. This certainly applies to other agile implementation projects that create close ties to very small supplier companies. No company can afford to make many mistakes in expenditures. However, simply a slow return on investment in a very small firm might force it into financial failure before the benefits can be seen. Options of training, hiring new employees, purchasing new equipment are more critically examined at a personal level by private owners of a small business. They do not necessarily look at whether to buy copy machine A versus copy machine B, they might be looking at whether to buy copy machine A for the business versus some type of personal purchase. Business and personal motivations become inseparably intertwined. This must be understood by any companies who wish to partner with such firms.

Table 7.3. Summary of Critical Barriers to Midsized-Small Company Alliances

• Lack of clear mandate for change for all participants	• Technical solution more involved than anticipated
• Ambiguous benefits of success	• Behavioral issues shortchange power levels of companies
• Non-technical issues not addressed adequately	• Economic limitations of small business
• Failure to maintain sufficient communication	• Constrained by Agility level and involvement of all suppliers

Lessons Learned

This project has important implications for agile initiatives as well as other business initiatives attempting similar partnerships (Table 7.4). This project was technically ambitious and in many respects could be considered a limited technical success. It was the lack of understanding of and consideration for the non-technical issues that has put the project at a standstill.

There is a clear need to create a strong sense of vision of where the project is going. This project had implications on the way everyday business tasks were performed. That implies that there must be a significant mandate for change that must be clearly defined for all parties. This change plan must be continuously revisited and amended as required. There needs to be buy in from all sides on how to resolve problems and differences. There also must be an ease of interactive communication where candid discussions and disagreements are encouraged.

It would be helpful to measure progress, remaining mindful that over measurement can hinder activities. At the project level, this project would have been better served with a more detailed schedule. Scheduled milestones would have tangible results and options for follow-on work would be considered up front. Scheduled items would not only consist of technical milestones, but milestones for skill creation, product familiarity, discussions of work environment impact and other such non-technical issues. Also, interviews revealed that perhaps more should have been made of Thompson draftsmen that completed Thompson's early in-house cycle time reductions. These resident experts were used up front but did not maintain strong communication over the course of project implementation. They were needed to closely monitor and suggest solutions to lesson the impact of ongoing problems that were being identified.

It must be realized that the high tech solution might not be the best solution for any given situation. The agile paradigm, which advocates highly sophisticated infrastructures, might in some cases be better served with low-tech solutions. Training is often key to maintaining highly skilled employees but cost considerations make this option difficult especially for smaller firms. Cost effective training options and alternatives need to be explored.

Two most important lessons were the importance of maintaining trust and noting how Agile procedures considered ideal in the abstract may in fact alter power/dependence relations between firms. Both sides needed to feel confident that the other could and would maintain a committed relationship. With the increasing dependence on one another, there needed to be a clear understanding of roles and responsibilities. Bilmo needs to maintain its ownership and control of its processes (its competitive advantage), and Thompson needs the internal flexibility to easily alter its production and design schedule as required. A win-win situation needed to be identified that all could agree upon and work towards.

Table 7.4. Summary of Lessons Learned for Midsized-Small Alliances To Apply to Other Agile Initiatives

• Need to create sense of buy-in from all participants which is monitored throughout the project	• Complete cost-benefit analysis before initiation of project to better monitor success
• Better define team member's responsibilities	• Do not assume that high tech solution is necessarily best
• Make use of non-management level employees on team	• Need to set clear boundaries of responsibility and work on ways to create trust and share risk

NOTE

1. This case study was conducted with the approval of the organizations named, yet the views presented are those of the author obtained through limited data collection sources (observation, interviews, 3rd party data) and should in no way be taken as representative of the entire organization.

CHAPTER 8

Agility and the Global Aerospace Industry

The aerospace industry has undergone dramatic transformations over the past decade. This chapter summarizes the current climate of the industry and addresses the unique factors within the aerospace industry that have propelled these changes. The chapter also points out why the concept of agile manufacturing is increasingly embraced by industry members as the business paradigm of the future.[1]

GLOBAL AEROSPACE INDUSTRY

US defense budget cuts following the end of the cold war coupled with the recessionary forces of the 1980s and its impact on commercial airlines' profitability adversely affected the growth of the aerospace industry. Aerospace firms were basically unprepared to respond to these significant challenges. It is estimated that over 150,000 jobs were lost in the US as a direct result of these industry changes. The downsizing or "rightsizing" that occurred during this period has not been restricted to the United States: the United Kingdom lost almost 50,000 aerospace jobs between 1989 and 1992 and France reduced its aerospace labor force to just over 100,000. According to most estimates, the industry as a whole suffered a 30% over-capacity in the early 1990s (Hayward, 1994 p. 1; *Flight*, 2/8/92:32 & 2/9/92:51).

The United States continues to dominate the global aerospace arena, commanding 60% of the world market. Europe, (mostly France, Germany and the UK) has captured a third of this market, while Canada, Japan and a few other countries in South America and Asia together make up the rest. The former USSR aerospace industry is now concentrated in Russia and Ukraine but is, at present, only a marginal player, especially in the commercial airplane arena. Seventeen of the 30 largest aerospace firms are US.

Internationalization of the aerospace industry is continuing at an ever increasing rate as many governments across the world view a vibrant domestic aerospace industry as a source of national prestige, national security and a key to future economic prosperity. Accordingly, these governments are aggressively pursuing the growth of their respective aerospace industries through increased R&D spending, subsidies and participation in collaborative and joint venture strategies. In the US the federal government has always played an influential but indirect role in the development and operation of the aerospace industry. Increased global competition has led some to call for the adoption of an interventionist trade strategy in order to protect US industrial pre-eminence (Senate Committee on Government Operations, 1992). Others call for increased R&D investments and for NASA to shift more of its focus to subsonic transport research and development (Senate Committee on Government Operations, 1992; General Accounting Office, 1993; Vadas, 1995).

The buzz-words in today's aerospace industry are rationalization, standardization, inter-operability, flexibility, burden-sharing, and co-operative defense programs. Joint ventures are becoming increasingly prevalent to increase market access and promote cross fertilization of technology. These ideas form a partial set of tools that might be used by companies who seek to become agile. Agility is an umbrella concept that, if adopted fully by industry, would allow it to anticipate and adjust quickly to changing circumstances and increased global competition. Agile companies are theoretically able to quickly assemble technology, employees and management in ways not possible with traditional hierarchical and mass production structures.

ECONOMICS OF THE AEROSPACE MARKET

The US aerospace industry is precariously perched between fortune and failure. In the US, firms in this industry often seem to be at the mercy of election results. They are constantly betting on designs that will satisfy the latest politically-inspired requirements and are slaves to time schedules. The market is a blend of the limited oligopoly of sellers including such key aerospace firms as Boeing, McDonnell Douglas and Lockheed and monopsonistic buyers such as the Air Force, the Navy and the few major commercial airlines. In this market price often plays a relatively minor role in acquisition decisions which are instead driven more by performance considerations, maintainability and most importantly, on-time delivery.

Entry to the market is restricted by enormous capital and R&D outlays. Market structure is far from the free-market model and all attempts to regulate it into such a structural framework have met with failure and unintended consequences. This structure which is peculiar to the aerospace industry will significantly impact the implementation of agile practices in ways yet to be fully investigated and understood.

DEFENSE AND COMMERCIAL MARKETS

In the United States no great distinction is made between the defense and commercial aerospace industries as the same firms cater to both segments of the market (William Perry, statement to Congress, Senate Committee on Government Operations, 1992). The defense sector is an integral part of the aerospace industry in the US as a majority of the US aerospace prime contractors are heavily dependent on defense contracts for their bottom-line. With the exception of Rockwell, UTC, Boeing and GE, all US aerospace prime contractors sell more than half of their output to the government (Hayward, 1994; Pint and Schmidt, 1994).

A Rand Corporation study of the financial condition of US military aircraft prime contractors established a correlation between the size, profitability, level of debt, R&D spending and dependence on defense contracts. The study stated that while sales of all firms fell over some period in the last five years, those firms least dependent on government sales were generally the most profitable (Pint, 1994). In the R&D area, those firms most heavily dependent on defense contracts slashed their budgets because of the demise of fixed-price development contracts. Fixed price development contracts had also led to defense contractors accruing major losses in the 1980s.

Considerable literature is available on defense acquisition management which is basically a form of cost-based regulation (Rogerson, 1994). One of the key issues here is whether existing rules create appropriate incentives for continued innovation. One of the latest works in this field, *Breaking the Mold* (National Research Council,

1993), strongly advocates a change in the process of defense acquisition and manufacturing to preserve the innovative function.

Another paper on defense acquisition policy, *Competition in Defense* (Pilling, 1989), states that aerospace companies are unlikely to be responsive to R&D needs if dual sourcing takes away their ability to make an acceptable rate of return on their investment.

The DoD's new acquisition strategy anticipates small product runs and to remain profitable, defense contractors will need to adopt flexible and agile manufacturing systems so that they can move quickly from making weapons to making commercial products.

SUBCONTRACTORS

The aerospace industry has a pyramidal structure with a very wide base. At the top of the pecking order are the few prime contractors, systems integrators and engine makers followed by more discrete systems and equipment firms. At the base there are thousands of medium and small suppliers commonly referred to as subcontractors. It should be noted here that sometimes prime contractors subcontract out to each other and are often referred to as subcontractors. However, most of the subcontractors in the industry are small operations, many with less than 250 employees (Bluestone, Jordan et al., 1981).

Airplane parts suppliers and subcontractors have also been adversely affected by defense cuts. At tiers lower than prime contractor, more and more firms are leaving the defense market. Many are making long term decisions not to return because of the associated high cost (Statement of James A. Blackwell to Congress, (Senate Committee on Banking Finance and Urban Affairs, 1989). A US Air Force Report titled *Lifeline Adrift* indicated that over 15,000 suppliers left the defense aerospace business between 1982 and 1987. Unfortunately, the supplier base has not experienced any resurgence in recent years. Several factors contribute to this phenomenon:

- decreased progress payment rates
- technical rights issues
- increased shares of business costs made unrecoverable
- unreasonable profit ceilings
- excessive auditing in the procurement process

In a prepared testimony before Congress in 1992, Mr. J. Michael Farren, under-secretary of International Trade Administration underscored the fact that the base of suppliers in the commercial aerospace sector had been reduced, but not from decreasing sales volumes (Statement of Michael Farren to Congress, Senate Committee on Government Operations, 1992). In this sector the reduction was brought on by a demand for greater efficiency. For example, over the last decade the supplier base for Boeing and McDonnell Douglas shrunk from over 11,000 to 4,000 subcontractors.

Other key impediments directly impact the operations and ultimately the success of aerospace firms. Collectively, these impediments tend to act as significant barriers to entry for subcontractors and suppliers to the aerospace industry. In fact, it is rare for new firms to enter this industry with its unique operating environmental constraints. Some of these barriers include (Gansler, 1982):

1. *Marketing problems* The oligopolistic-monopsonistic structure of the market makes it difficult for new entrants to break through.

2. *Inelastic demand* The demand is basically fixed either by government's requirements or by major airlines' requirements, and reductions in price are unlikely to increase quantities demanded.

3. *"Brand loyalty"* Contractors who do not demonstrate some level of prior experience are frequently disallowed from the bidding process.

4. *Demand for higher performance* Technical characteristics are usually the most important selection criteria, and new suppliers frequently are unable to prove their products' qualifications.

5. *Need for significant scientific and engineering capability* Because of the very high ratio of R&D to production, the engineering and scientific staffs must be larger than in a commercial firm of comparable size.

6. *Existence of expensive specialized equipment* For the small competing firms, technological advances exacerbate the

problem of the cost of acquiring the latest equipment and machinery

7. *Need for capital* Subcontractors and parts suppliers have found it very difficult to obtain adequate amounts of financing due to the views of the investment community.

8. *Market environment* Shrinking markets, low volumes and low initial profits make entry to this business extremely unattractive.

9. *Necessity of "buying in" at the beginning of the program* Small companies with good ideas are usually bought out by firms with greater financial clout.

10. *Probability that a project will not remain sole source throughout its life* Subcontractors that often make large investments in the development phase are frequently replaced, especially in defense contracts and therefore do not have much assurance of getting the contract for the high volume full production run.

Over half the aerospace defense dollars are spent on the lower tiers of the industry, yet the government has often failed to recognize differences in structure, conduct and performance between the business done with the subcontractors and parts suppliers and that done with the large prime contractors. More damaging is the government assumption that the lower tiers are taken care of by the prime contractors. As defense and airline acquisition budgets have been cut, the primes contractors have tended to vary their make/buy ratios counter-cyclically in order to stabilize their own employment at the expense of their vendors (Bluestone, 1981). Survival of subcontractors is thus precarious and based upon these firms' ownership and unique ability over a product or process.

POLICY-MAKERS' CONCERNS

The status and health of the domestic aerospace industry has been increasingly impacted by outside sources. For example, European subsidies towards sustaining the presence of Airbus has steadily increased its share of the commercial airplane market. Such events have resulted in considerable concern and debate among US policy-makers. The aerospace industry had been a beacon in an era of declining US industrial competitiveness throughout the early 80s, contributing a positive $20-30 billion to the balance of trade figures every year. Losing pre-eminence in this industry is a terrifying prospect to US legislators. Aerospace is not a low-technology industry that the US inevitably has to relinquish in the face of lower off-shore labor cost. It is precisely the kind of high-tech industry that is supposed to lead the resurgence in US economic competitiveness.

Unfortunately, the decline in the number of US aerospace subcontractors and parts suppliers has largely gone unnoticed. Much of the import penetration in the aerospace industry has occurred at the lower tiers, in components and sub-assemblies, where the penetration rates are reaching 20%. Increasingly, parts and subsystems are being sourced from foreign suppliers. The ITA estimates that the percentage of foreign products installed in the Boeing 777 will be close to 30% compared with the approximately 2% for the 727 and 15% for the 767.

Three factors contributing to the internationalization of subcontracting work in aerospace are:

1. prime contractors are generally manufacturing less in-house,

2. improved communication and transportation links allow widely dispersed companies to make competitive bids and,

3. international politics and finance, mainly offset agreements whereby customers make their aircraft purchase contingent on manufacturing or servicing agreements and foreign governments' subsidies for their domestic aerospace industry.

Concerns over the possible loss of competitiveness in the US aerospace industry led law-makers to table the Aeronautical Technology Consortium Act of 1993 which would place nearly $10 billion of Federal aerospace R&D funds under a single roof. These funds are currently spread across a multitude of programs and agencies, and, as claimed by an increasing number of critics, these expenditures are not effectively doing the job. A central feature of the proposed legislation introduced by Senator Danforth (R-Missouri) is that the bill would enable aerospace firms to work together in a consortium to develop joint approaches to a variety of technological challenges that lie ahead. This consortium is to be closely modeled after SEMATECH. If successful, the bill would mandate an aircraft technology coordinating process, the effort to be led by the Office of Science and

Technology Policy with additional input from the Department of Transportation, the Department of Defense, NASA, and the Department of Commerce.

CONCLUDING REMARKS

Although the aerospace industry is currently witnessing a significant downturn, the long range prospects of the industry can be considered excellent. The long term demand for large transport aircraft over the next 20 years is forecasted to be in the region of 13,000 airplanes, which is twice the number that US companies have supplied over the last 20 years. However, with this increasing market comes increasing competition, most currently, in the form of Airbus. The majority of these airplanes will be sold in foreign markets, particularly in the fast-growing economies of Asia. There will be even greater competition in the supplier markets as companies scramble to gain market access in these countries.

In this environment US companies must focus on an improved export strategy involving more direct exports and more participation in international business alliances. Further investment must also be made to enhance product capabilities, reduce research and production costs and shorten the time between product development and delivery, all essential elements of agility (Vadas, 1995).

On an encouraging note, Congress is beginning to recognize some of the out-of-date legal constraints that have been impeding the industry. More and more lawmakers are becoming amenable to a change in the legal structure to encompass intellectual property rights, anti-trust issues, product-liability laws and procurement processes.

The combination of constraints and barriers imposed upon aerospace firms make the application of the practices of agility especially difficult. Interpretations of agility to date have primarily focused on firms operating in open markets with easily interchangeable suppliers and a large customer base. Clearly, this industry requires special considerations and adjustments before agility can be implemented fully.

NOTE

1. This chapter utilizes material from a white paper developed by the Agile Aerospace Manufacturing Research Center team in 1995 by Sunil Tankha, Jeff Amos, and David Gibson (1995).

CHAPTER 9

Creating a Measure of Agility

A key difficulty with the study of agility is that it encompasses a cross section of traditional business topics such as management, marketing, accounting, and information systems along with lesser defined yet critical aspects such as flexibility, teaming, trust, and interpersonal communication. The antecedent variables in the proposed model are theorized to be interrelated and that some factor or overarching concept is present that ties them together. This concept is agility. Many authors have called for measures of agility (Vasilash, 1993; Burgess, 1994; Groover, Meixell et al., 1995; Kumar and Motwani, 1995; Booth, 1996). However, to date, no way has been found to quantify a measurement that may allow the comparison of one firm's "agility" to another. Only anecdotal information has been presented to possibly explain the differences in agility levels.

In this chapter the author attempts to use the method of Data Envelopment Analysis (DEA) to suggest a possible quantifiable measure of agility. The analytical DEA method was first presented by Edwardo Rhodes as part of his dissertation in 1978 (Rhodes, 1978). The method relates individual company performance to a piecewise linear production frontier which is an empirically estimated production function based upon multiple inputs and outputs of each company in a selected sample. The present research uses the publicly reported financial data of companies in the U.S. aerospace industry as well as a number of international aerospace companies.

This chapter has been organized to accomplish several purposes. First, present a background on DEA and its theory development. In addition, descriptions of models and computer techniques utilized in the analysis will be presented. Data was acquired from domestic and international aerospace companies (as determined by SIC code). Implications of the results and the potential of this method to serve as an effective measure of agility is presented in the final section along with future directions required for a more comprehensive analysis of agility in the aerospace industry.

BACKGROUND ON DATA ENVELOP ANALYSIS (DEA)[1]

Data Envelop Analysis can find its deepest roots in an article entitled "The Measurement of Productive Efficiency" by M. J. Farrell (1957) in which he presented an optimization method of mathematical programming. He developed a single-input/single output technical-efficiency measure in his research. Key developments were not made however until the dissertation research conducted by Edwardo Rhodes at Carnegie Mellon University under the direction of W. W. Cooper. In 1978 based upon this research, Charnes, Cooper, and Rhodes developed a multiple-output/multiple-input form of the Farrell model. They constructed a single "virtual" output to a single "virtual" input relative efficiency measure. They were able to effectively link the estimation of technical efficiency and production frontiers.

Rhodes' project began with a study which required the estimation of the relative "technical efficiency" of public schools where multiple outputs and inputs were used and where traditional analysis data such as price was not relevant. The goal of this 1978 study was to develop a new Management Science tool for technical-efficiency analysis of public-sector decision-making units which were termed DMUs. The non-profit entities that were analyzed were essentially a resource allocation type of problem in which the DEA solution technique was developed by the application of standard Operations Research / Management Sciences methodologies in heuristics and optimization.

The general goal of data analysis is to extract useful information from a population of observations. Traditional single-optimization statistical approaches focus on the averages and estimation of parameters. Using a sample to estimate a population parameter is one of the most common forms of statistical inference. There exist multiple tools in statistical estimation analysis which are better suited for different problems. For example, the sample mean is a particularly good estimator for the population mean. In addition, the parametric approach is used to optimize on individual observations with an objective of optimizing a single regression plane through the data. Results from non-parametric (mathematical-programming) DEA techniques suggest that it is best suited to the analysis of individual observations as represented by one optimization for each observation. The DEA method optimizes on each individual observation with an objective of calculating a discrete piecewise frontier determined by the set of Pareto-efficient DMUs. Both methods (parametric and non-parametric) use all information contained in the data; however, in parametric analysis, the single optimized regression equation is assumed to apply to each DMU. DEA, in contrast, optimizes the performance measure of each DMU. This allows an understanding of a each single DMU as opposed to an average DMU that doesn't really exist.

A potential problem of parametric solution methods is that the solution must be tied to a specific functional form. That is, there must exist a regression equation or a particular production function which relates independent variables to dependent variables. Also, specific assumptions about the distribution of error terms must be applied, such as whether error terms are independently distributed or identically normally distributed.

DEA has the advantage that no assumptions are required on the functional form. The technique is able to find the maximal performance measure for each DMU relative to all DMUs in the observed population. All DMUs are defined to lie on or below an extremal frontier. The DEA analysis produces a piecewise empirical extremal production surface which is interpreted as the "revealed" best practice production frontier. This frontier defines the maximum output empirically obtainable from any DMU in the observed population based upon its inputs. All of the DMUs utilize different amounts of a single input to product various amounts of a single output. It must be noted that these efficiency measures are only relative to all other DMUs included in the analysis. This does not allow for extrapolation of DMUs not originally included in the analysis as is possible in typical parametric analysis.

The straightforward DEA method utilized in this research calculates the relative technical efficiency of decision making units (DMUs) (aerospace companies this case). The calculation is made by the formation of a ratio of weighted sum of outputs to weighted sum of inputs. The weights are multipliers for both inputs and outputs. These weights are selected subject to a constraint that no DMU can have a relative efficiency score greater than unity. No specific knowledge of a priori weights for inputs or outputs are required.

The extremal frontier that results from the analysis can be used to identify the DMUs that are "efficient" (i.e. lying on the frontier) vs the "inefficient" (lying below the frontier). Sources and levels of inefficiencies for each of the inputs and outputs can be found for each inefficient DMUs in the sample population. Efficient firms will utilize the same level of inputs as inefficient firms yet sustain higher levels of outputs. Comparison to other inefficient DMUs can lead to the determination of the level of inefficiency. Calculations of potential improvements can be made by requiring solutions to satisfy inequality constraints that can increase some outputs (or decrease some inputs) without worsening the other inputs or outputs. These calculations are indicative of potential improvements obtainable which is based upon the revealed best-practice performance or "comparable" DMUs located on the efficient frontier.

Charnes and Cooper (1994) describe three key features of the DEA method which make it of importance to operations analysts, management scientists, and industrial engineers:

1. characterization of each DMU by a single summary relative-efficiency score,

2. DMU-specific projections for improvements based on observable referent revealed best-practice DMUs, and

3. obviation by DEA of the alternative and indirect approach of specifying abstract statistical models and making inferences based on residual and parameter coefficient analysis.

The long term effects of the original 1978 study and the presentation of the Charnes, Cooper, and Rhodes (CCR) model has been to open a plethora of research in which this technique has been applied to wide ranging problems. According to Seiford (1994) over 472 articles have been published with topics relating to data envelop analysis between 1978 and 1992. There is an enormous range of applications in a wide range of contexts, such as education (public schools and universities), health care (hospitals, clinics, physicians), banking, armed forces (recruiting, aircraft maintenance), auditing, sports, market research, mining, agriculture, siting and spatial studies, organizational effectiveness, and benchmarking.

MATHEMATICAL FORMULATION OF THE MODEL USED

The purpose of this portion of research was to see if DEA could be applied to financial data of the aerospace industry and determine a measure of agility.

In the research in this section there existed a specific number, n, of domestic companies and international companies. The number, n, was simply determined by the data that was available from the internationally recognized COMPUSTAT or GLOBAL VANTAGE databases. The specific companies and data used in the analysis are presented in the following section.

There are four basic models of DEA: the CCR ratio model developed in 1978, the BCC model (1984), the Multiplicative models (1983), and the Additive model (1985). Each models seeks to establish which subsets of n DMUs determine parts of an envelopment surface. The BCC model was chosen for this research as it distinguishes between technical and scale inefficiencies. The model estimates pure technical efficiency at the given scale of operations and identifies whether increasing, decreasing or constant returns to scale possibilities are present.

Each of n companies correspond to the Decision Making Units (DMU). Using the terminology developed by Charnes et al (1994), each company is perceived to consume varying amounts of m different inputs and s different outputs. A matrix of $(m \times n)$ inputs, $\mathbf{X}$, can be formed such that $\mathbf{X}_j = \{x_{ij}\}$, $x_{ij} > 0$ where $j = 1,...,n$)and $(i = 1,...,m)$. Similarly, the output matrix, $(s \times n)$, can be formulated such that $\mathbf{Y}_j = \{y_{rj}\}$, $Y_{rj} > 0$ where $(j = 1,...,n)$ and here and $(r = 1,...,s)$. These inputs and outputs are generally taken as constants and based upon the observations.

The geometry of the envelopment surface which characterizes efficiency and identifies inefficiencies is prescribed by the specific DEA model employed. To be efficient, a point P_j corresponding to Company j must lie on this surface. Companies that do not lie on the surface are termed inefficient, and the DEA analysis identifies the sources and amounts of inefficiency providing a summary measure of relative efficiency.

The linear equations for the input oriented BCC Primal are given below. Primal refers to the *envelopment form* as opposed to an alternative form for the BCC model which is termed "Dual" and provides the *multiplier form*. Only the Primal form was used in the current research.

Input Oriented BCC Primal (BCC$_P$ - I)

$$\min_{\theta, \lambda, s^+, s^-} z_0 = \theta - \varepsilon \overline{1} \bullet s^+ - \varepsilon \overline{1} \bullet s^- \qquad \text{4.1}$$

s.t.
$$\mathbf{Y}\lambda - s^+ = \mathbf{Y}_0 \qquad \text{4.2}$$

$$\theta \mathbf{X}_0 - \mathbf{X}\lambda - s^- = 0 \qquad \text{4.3}$$

$$\lambda, s^+, s^- \geq 0 \qquad \text{4.4}$$

$$\overline{1}\lambda \geq 1 \qquad \text{4.5}$$

As detailed by Charnes et al (1994), the scalar variable θ is the proportional reduction applied to all inputs of the current company (DMU) under evaluation. This reduction is to determine an improved efficiency and is applied simultaneously to all inputs and results in a radial movement toward the envelopment surface. There is also a non-Archimedean (infinitesimal) constant ε that effectively allows the minimization over θ to preempt the optimization involving the slacks (s^+ and s^-). The optimization is computed in a two-stage process with maximal reduction of inputs being achieved first, via the optimal θ^*, then movement onto the efficient frontier is achieved via the slack variables. Nonzero slacks and the value of $\theta^* \leq 1$ identify the sources and amount of any inefficiencies that may be present.

DATA SOURCES AND LISTS OF INPUTS AND OUTPUTS

The wealth of data available now readily available via such database services as GLOBAL VANTAGE and COMPUSTAT makes the choice of inputs and outputs particularly challenging. However, as this research is simply attempting to establish the feasibility of DEA for use in measures of agility, alternative sets of inputs and outputs were not considered. The input and output sets chosen are listed below. For the domestic companies the COMPUSTAT database was used along with the acronyms accepted in that database.

inputs: COGS, XSGA, EMP
outputs: SALE, NI

where

COGS—Cost of Goods Sold
XSGA—Selling, general, and administrative expenditures
EMP—Labor force, in thousands of workers, at end of year
SALE—Gross sales revenue
NI—Net Income

The variables are listed in millions of dollars. For the international companies the GLOBAL VANTAGE database was used. The variables used were

inputs: COGS, XSGA, EMP
outputs: SALES, REVT

where

COGS—Cost of Goods Sold
XSGA—Selling, general, and administrative expenditures
EMP—Labor force, in thousands of workers, at end of year
SALE—Gross sales revenue
REVT—Revenue before taxes.

Dollars are used for international companies based upon year-end conversions primarily for the ease of computation and comparison. Certainly, more input and output variables could have been used in the analysis but was not necessary to achieve the present objectives. The GAMS (General Algebraic Modeling System) computer program used in many economic modeling applications was used on a 486 PC to solve the linear equations in the current analysis. GAMS was created for use in the World Bank by David Kendrick and Alexander Meeraus among others in the mid 1980s (Kendrick, 1983).

Companies were chosen from the databases based upon Standard Industrial Classification (SIC) code. Any companies that fell into the range from 3720 to 3728 were included in the analysis. These are companies that manufacture any type of aircraft, aircraft component, or supporting devices ultimately to be used in an aircraft. Table 9.1

Table 9.1. Listing of Domestic Aircraft Companies Used in DEA Study

Company Code	Company Name	SIC Code	Ticker Symbol
CO1	TEXTRON INC.	3720	TXT
CO2	TEXTRON INC-PRE FASB	3720	TXT.F
CO3	AIRSHIP INDS LTD -ADR	3721	AIRSY
CO4	AMERICAN AIRCRAFT CORP	3721	3AARC
CO5	BANGOR PUNTA CORP	3721	BNK
CO6	BEECH AIRCRAFT CORP	3721	BCX
CO7	BELLANCA AIRCRAFT CORP	3721	1474B
CO8	BOEING CO	3721	BA
CO9	CESSNA AIRCRAFT CO	3721	CEA
CO10	COMMANDER AIRCRAFT CO	3721	CMDR
CO11	ENSTROM HELICOPTER CORP	3721	1318B
CO12	GATES LEARJET CORP	3721	GLJ
CO13	GRUMMAN AMERICAN AVIATION CP	3721	1360B
CO14	GRUMMAN CORP	3721	GQ
CO15	GULFSTREAM AEROSPACE CORP	3721	GA.
CO16	HILLER AVIATION INC	3721	HIL.2
CO17	LOCKHEED MARTIN CORP	3721	LMT
CO18	MCDONNELL DOUGLAS CORP	3721	MD
CO19	NORTHROP GRUMMAN CORP	3721	NOC
CO20	PIASECKI AIRCRAFT CORP	3721	2260B
CO21	PRECISION STANDARD INC	3721	PCSN
CO22	QUICKSILVER ENTRP	3721	3QEIC
CO23	VOUGHT CORP	3721	LTV1
CO24	WHITEHALL CORP	3721	WHT
CO25	A.B.A. INDUSTRIES INC	3724	ABA.2
CO26	AERODEX INC	3724	AOX
CO27	AVCO CORP	3724	TXT1
CO28	CADE INDUSTRIES INC	3724	CADE
CO29	CHEM-TRONICS INC	3724	CTRN.
CO30	EDAC TECHNOLOGIES CORP	3724	EDAC
CO31	HEICO CORP	3724	HEI
CO32	KREISLER MANUFACTURING CORP	3724	KRSL

Table 9.1 (continued)

Company Code	Company Name	SIC Code	Ticker Symbol
CO33	MACRODYNE INDS	3724	4711B
CO34	PIPER AIRCRAFT CORP	3724	PPA.
CO35	SEQUA CORP -CL A	3724	SQA.A
CO36	SIFCO INDUSTRIES	3724	SIF
CO37	SIGNAL COS	3724	SGN
CO38	TAT TECHNOLOGIES LTD -ORD	3724	TATTF
CO39	TELEDYNE INC	3724	TDY
CO40	UNC INC	3724	UNC
CO41	UNITED AIRCRAFT PRODUCTS INC	3724	UAP
CO42	UNITED TECHNOLOGIES CORP	3724	UTX
CO43	WALBAR INC	3724	WBR
CO44	AERONCA INC	3728	ARN.
CO45	AMERICAN WELDING & MFG CO	3728	AWLD
CO46	BALLISTIC RECOVERY SYSTEMS	3728	3BRSI
CO47	BERTEA CORP	3728	BTA
CO48	CANOGA INDS	3728	CGA.1
CO49	CHALCO INDUSTRIES INC	3728	3CLCO
CO50	CPI AEROSTRUCTURES INC	3728	CPIA
CO51	CRITON CORP	3728	CN.1
CO52	DATRON SYSTEMS INC	3728	1114B
CO53	DUCOMMUN INC	3728	DCO
CO54	EANCO INC	3728	1557B
CO55	FLEET AEROSPACE INC	3728	3FLAI
CO56	HENLEY GROUP INC/DEL	3728	HENG.
CO57	K & F INDUSTRIES INC	3728	6659B
CO58	KEENE CORP	3728	3KEENQ
CO59	KINEMOTIVE CORP	3728	3KINE
CO60	LTV AEROSPACE & DEFENSE CO	3728	QLTV4
CO61	MENASCO MFG CO	3728	MEN.
CO62	PRECISION AEROTECH INC	3728	3PAER
CO63	ROHR INC	3728	RHR
CO64	SIERRACIN CORP	3728	SER.2
CO65	STANLEY AVIATION CORP	3728	SAC
CO66	SUNDSTRAND CORP	3728	SNS
CO67	TELEFLEX INC	3728	TFX
CO68	TRE CORP	3728	TRE.1

Table 9.2. Listing of International Aircraft Companies Used in DEA Study

Company Code	Company Name	SIC Code	Ticker Symbol
CO1	AEROSPATIALE	3720	
CO2	HUREL-DUBOIS	3720	
CO3	KAWASAKI HEAVY INDUSTRIES LT	3720	
CO4	PIPER GENERALVERTRETUNG DEUT	3720	
CO5	SNECMA SA	3720	
CO6	SUMITOMO PRECISION PRODUCTS	3720	
CO7	TEXTRON INC	3720	TXT
CO8	BOEING CO	3721	BA
CO9	BOMBARDIER INC	3721	BBD.B
CO10	BRITISH AEROSPACE PLC	3721	
CO11	DASSAULT AVIATION SA	3721	
CO12	ENICHEM AUGUSTA SPA	3721	
CO13	FOKKER NV	3721	
CO14	HONG KONG AIRCRAFT ENGINEERI	3721	
CO15	LOCKHEED MARTIN CORP	3721	LMT
CO16	MCDONNELL DOUGLAS CORP	3721	MD
CO17	NORTHROP GRUMMAN CORP	3721	NOC
CO18	SINGAPORE TECHN AEROSPACE LT	3721	
CO19	WESTLAND GROUP PLC	3721	
CO20	WHITEHALL CORP	3721	WHT
CO21	HEICO CORP	3724	HEI
CO22	ROLLS-ROYCE PLC	3724	
CO23	SEQUA CORP	3724	SQA.A
CO24	SIFCO INDUSTRIES	3724	SIF
CO25	TELEDYNE INC	3724	TDY
CO26	UNC INC	3724	UNC
CO27	UNITED TECHNOLOGIES CORP	3724	UTX
CO28	DUCOMMUN INC	3728	DCO
CO29	INTERTECHNIQUE (GROUPE)	3728	
CO30	IPECO HOLDINGS PLC	3728	
CO31	JAPAN AIRCRAFT MFG CO LTD	3728	
CO32	PRECISION AEROTECH INC	3728	3PAER
CO33	ROHR INC	3728	RHR
CO34	SUNDSTRAND CORP	3728	SNS
CO35	TELEFLEX INC	3728	TFX
CO36	ZODIAC GROUP	3728	

provides a listing of domestic aerospace companies and Table 9.2 provides the international listing. Included in the tables are the company identification codes used for the rest of the analysis.

INDUSTRY SALES DATA

The data used in the research covers 15 years from 1979-1994. As mentioned in the previous chapter, the aerospace industry has undergone tremendous turmoil during this period. However, it is interesting to note that the decline in sales had a much more noticeable impact on firms with cumulative sales less than 1 billion dollars. Figure 9.1 shows the total sales over the period for all domestic companies with available data in the COMPUSTAT database. Figures 9.2 and 9.3 show the total sales for domestic companies with less than 1 billion in sales and greater than 1 billion in sales respectively. There is a visible decline in sales for smaller firms between 1985 to 1989 as opposed to a continual increase for larger firms.This trend is not the same for international firms over the same period which can be noted in Figures 9.4-9.6. (Data was only available from 1985-1994 for international firms.)

RELATING EFFICIENCY MEASURE TO AGILITY

DEA analysis provides a relative efficiency rating of companies. Various management implications can be applied when reviewing the efficiency of companies. The author extends these management connotations to the concept of agility. The author proposes the following propositions:

P1: The company that maintains consistent efficiency during times of fluctuating inputs and outputs has a high level of agility.

P2: Conversely, the company in which efficiency closely tracks the fluctuation in inputs and outputs has a low level of agility.

The problem then becomes one of the determination of how closely related the efficiency of a firm is with its inputs or outputs. Standard correlation analysis was used to measure the *degree* to which the variables are related to efficiency. Three variables were chosen to

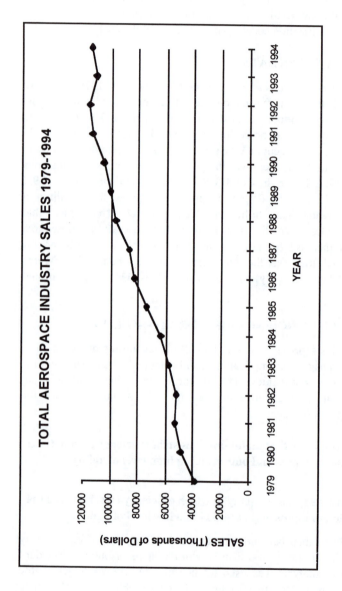

Figure 9.1. Domestic Aerospace Industry Sales for all Firms 1979-1994.

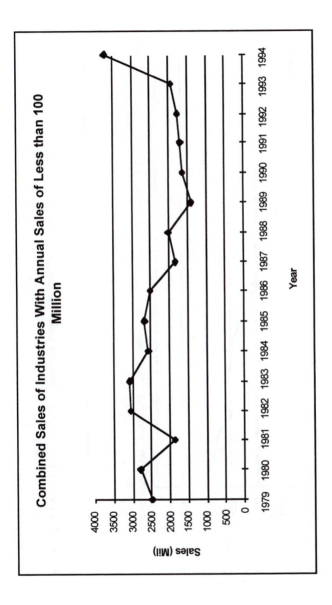

Figure 9.2. Domestic Aerospace Industry Sales for Small Firms 1979-1994.

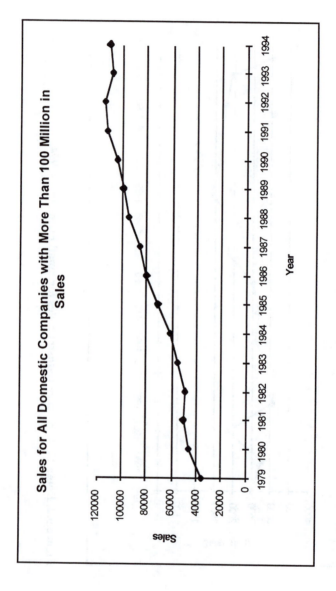

Figure 9.3. Domestic Aerospace Industry Sales for Large Firms 1979-1994.

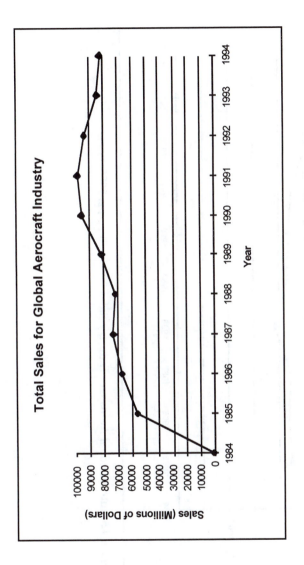

Figure 9.4. International Aerospace Industry Sales for All Firms 1985-1994.

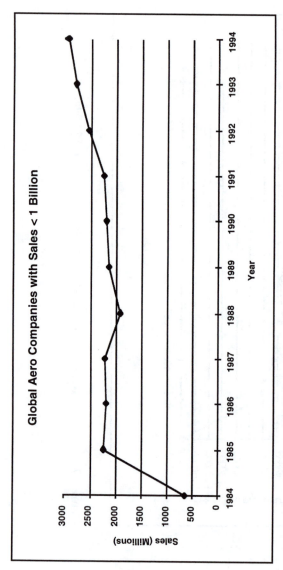

Figure 9.5. International Aerospace Industry Sales for Small Firms 1985-1994.

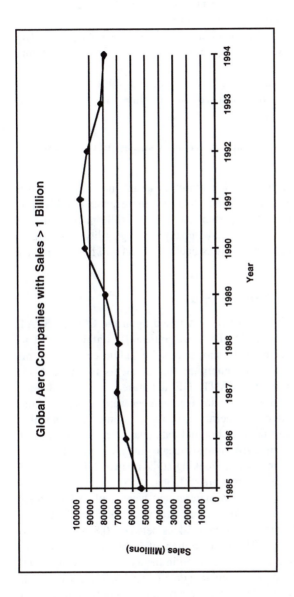

Figure 9.6. International Aerospace Industry Sales for Large Firms 1985-1994.

consider in the analysis: sales, change in sales and the absolute value of the change in sales. Following the propositions, those companies which are most agile will have correlation coefficients approaching zero. The sluggish companies, or least agile, will have correlation coefficients approaching unity.

If a company's agility can be determined, the more important larger question can be proposed and is stated in the following proposition:

P3: Companies with high agility are more successful than those with lower agility.

The measure for success in this research is net income. Therefore, if a company is agile, which means that it can respond quickly and anticipate changing environmental conditions, while maintaining or even increasing profits, then that company is using agility successfully as a component or tool of business operations and will have rising net income.

PRESENTATION OF DEA RESULTS

The data used in DEA analysis was based upon the COMPUSTAT (domestic) and VANTAGE (international) databases. The COMPUSTAT database only shows data for public companies and even that published data sometimes has elements missing. Also, international data in the VANTAGE database was inconsistent; therefore data from these international companies were not a part of the remainder of the study. Furthermore, of the 67 domestic companies only 34 had complete input and output data available. The absence of data from the complete DEA analysis means that a true frontier is not achieved; however, since we are looking at the relative agility levels of companies, the existing samples are sufficient.

The correlations that were determined were analyzed for their proximity to zero or unity. Correlations with values less than |0.2| were classified "agile." Correlations with values between |0.8| and 1.0 were considered "sluggish." The first column of Table 9.3 presents the companies according to their code used in the analysis. (The company names which apply to the particular code are listed in Table 9.1 as well as in Figures 9.7-9.40.) The second column provides only an indication towards how the company is maintaining its efficiency with overall increases or decreases in sales. This column is calculated based upon sales and efficiency. Figures 9.7-9.40.b graph these data over time in years. This consideration is most recognizable in Figures 9.7-9.40.a wherein the tracking of sales and efficiency can be visibly noted.

Since agility concerns business operations in the face of unanticipated change, a more relevant measure would be how that company responds in the face of yearly *changes* in sales. Those correlation coefficients are presented in column 3 of Table 9.3 and in Figures 9.7-9.40.c. A bar chart of these correlation coefficients is presented in Figure 41. Fourteen companies have correlation coefficients which are less than |0.2| in this category (8, 18, 19, 21, 24, 31, 40, 42, 46, 50, 57, 63, 66, 67). This might be an indication of their agility in the face of changing sales.

Based on the graphs and data, many companies seem to be able maintain efficiency when faced with continuously increasing sales. But, do these companies operate as well when sales are falling? Column 4 of Table 9.3 (corresponding to Figures 9.7-9.40.d is perhaps the most effective measure in the current analysis. The assertion could be made that if a company could maintain its efficiency regardless of changes in sales, positive and negative, then that company could be classified agile. Fifteen companies meet this criterion (8, 14, 18, 24, 31, 32, 35, 36, 42, 50, 57, 62, 63, 66, 67)

Of the companies in this analysis, five had efficiency ratings of unity in every year measured. These companies were the lead or frontier companies for this sample. The value of efficiency as 1 automatically assigns a value of 0 to the correlation coefficients inferring agility under this measurement conceptualization. Two of these were large companies and three small: Boeing (CO8), United Technologies (CO42), CPI Aerostructures (CO50), K&F Industries (CO57), Sundstrand Corp (CO66). This is particularly interesting in the case of Boeing in that the company laid off thousands of workers during this period. The company was able to maintain output and keep costs and expenditures under control in relation to that output. Each of these firms were maintaining efficiency while undergoing radical changes in revenue and employment.

In addition to the five companies above, only one company maintained a correlation coefficient value of less than |0.2| in all three correlation measurement types. That was Company 31, Heico Corp.

This small company was able to maintain high efficiency with sales changing by plus and minus $15 million.

Only three firms came out with high correlation coefficients of greater than |0.8|: Textron (CO2, a large company), Commander Aircraft (a small company), and Northrop Grumman (CO19, a large company). Figure 9.14 shows the plots for Northrop Grumman.[2] Efficiency goes up and down right along with sales. According to the premise of this chapter, the company overall cannot maintain efficiency levels consistent in an environment of changing sales. The same could be said for Textron (Figure 9.7) but only for years preceding 1987. Notice that in Textron the company suffers greatly in the early 80s, but appears to recover it momentum and is able to withstand the tumultuous changes in sales in the late 80s. Even with a drop of $ 600 million in sales in 1987 and with a jump in sales of $ 600 million in 1991, the company maintains a steady efficiency. The amount of data for Commander Aircraft (CO10) is limited to three years and little should be inferred from this data.

In figures 9.7-9.40 note that LTV Aero & Defense (CO60) was sold to separate companies in 1992 and 1993. The Aircraft construction facility became the Arrowplane Aircraft Company and was the component that is described in the case study. The Defense portion was purchased by Loral Corp (omitted in this study). Also, note that the Grumman corporation (CO14) held large cash reserves which made it ripe for the takeover in 1993 by Northrop Corp. It will be interesting to see how these different companies with different historical agility ratings will proceed in the future. Northrop Grumman Corp President Ken Kresa has stated that agility is a key operational goal of the company in the next few years (Kresa, 1995).

IMPLICATIONS OF RESULTS

As stated in proposition **P3**, a high level of agility should imply a high level of performance. The measure of high performance in this DEA feasibility study is net income. Graphs for Companies 8 (Boeing), 31 (Heico), 42 (United Technologies) and 66 (Sundstrand Corp) are presented in Figures 9.42-9.45. Unfortunately, the Net Income figures for each of these companies is insufficient to demonstrate the "success" of the company. Values vary significantly, as much as $100 million in the case of Sunstrand.

Table 9.3. Correlations Between Efficiency and Sales

Company Code	Correlation Coefficient (Sales vs. Efficiency)	Correlation Coefficient (Change in Sales vs. Efficiency)	Correlation Coefficient (ABS[Change in Sales] vs. Efficiency)
CO2	0.925	0.435	0.283
CO4	0.329	-0.472	0.618
CO8	0.000	0.000	0.000
CO10	0.890	-1.000	-1.000
CO14	0.407	0.000	0.000
CO17	0.036	0.267	0.315
CO18	0.429	-0.141	0.124
CO19	0.826	0.064	0.288
CO21	0.340	0.102	0.299
CO22	-0.300	0.767	0.796
CO24	0.614	0.012	-0.024
CO28	-0.058	-0.590	-0.324
CO30	-0.053	0.223	0.205
CO31	0.106	-0.139	0.148
CO32	0.330	0.317	0.056
CO35	-0.314	0.432	0.003
CO36	0.558	0.512	-0.103
CO38	0.202	0.369	0.469
CO39	0.300	0.258	0.225
CO40	0.452	-0.108	0.213
CO42	0.000	0.000	0.000
CO46	0.038	-0.067	-0.341
CO49	0.550	0.403	0.266
CO50	0.000	0.000	0.000
CO53	0.447	0.690	-0.447
CO55	-0.396	0.851	-0.930
CO56	0.055	-0.255	0.292
CO57	0.000	0.000	0.000
CO58	0.004	-0.591	0.449
CO60	0.371	0.717	0.323
CO62	-0.027	-0.398	0.125
CO63	-0.375	0.104	0.165
CO66	0.000	0.000	0.000
CO67	0.282	0.155	0.155

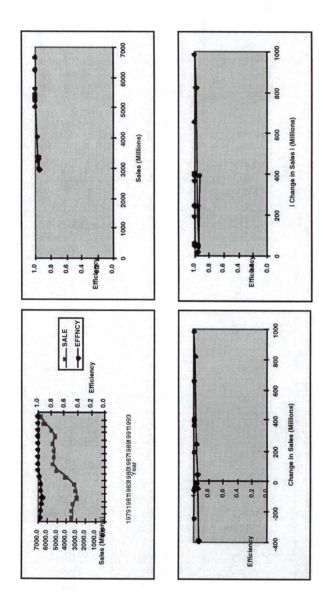

Figure 9.7. a. Sales, Efficiency vs Year, b. Efficiency vs Sales, c. Efficiency vs Change in Sales, d. Efficiency vs Abs(Change in Sales) for Textron Inc (Company 2)

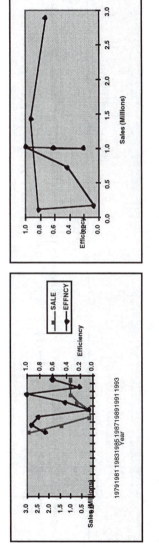

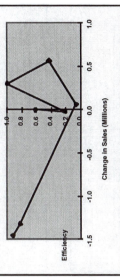

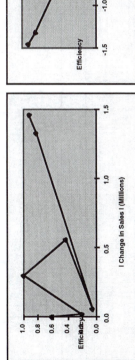

Figure 9.8. a. Sales, Efficiency vs Year, b. Efficiency vs Sales, c. Efficiency vs Change in Sales, d. Efficiency vs Abs(Change in Sales) for American Aircraft (Company 4)

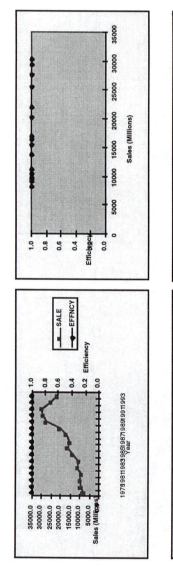

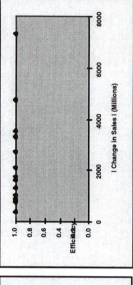

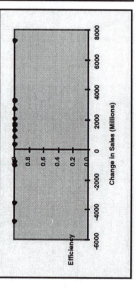

Figure 9.9. a. Sales, Efficiency vs Year, b. Efficiency vs Sales, c. Efficiency vs Change in Sales, d. Efficiency vs Abs(Change in Sales) for Boeing (Company 8)

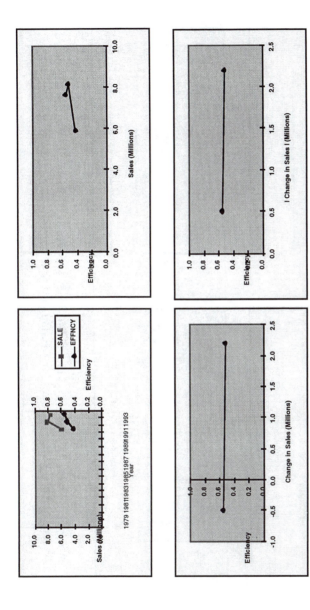

Figure 9.10. a. Sales, Efficiency vs Year, b. Efficiency vs Sales, c. Efficiency vs Change in Sales, d. Efficiency vs Abs(Change in Sales) for Commander Aircraft Co. (Company 10)

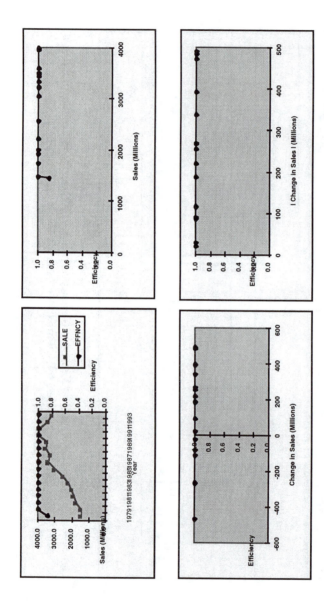

Figure 9.11. a. Sales, Efficiency vs Year, b. Efficiency vs Sales, c. Efficiency vs Change in Sales, d. Efficiency vs Abs(Change in Sales) for Grumman Corp. Company 14

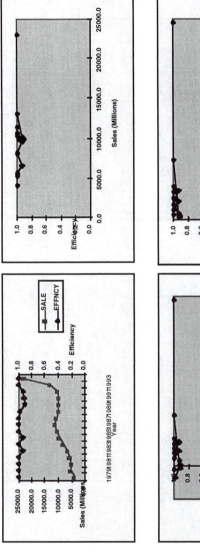

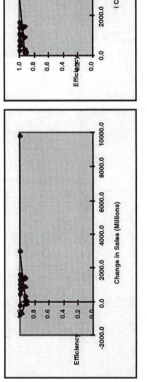

Figure 9.12. a. Sales, Efficiency vs Year, b. Efficiency vs Sales, c. Efficiency vs Change in Sales, d. Efficiency vs Abs(Change in Sales) for Lockheed Martin Corp. Company 17

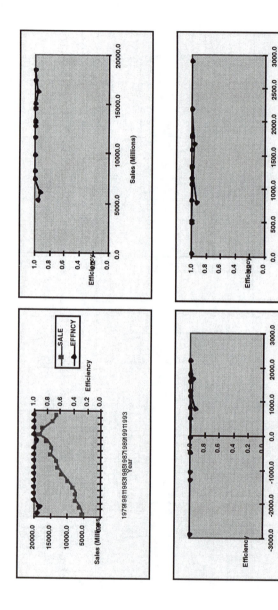

Figure 9.13. a. Sales, Efficiency vs Year, b. Efficiency vs Sales, c. Efficiency vs Change in Sales, d. Efficiency vs Abs(Change in Sales) for McDonnell Douglas Corp. Company 18

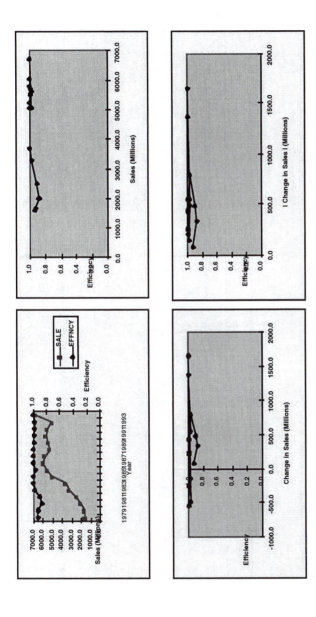

Figure 9.14. a. Sales, Efficiency vs Year, b. Efficiency vs Sales, c. Efficiency vs Change in Sales, d. Efficiency vs Abs(Change in Sales) for Northrop Grumman Corp. Company 19

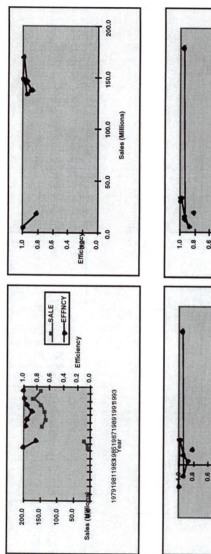

Figure 9.15. a. Sales, Efficiency vs Year, b. Efficiency vs Sales, c. Efficiency vs Change in Sales, d. Efficiency vs Abs(Change in Sales) for Precision Standard, Inc. Company 21

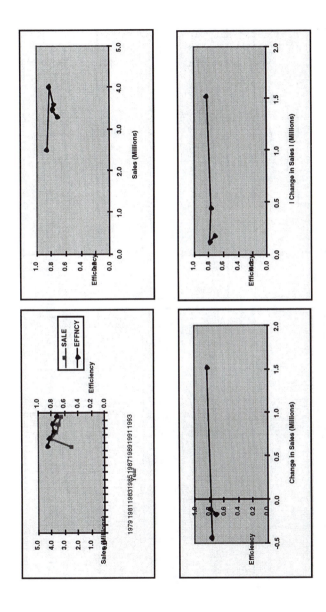

Figure 9.16. a. Sales, Efficiency vs Year, b. Efficiency vs Sales, c. Efficiency vs Change in Sales, d. Efficiency vs Abs(Change in Sales) for Quicksilver Enterprises Company 22

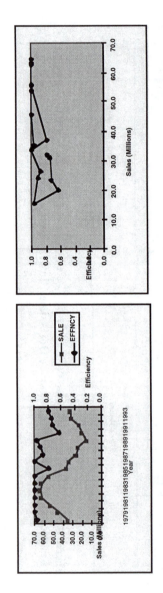

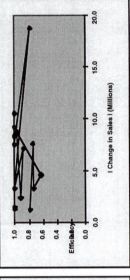

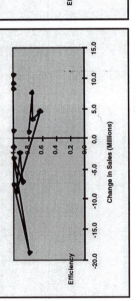

Figure 9.17. a. Sales, Efficiency vs Year, b. Efficiency vs Sales, c. Efficiency vs Change in Sales, d. Efficiency vs Abs(Change in Sales) for Whitehall Corp. Company 24

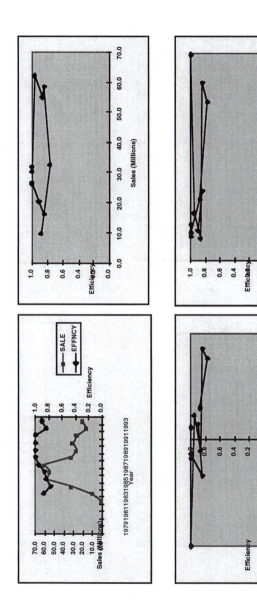

Figure 9.18. a. Sales, Efficiency vs Year, b. Efficiency vs Sales, c. Efficiency vs Change in Sales, d. Efficiency vs Abs(Change in Sales) for CADE Industries, Inc. Company 28

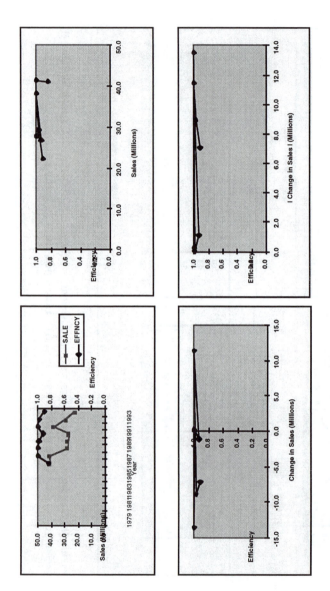

Figure 9.19. a. Sales, Efficiency vs Year, b. Efficiency vs Sales, c. Efficiency vs Change in Sales, d. Efficiency vs Abs(Change in Sales) for EDAC Technologies Corp. Company 30

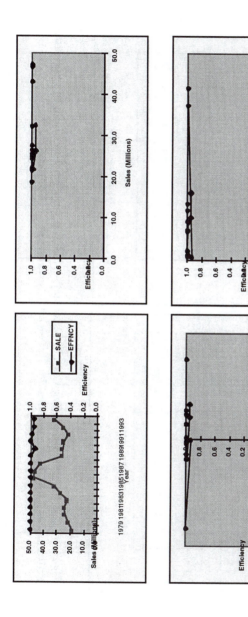

Figure 9.20. a. Sales, Efficiency vs Year, b. Efficiency vs Sales, c. Efficiency vs Change in Sales, d. Efficiency vs Abs(Change in Sales) for Heico Corp. Company 31

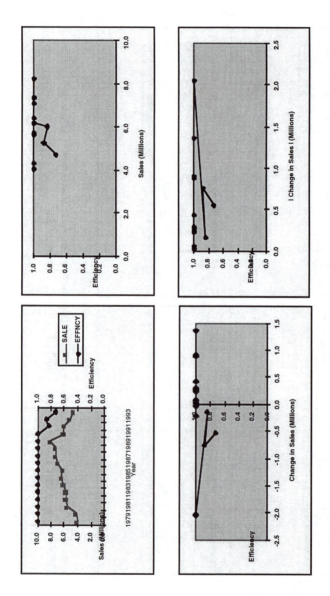

Figure 9.21. a. Sales, Efficiency vs Year, b. Efficiency vs Sales, c. Efficiency vs Change in Sales, d. Efficiency vs Abs(Change in Sales) for Kreisler Manufacturing Co. Company 32

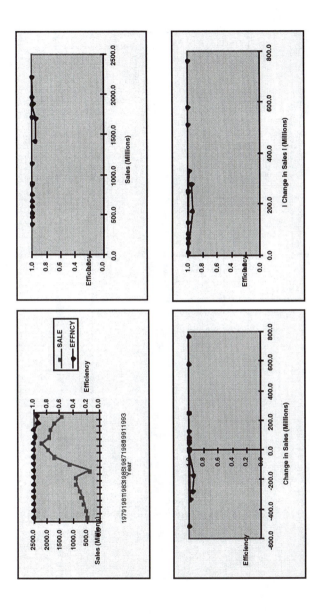

Figure 9.22. a. Sales, Efficiency vs Year, b. Efficiency vs Sales, c. Efficiency vs Change in Sales, d. Efficiency vs Abs(Change in Sales) for Sequa Corp. Company 35

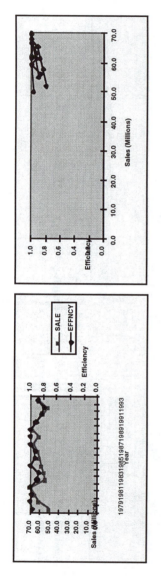

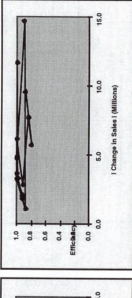

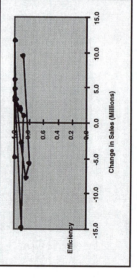

Figure 9.23. a. Sales, Efficiency vs Year, b. Efficiency vs Sales, c. Efficiency vs Change in Sales, d. Efficiency vs Abs(Change in Sales) for SIFCO Industries Company 36

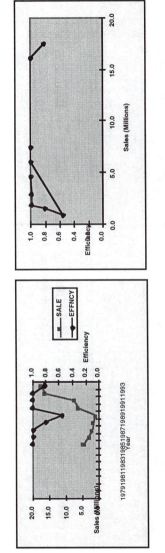
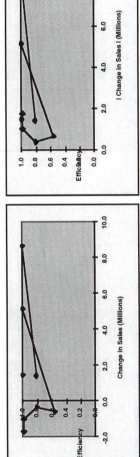

Figure 9.24. a. Sales, Efficiency vs Year, b. Efficiency vs Sales, c. Efficiency vs Change in Sales, d. Efficiency vs Abs(Change in Sales) for TAT Technologies Ltd. Company 38

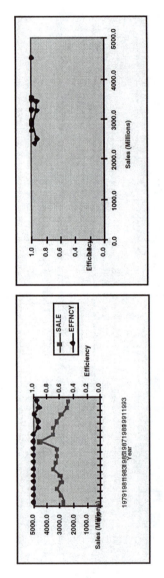
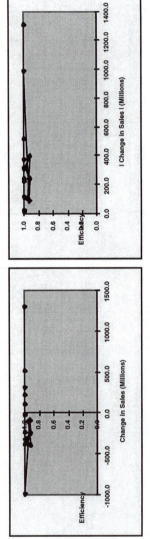

Figure 9.25. a. Sales, Efficiency vs Year, b. Efficiency vs Sales, c. Efficiency vs Change in Sales, d. Efficiency vs Abs(Change in Sales) for Teledyne, Inc. Company 39

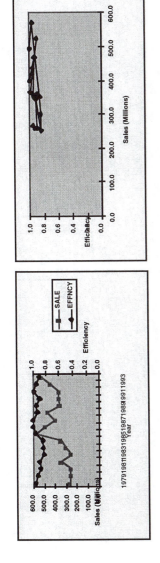

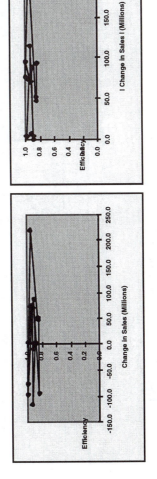

Figure 9.26. a. Sales, Efficiency vs Year, b. Efficiency vs Sales, c. Efficiency vs Change in Sales, d. Efficiency vs Abs(Change in Sales) for UNC Inc. Company 40

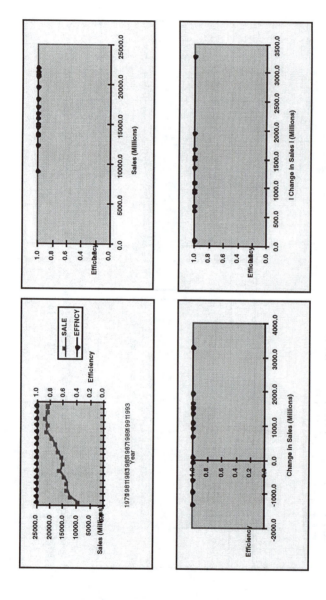

Figure 9.27. a. Sales, Efficiency vs Year, b. Efficiency vs Sales, c. Efficiency vs Change in Sales, d. Efficiency vs Abs(Change in Sales) for United Technologies Corp. Company 42

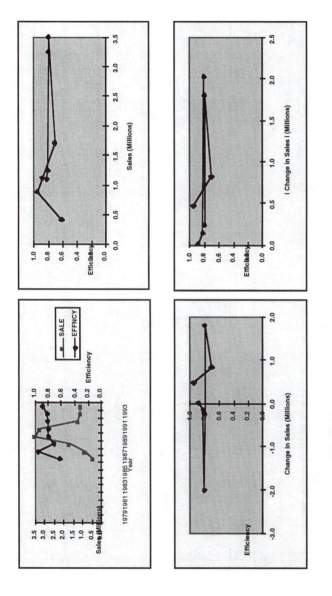

Figure 9.28. a. Sales, Efficiency vs Year, b. Efficiency vs Sales, c. Efficiency vs Change in Sales, d. Efficiency vs Abs(Change in Sales) for Ballistic Recovery Systems Company 46

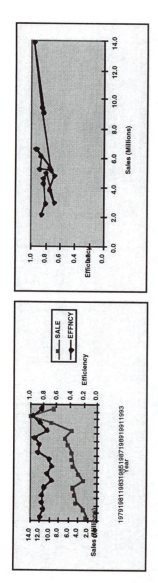

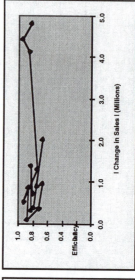

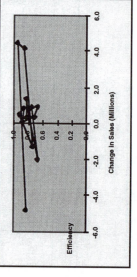

Figure 9.29. a. Sales, Efficiency vs Year, b. Efficiency vs Sales, c. Efficiency vs Change in Sales, d. Efficiency vs Abs(Change in Sales) for Chalco Industries. Company 49

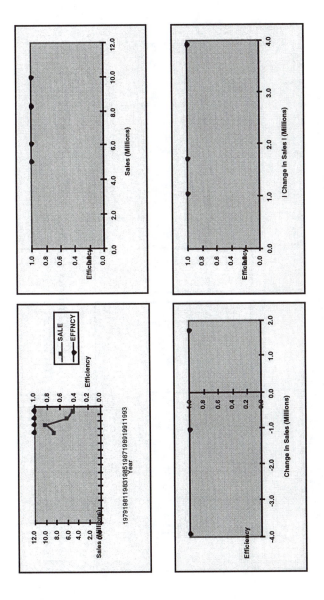

Figure 9.30. a. Sales, Efficiency vs Year, b. Efficiency vs Sales, c. Efficiency vs Change in Sales, d. Efficiency vs Abs(Change in Sales) for CPI Aerostructures Inc. Company 50

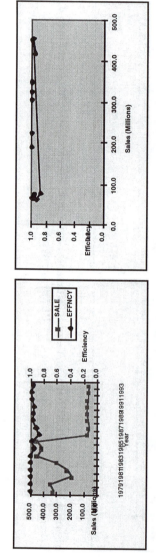
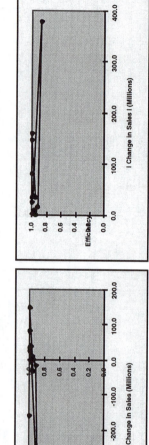

Figure 9.31. a. Sales, Efficiency vs Year, b. Efficiency vs Sales, c. Efficiency vs Change in Sales, d. Efficiency vs Abs(Change in Sales) for Ducommun Inc. Company 53

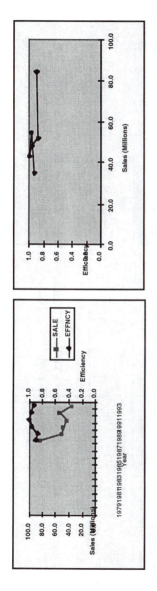

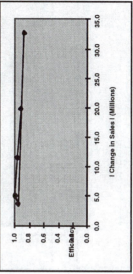

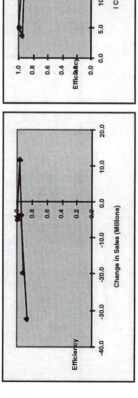

Figure 9.32. a. Sales, Efficiency vs Year, b. Efficiency vs Sales, c. Efficiency vs Change in Sales, d. Efficiency vs Abs(Change in Sales) for Fleet Aerospace Inc. Company 55

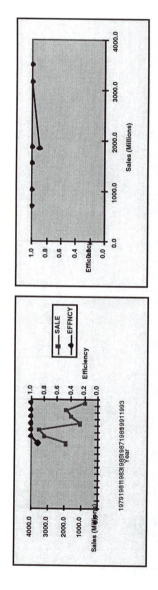
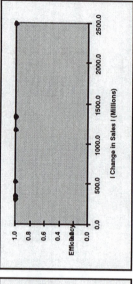
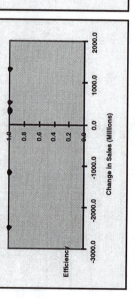

Figure 9.33. a. Sales, Efficiency vs Year, b. Efficiency vs Sales, c. Efficiency vs Change in Sales, d. Efficiency vs Abs(Change in Sales) for Henley Group Inc. Company 56

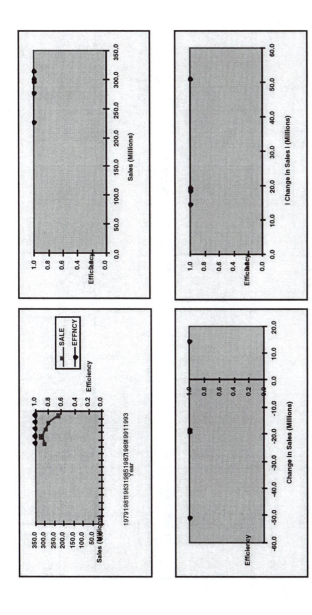

Figure 9.34. a. Sales, Efficiency vs Year, b. Efficiency vs Sales, c. Efficiency vs Change in Sales, d. Efficiency vs Abs(Change in Sales) for K&F Industries Inc. Company 57

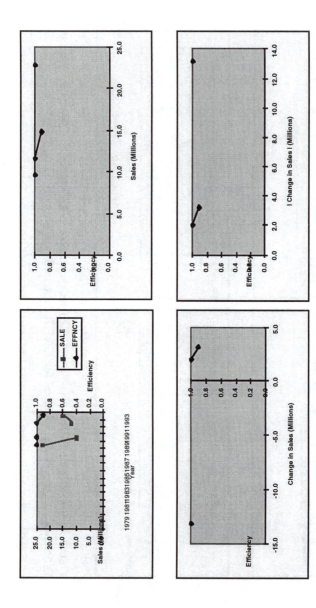

Figure 9.35. a. Sales, Efficiency vs Year, b. Efficiency vs Sales, c. Efficiency vs Change in Sales, d. Efficiency vs Abs(Change in Sales) for Keene Corp. Company 58

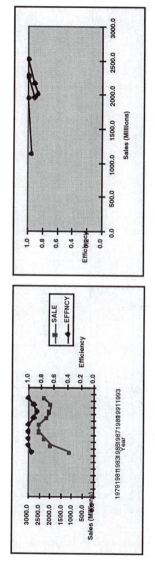

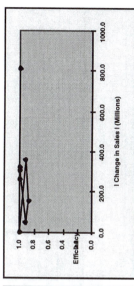

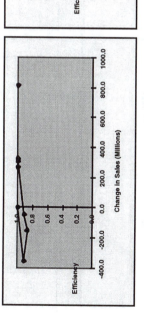

Figure 9.36. a. Sales, Efficiency vs Year, b. Efficiency vs Sales, c. Efficiency vs Change in Sales, d. Efficiency vs Abs(Change in Sales) for LTV Aerospace & Defense Co. Company 60

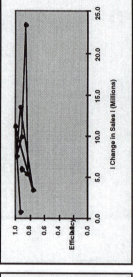

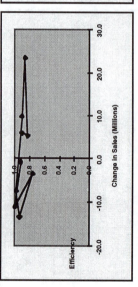

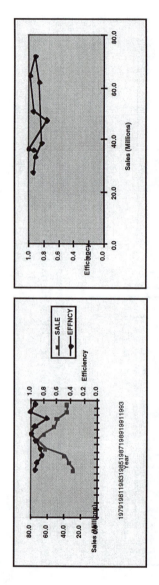

Figure 9.37. a. Sales, Efficiency vs Year, b. Efficiency vs Sales, c. Efficiency vs Change in Sales, d. Efficiency vs Abs(Change in Sales) for Precision Aerotech Inc. Company 62

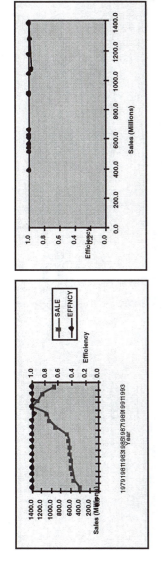
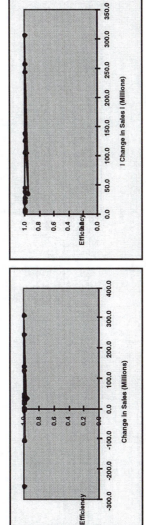

Figure 9.38. a. Sales, Efficiency vs Year, b. Efficiency vs Sales, c. Efficiency vs Change in Sales, d. Efficiency vs Abs(Change in Sales) for Rohr Inc. Company 63

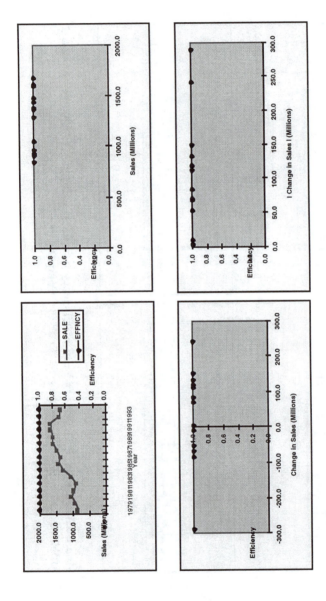

Figure 9.39. a. Sales, Efficiency vs Year, b. Efficiency vs Sales, c. Efficiency vs Change in Sales, d. Efficiency vs Abs(Change in Sales) for Sundstrand Corp. Company 66

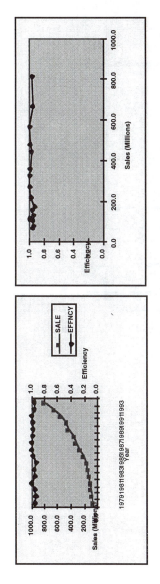

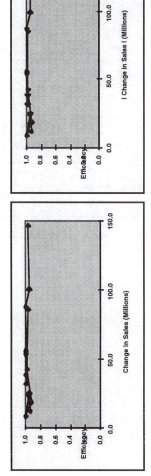

Figure 9.40. a. Sales, Efficiency vs Year, b. Efficiency vs Sales, c. Efficiency vs Change in Sales, d. Efficiency vs Abs(Change in Sales) for Teleflex, Inc. Company 67

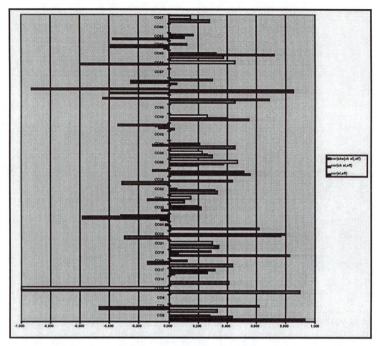

Figure 9.41. Correlation Coefficients: Agile, 0 < (< |0.2|; Sluggish, |0.8| < (< 1.0

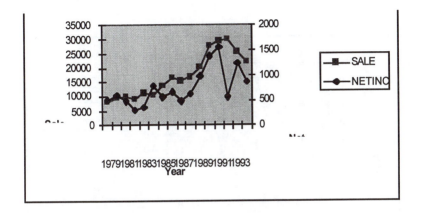

Figure 9.42. Company 8, Boeing Sales and Net Income

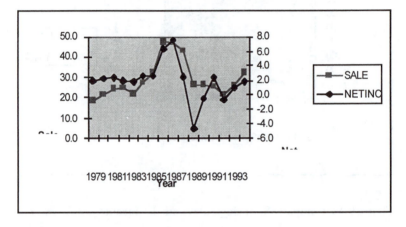

Figure 9.43. Company 31, Heico Sales and Net Income

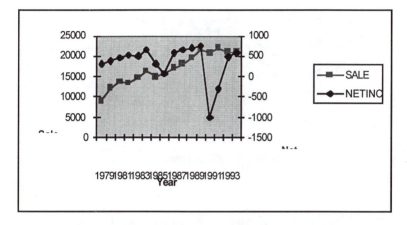

Figure 9.44. Company 42, United Technologies Sales and Net Income

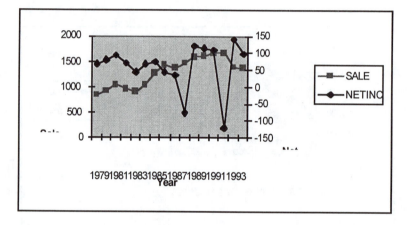

Figure 9.45. Company 66, Sunstrand Sales and Net Income

In each of these "agile" companies it is notable that the efficiency remains high in spite of the fluctuating sales and net income; however, this evidence does not bring researchers any closer to linking agility with corporate success.

FUTURE DIRECTIONS FOR THE AIRCRAFT INDUSTRY DEA RESEARCH

The research in this chapter attempts to determine a method to create a measure for agility. The potential for DEA to be an effective measure remains great. The capability to analyze the extensive public data on companies without depending on a particular formulation of a production function or regression equation would seem especially suited to the concept of agility. Following are some descriptions of potential problems with this method and recommendations for future DEA research on agility.

Unfortunately, this chapter's formulation did not lead to a conclusive measure of agility. This is not necessarily an elimination of the potentials for DEA analysis applied to agility, further examination of various input and output measures is required. For example, a company might maintain high efficiency simply by keeping the inputs matched with the outputs. That is, if sales were significantly decreasing and an equivalent reduction in employees was made, then that company would still maintain its efficiency score.

When addressing agility, the particular inputs chosen become critical. For example, it may not necessarily be in the best interest of the company to reduce the workforce drastically in an agile environment. Yet, if that is a primary input used in the measure, such a reduction would be recommended as a means to increase agility. This formulation only had three major inputs, a more complete selection of inputs should allow for a better calculation. Other important inputs might be number of new products developed per year or number of new technologies developed. Each one along might have particular dangers. For example, if an input was number of new products introduced a company could appear to be agile it just continued to produce multiple products— whether or not successfully introduced. Such problems could be counteracted with more inclusive inputs and outputs. This should be a primary goal of future application.

The method employed in this DEA technique was the most basic BCC model. Other models (Multiplicative, Additive, CCR) each have benefits which might improve the agility measure. One of the more likely would be an output oriented measure such as the differential CCR method which might reflect more stability in the measurement correlations.

NOTES

1. The background material for this section relies heavily upon a variety of sources including Thore, Kozmetsky, Phillips (1994), personal interviews with Dr. Sten Thore, and from material provided in *Data Envelopment Analysis: Theory, Methodology, and Applications*, edited by Charnes, Cooper, Lewin, and Seiford (1994).

2. The data for all of the years preceding 1993 is for Northrop Corporation alone before the acquisition of Arrowplane and Grumman.

CHAPTER 10

Analysis and Model Revisions

CASE AND MODEL ANALYSIS

In order to revise the model on agility and see where it can be applied more effectively, a review of the case material is presented in the context of the proposed antecedent model (Figure 5.6). Accordingly, it is important to relate the lessons learned from the cases and the present research.

LINKING CASE STUDY 1 LESSONS AND OBSERVATIONS WITH PROPOSED MODEL ON AGILITY

Communication Connectedness. The electronic connection between Arrowplane and Composit Labs (CL) enabled a richer communication link between the two companies. Composit representatives can look into relevant aspects of Arrowplane's production system and identify their orders. Arrowplane can look at the status of any work order that is in the system (whether physically at Arrowplane or actually in progress at CL. This collaboration also requires the updating and linking of many unrelated systems including: inventory control, procurement, receiving, accounts payable, and the manufacturing control systems. Communication connectedness also applies to non-technical or project specific aspects of communication. Success is hindered without "buy-in" from all personnel involved with or even tangent to the project.

Interorganization participation. The prior relationship between Arrowplane and Composit had been based upon relatively impersonal purchase orders and invoices. Interorganization participation was "not rich" and was centered on purchase orders. With the EDI project, face to face meetings, trust and understanding became high priority. Now the companies have contingency plans identified in case of material shortfalls and order mistakes. Employees other than sales representatives have personal, daily contacts with members of the other company that enhance their dedication to each other and instills personal pride in the success of the project. This level of interaction would indicate extremely high interorganizational participation. *Trust* between employees as well as between functional areas of both the companies has also increased from before and would be considered high. This factor may change depending on the continued ability of the CL to meet its commitments to Arrowplane given ongoing problems at the Composit mill. The intervening variable of *dependence* is exemplified when recalling Composit's backlog of orders at the mill. This potential problem was emphasized by nay-sayers at the outset of the Arrowplane-Composit project. In spite of this, trust and commitment between the two companies encouraged the search for mutually acceptable solutions rather than allowing the problem to fracture the EDI system.

Production Flexibility. In the current case, the ability of Arrowplane or other company's design engineers to change material orders up to the last minute before delivery allowed for design changes to be implemented at least six months earlier than would have been possible before this project. Unfortunately, due to the limited scope of the project, only inferences can be made on the flexibility this new program might provide to Arrowplane production systems.

Management involvement. Many individuals within Arrowplane had promoted the benefits of agility, JIT, EDI or other program improvements to internal processes, but it was the push from top management that finally cleared the way for dedicated resources necessary to implement the project. The unexpected changes due to restructuring the company after the buy-out by Northrop-Grumman left many team members feeling like their work had lost momentum. Once employees had bought into the EDI concept they wanted to continue to quickly apply the lessons learned to other projects. The cross-functional team that had been formed felt a strong sense of achievement as a result of the success of the EDI project. Having felt a strong sense of mission, they believed that their frustration level at the unclear future of the project grew more quickly than it had in the past. (The team was disbanded upon project completion and assigned to other tasks.)

Employee empowerment. The creation of cross-functional inter-departmental teams, as well as inter-organizational teams, was a first for the employees at Arrowplane and this teaming was a critical factor to success. While the Arrowplane team commented that they *felt* a strong sense of authority and empowerment, they frequently commented that they spent too much time waiting for approval at each step during implementation of the processes. This would indicate only a medium level of empowerment and indicates low *autonomy*. Some *training* was required although it was considered unnecessary for project success. The *teaming* aspect of the project appeared successful and high. The team formed a sense of independent identity, enjoying a high profile in the company during project implementation. They felt a loss when the project was not expanded to other areas.

LINKING CASE STUDY 2 LESSONS AND OBSERVATIONS WITH PROPOSED MODEL ON AGILITY

Communication Connectedness. Principally, the Thompson-Bilmo project was to link the supplier more directly with the designer, draftsmen, and engineers at Thompson, to increase *communication connectedness* across organizations. However, the focus of the project was technical, and while that component was accomplished it has been stalled due to behavioral considerations. The behavioral component of was under appreciated and resulted in a technical success that may never be fully utilized.

Interorganizational Participation. Both companies undertook this agile initiative to begin to try methods of operations that extended their interorganizational collaboration. The old relationship was superficial. The new project called for expanded elements of *trust*. This trust was based upon increasing dependence on one another, that concept was recognized and vocalized by the team but did not carry over to effective implementation.

Product Flexibility. Thompson needs to product more products in shorter time. Internal processes need to link all systems together. Thompson is worked to include Bilmo in this linkage. The technical programming of machines to interpret drawings and program themselves to produce products allows for excellent flexibility.

Management Involvement. Both Thompson and Bilmo enjoy high management involvement in day to day operations as well as this specific alliance. The quality programs and the preferred supplier programs affected the way the organization operated. An aspect of this factor which leads to increased agility is that once new programs or processes are implemented, management changes make it difficult for the company to operate with the old methods. Employees who did not change to adapt to new methods of working when Thompson instituted new quality programs are no longer with the company. They did not need to be fired, they simply could not continue with their past work roles. While both companies have high internal levels of management involvement, this factor was not overtly recognized as a vital component in this project. Changes that did occur were essentially pushed through. There was little gathering of consensus or buy in. Thompson dictated the method in which cycle time would be reduced. This is certainly an historically effective method of management for many situations. However, when attempting to employ agile practices, management must often interact more with project participants and let employees determine for themselves how to best accomplish new objectives.

Employee Empowerment. Both companies are led by traditional strong leaders with employees expected to accomplish the objectives that they are assigned. In the *teaming* aspect, the machinists were not included on the project team. The draftsmen who completed the similar internal programs within Thompson were only involved in a cursory manner. While *training* is considered vital within Thompson, that idea did not carry over to the partner company. Thompson could use its good experiences with training to assist in the execution of this important aspect. There appear to be many checks within Thompson to avoid exposure to risk. This is natural for most companies, but it reflects a low level of *autonomy*. Overall, the fact that the machinists refused to use the new methods, effectively killed the project which could be considered high empowerment. However, the level of empowerment across the project team would be considered low. The UniSci technicians, as outsiders, had no empowerment to implement changes in behavior within the firm. The critical factor is that the project team personnel must have a high empowerment level to implement a new idea, process or plan. This case demonstrates that when technical and especially behavioral obstacles are encountered some recognized authority must be available to effectively see the problem through resolution. This recognized authority should be rooted in higher management and has provided evidence of the transferred authority to the empowered project team.

CROSS CASE ANALYSIS

The two cases investigated in this research were not concerned with identical issues of agility or supplier integration. However, each agile project was similar enough that comparisons are useful in trying to identify which antecedent components and/or other aspects of agility might have been revealed.

Project Similarities

Even though the cases were applied for somewhat different objectives the problems encountered were remarkable similar. The primary concern of both companies was the reduction of cycle time. The issue of speed in the face of quickly changing environmental circumstances, which is a defining aspect of agility, is strongly evidenced in these cases. Both sets of project decided that one way to achieve their objectives was through a supplier integration/management type of project. In each case, the companies were building upon technologies, designs and implementations that had been successfully implemented internally. Each project chose to work with one supplier, small and non-union. In both cases there were individuals within and without the project team that had serious reservations about the ultimate chances for success.

Project Differences

The differences between the two projects may have impacted the overall outcome. Thompson and Bilmo both would be considered prime examples of entrepreneurial companies. Upon first glance, it would seem reasonable that both would be more agile than either Arrowplane or Composit. Indeed, overall Thompson and Bilmo demonstrated more characteristics of agility; however, these characteristics were not readily apparent in this particular pilot project. Interestingly, Thompson and Bilmo had an existing relationship extending beyond the work environment, while Arrowplane and Composit were only buyer and seller with only the most cursory relationship. The closer relationship did not seem to add any help the Thompson and Bilmo problems, nor conversely, did the more distant relationship hinder Arrowplane and Composit.

A vital difference emerging from Arrowplane was that the success of this project was seen to have implications on the success of the overall business. These implications also extended to the professional success of the team participants. While not fearing for their jobs, "we knew we had to show [top management] that our ideas could work" (Smith, 1995). These team members had had enough with bureaucratic procedures and overwork; they felt that these measures could make a big difference in their work. Similarly, member of the Composit team felt that they were continuing to "prove" themselves and the worth of their "independent" facility to the corporate management of Composit (Barry, 1995). The project at Thompson was seen as quite useful with important implications, yet with little impact on overall operations. This attitude was different between top management and personnel working to implement the project. Its relative importance, however, failed to disseminate throughout the project.

The difference in project team may have held the secret to the overall success of the Arrowplane project and the limited success of the Thompson project. The Arrowplane team consisted of members from throughout multiple departments at Arrowplane and Composit who worked on and were actively involved in the project from design well into implementation. The Thompson team consisted of members from Thompson, Bilmo and UniSci; however, the actual implementation of the project was left to UniSci, the "outside" team. The Thompson project was more modularized that the Arrowplane project and more barriers appeared between the modules.

In fairness, the Arrowplane project was more visible and had more inertia than the Thompson project. The Thompson project was more to fulfill the needs of UniSci membership than fulfill a pressing problem within the company. Yet, generalizations might be made here that the move to agility cannot be made half-heartedly. A full dedication and a sense that you cannot go back seems to be required in projects of this nature. Perhaps, the use of an outside company such as UniSci to implement agile projects might not be the best method as they "take off the weight" of those who need the new concepts.

Table 10.1. Similarities and Differences Between the Cases Investigated

Similarities	Differences
• Reasons for wanting agility	• Small entrepreneurial company (Thompson & Bilmo); Large bureaucratic company (Arrowplane)
• Internal successes of some design concepts	• Existing relationship between Thompson and Bilmo, virtually none between Arrowplane and Composit
• Use of small, non-union supplier companies for pilot studies	• Feeling of company future riding on successful implementation of pilot (Arrowplane)
• Skepticism of project success	• Active project team consisting of members from both companies working project through fruition (Arrowplane). Project handed off to outside team (Thompson).

GRID OF RESEARCH FINDINGS

The grid of Figure 10.1 summarizes the relationships that appeared evident over the course of the research. The grid relates each case investigated to the proposed antecedent variables on agility a well as the key variables used in the Agility Forum's depiction of agility. The ratings are simply H (high), M (medium) and L (low). Each variable was rated on the evidence of it appearing in the particular case.

MODEL REVISION AND FUTURE RESEARCH RECOMMENDATIONS

The four variables from the Agility Forum are more variables which describe the attributes of agility. The antecedent variables can easily be viewed as leading to the desirable attributes. Further studies might look at how the antecedent variables might lead to the specific agile attributes. Such a formulation might make a survey, quantitative investigation more feasible as opposed to trying to examine the encompassing aspects of agility.

	Communi-cation Connected-ness	Interorgani-zational Participa-tion	Production Flexibility	Manage-ment Involve-ment	Empower-ment	Reconfig-urability	Enriching Customer	Integration	Cooper-ation
Case 1: Arrowplane	H	H	M	H	M	M	M	H	H
Case 1: Composit Materials	H	H	M	H	M	M	H	H	H
Case 2: Thompson Enterprises	H	M	H	M	M	M	M	H	H
Case 2: Bilmo	M	H	M	H	M	M	M	H	H

Figure 10.1. Summary Grid of Cases versus Antecedent Variables and Other Variables on Agility from Literature

Empowerment seems to be a weak variable in the current depiction of agility. It is overused and under-defined, stated in every description of what the corporate future will look like in the Agile world. While the term itself remains vague, a central aspect is that each employee will increasingly have the authority and responsibility to make localized decisions that contribute to the good of the entire company. As management layers are removed and the need for quicker corporate response times increases, employees will be making decisions regarding issues that were formerly handled by their supervisors two or three levels above them. Employees' value added potential should be enhanced by new information systems and the unlocking of the individual's creative abilities. The tools and training required to make good decisions will be made available to all employees. Employees will be expected to make maximum usage of these tools and will maintain responsibility for their actions. Future research should identify a more succinct term to describe these issues or break up the concept further.

An added aspect of control should be applied in this configuration as well. New technologies and management processes are touted as the key that will unlock this environment unencumbered by management bureaucracy. Yet, there remain serious questions that must be addressed before such lofty plans can be instituted. How is this "useful" information to be transmitted around the company? Who determines what information is useful? How can employees, who have never been allowed to make critical business decisions, gain the experience necessary to make wise decisions? Each of these critical questions cannot be answered today.

Another aspect that is not sufficiently highlighted in the proposed model is leadership. This might be considered a part of empowerment or management involvement. Neither one as depicted in the current research clearly define this role as well as it may have warranted upon review of the various case material. Historically they leader concept has undergone great transitions. The early type of motivation was 'we'll make them do it' (authoritarian), then in the first half of the 20th century 'we'll make them want to do it' via persuasion and rewards (participative), during the 1960s and 70s the idea became 'we'll make them happy doing it' attempting to draw upon ideas of cooperation. While the ideas of cooperation still hold true, it is an illusive goal and unlikely that people can be "made" happy (Moore, 1958; Newman, 1978; Bowen, 1994). The most popular definition of a leader and business leadership today is those who have ability to see future, to frame it in compelling terms, and to translate it into action-oriented missions both for the members of the project team and for people in specialized areas who support the team (Bowen, 1994). This concept is especially evident in the supporting case material and should be included overtly in the antecedent model.

The importance of trust in an agile environment cannot be overestimated. In every case and supplemental case investigated this factor would seem to be the make or break aspect of the team or project. It is certainly not sufficient for agility, but agility cannot exist without it in the highest levels. The nature and aspects of this variable should be heavily investigated.

Motorola, Xerox, Johnson & Johnson, MCI, Composit, and 3M stay at the top because they show long-term commitment to planning for and managing changing business conditions (Want, 1993). These companies have worked many aspects that are directly applicable to agility: attitude of teamwork, revamped corporate culture, non-traditional reward systems, skills and knowledge used as competitive resource. a fostering of shared motivations and common goals, superior communication (primarily between people within and without the organization. A new paradigm has indeed replaced mass manufacturing. The skills and techniques required to competitively master this new paradigm successfully, whether or not recorded by history as "Agility", must be achieved. Table 10.2 lists some final conclusions on what the lessons learned in this research mean to agility.

Table 10.2. What Lessons Learned Mean to Agility

• Companies must actively pursue agility
• Expected benefits of agility must be anticipated before adoption
• All resources should be used to achieve agility (Technology, Employees, Partner Companies, Government, Academia)
• Implements must be the creators of agile initiatives
• Must achieve high risk tolerance interactively between and to internal staff, external partners and customers
• Agility can only be achieved through efforts that simultaneously address people, process and technology

REVIEW OF RESEARCH CONTRIBUTIONS

This dissertation makes many important contributions (Table 10.3). First, a body of knowledge on agility was developed that pulls together and builds upon the multifaceted issues that comprise agility. Second, this dissertation is the first to attempt to link antecedent variables to the agility level within firms. The existing models described the attributes of agility and do not necessarily provide factors that may be manipulated to increase the level of agility. Third, this research provides better grounding of the issues surrounding agility through the grounded theory approach and paves the way for more quantitative research aligned along the antecedent factors. Also, this dissertation was the first to apply the potentially useful techniques of Data Envelopment Analysis to the problem of agility. Further work may allow each of the antecedent variables to be measured accurately for useful manipulation. Finally, this dissertation research was conducted based primarily upon data within the aerospace industry. This look into the aerospace industry allowed for some unique and generalizable perspectives to agility that may not have been possible when studying other industries.

Table 10.3. Research Contributions

- Create body of knowledge consisting of literature that builds to conceptual framework for agility
- Development of antecedent factors leading to agility
- Grounded research case studies illuminating issues critical to agility
- Initial application of DEA to agility
- Early focus on implementation activities specifically directed at the aerospace industry

FUTURE DIRECTIONS

This research has allowed the generation of the information that will prove critical to future research (Table 10.4). Many projects have developed due to this work and learning from the research results has defined a path for future work. The first area of study will be the development of a sequence for the antecedent factors. It was noted in the research that all antecedent areas must be addressed when attempting agile implementation projects; however, how does a company balance limited resources during such a move? Also, how does a company show early success in one area when the expansion of a 'pilot' project often results in different and sometimes unexpected outcomes. Work on this area as it relates to the 'people' side or cultural side of companies is the focus of the "People in Agile Organizations" project. This project which provides useful data for several institutions and companies. The project currently has 12 sponsors including: Hughes, Rockwell, Sandia National Labs, Northrop Grumman, Kodak, Delphi Saginaw Systems, GPU Energy, Colgate-Palmolive, Silicon Graphics, Einstein Health Care Network, and New York State Electric and Gas.

Another important development of follow-on research is to develop a way to effectively measure the antecedent variables. An upcoming project with UniSci will allow for the determination of agile baselines. Quantifiable baseline data was unavailable in the current research and this was seen as clearly important in future work. Companies participating in the project will be assessed on several agility aspects as identified in the current research. This project will also be looking at the effects of moving from small scale implementation to larger scale implementation. Important factors might be missed in small projects that may prove to be critical in larger implementations.

Finally, there were many observations during the research that agility might have a different framework or different drivers when viewed from lessor developed nations. Future work especially focusing on the aerospace industry and their agile relationships with Asian partners/suppliers/customers will be the subject of research for the upcoming year.

Table 10.4. Future Directions

• Development of sequencing plan for agile implementation projects
• Development of metrics on antecedent variables
• Examinations of limited scope implementation vs. wide scale implementation
• Examination of non-North American centric drivers to agility
• International dimensions of agility; transformation requirements for countries wanting to miss the 'mass manufacturing' path

Gams Programs Used in Chapter 9, Figures 9.7-9.40

The data are for the international aircraft industry, 1979-1994

```
$OFFSYMXREF OFFSYMLIST
OPTION SOLPRINT = OFF;
OPTION LIMROW = 0, LIMCOL = 0;
OPTION SYSOUT = OFF;
```

*This is the 000000 version where companies are deleted if ANY values are 0.

```
SET DMU full list of companies  / CO1*CO36/
DMU84(DMU) /CO21, CO24, CO33/
DMU85(DMU) /CO7*CO8, CO16*CO17, CO20*CO21, CO23*CO27, CO32*CO35/
DMU86(DMU) /CO3, CO6, CO7*CO8, CO16*CO17, CO20*CO21, CO23*CO27,CO31*CO35/
DMU87(DMU) /CO3, CO6, CO7*CO8, CO16*CO17, CO20*CO28, CO30*CO35/
DMU88(DMU) /CO3, CO6, CO8, CO16*CO17, CO19*CO24, CO26*CO28, CO30*CO35/
DMU89(DMU) /CO3, CO6, CO8, CO16*CO17, CO19*CO28, CO30*CO35/
DMU90(DMU) /CO3, CO6, CO8, CO16*CO17, CO19*CO28, CO30*CO35/
DMU91(DMU) /CO3, CO6, CO8, CO16*CO17, CO19*CO28, CO30*CO35/
DMU92(DMU) /CO3, CO6, CO8, CO16*CO17, CO19*CO21, CO23*CO28, CO30*CO35/
DMU93(DMU) /CO3, CO6, CO8, CO16*CO17, CO20*CO21, CO23*CO28, CO31*CO35/
DMU94(DMU) /CO3, CO6, CO8, CO16*CO17, CO20*CO21, CO23*CO28, CO31*CO35/

$ONTEXT
```

*This is the 99999 version where companies are deleted if ANY values are 0.

```
SET DMU full list of companies  / CO1*CO36/
DMU84(DMU) /CO21, CO24, CO33/
DMU85(DMU) /CO1,CO7*CO10,CO14*CO17, CO20*CO21, CO23*CO28, CO32*CO35/
```

```
DMU86(DMU) /CO1,CO3, CO5*CO11, CO13*CO17, CO20*CO29, CO31*CO35/
DMU87(DMU) /CO1,CO3, CO5*CO11, CO13*CO17, CO20*CO36/
DMU88(DMU) /CO1,CO3, CO5*CO11, CO13*CO17, CO19*CO36/
DMU89(DMU) /CO1,CO3*CO11, CO13*CO17, CO19*CO36/
DMU90(DMU) /CO1*CO11, CO13*CO36/
DMU91(DMU) /CO1*CO11, CO13*CO36/
DMU92(DMU) /CO1*CO11, CO13*CO36/
DMU93(DMU) /CO1*CO36/
DMU94(DMU) /CO1*CO36/
$OFFTEXT
```

```
DATANAMES list of data
        /SIC sic code
        SALE annual sales
        REVT revenues total
        COGS costs of goods sold
        EMP number of employees
        XSGA administrative and selling overhead/

I(DATANAMES) list of inputs /COGS, EMP, XSGA/
R(DATANAMES) list of outputs /SALE, REVT/;
```

TABLE DATA84(DMU,DATANAMES)

	SIC	SALE	REVT	COGS	EMP	XSGA
CO1	3720	0	0	0	0	0
CO2	3720	0	0	0	0	0
CO3	3720	0	0	0	0	0
CO4	3720	0	0	0	0	0
CO5	3720	0	0	0	0	0
CO6	3720	0	0	0	0	0
CO7	3720	0	0	0	0	0
CO8	3721	0	0	0	0	0
CO9	3721	0	0	0	0	0
CO10	3721	0	0	0	0	0
CO11	3721	0	0	0	0	0
CO12	3721	0	0	0	0	0
CO13	3721	0	0	0	0	0
CO14	3721	0	0	0	0	0
CO15	3721	0	0	0	0	0
CO16	3721	0	0	0	0	0
CO17	3721	0	0	0	0	0
CO18	3721	0	0	0	0	0
CO19	3721	0	0	0	0	0
CO20	3721	0	0	0	0	0
CO21	3724	32.313	32.313	18.421	0.4	7.136
CO22	3724	0	0	0	0	0

CO23	3724	0	0	0	0	0
CO24	3724	9.255	59.255	49.693	0.597	8.317
CO25	3724	0	0	0	0	0
CO26	3724	0	0	0	0	0
CO27	3724	0	0	0	0	0
CO28	3728	0	0	0	0	0
CO29	3728	0	0	0	0	0
CO30	3728	0	0	0	0	0
CO31	3728	0	0	0	0	0
CO32	3728	0	0	0	0	0
CO33	3728	607.139	607.139	485.367	7.6	26.52
CO34	3728	0	0	0	0	0
CO35	3728	0	0	0	0	0
CO36	3728	0	0	0	0	0

TABLE DATA85(DMU, DATANAMES)

	SIC	SALE	REVT	COGS	EMP	XSGA
CO1	3720	3918.01	3918.01	2355.62	999999	999999
CO7	3720	4038.50	4038.50	3076.30	56	571.8
CO8	3721	13636.00	13636.00	11781.00	104	886
CO9	3721	478.574	478.574	406.363	999999	40.961
CO10	3721	3502.40	3502.40	2067.55	75.645	999999
CO14	3721	108.771	108.771	999999	999999	999999
CO15	3721	9535.00	9535.00	999999	87.8	999999
CO16	3721	11617.70	11617.70	9102.63	97.067	1614.30
CO17	3721	5056.56	5056.56	4012.00	46.9	543.4
CO20	3721	55.721	55.721	29.741	1.366	7.038
CO21	3724	47.346	47.346	25.027	0.5	8.587
CO23	3724	883.864	883.864	620.083	8	178.384
CO24	3724	61.323	61.323	48.228	0.574	7.84
CO25	3724	3256.20	3256.20	2423.70	47.2	431.5
CO26	3724	352.927	352.927	310.114	6.175	27.606
CO27	3724	14991.60	14991.60	10472.20	184.8	2919.42
CO28	3728	417.034	417.034	314.099	999999	96.072
CO32	3728	27.445	27.445	20.514	0.332	3.711
CO33	3728	626.124	626.124	505.353	8.4	33.59
CO34	3728	1284.14	1284.14	785.114	16.1	296.379
CO35	3728	171.816	171.816	114.795	2.864	31.684

TABLE DATA86(DMU, DATANAMES)

	SIC	SALE	REVT	COGS	EMP	XSGA
CO1	3720	4895.66	4895.66	3175.23	999999	999999
CO3	3720	4322.52	4322.52	3845.37	20.616	299.9

CO5	3720	2227.87	2227.87	1115.37	13.888	999999
CO6	3720	101.727	101.727	77.159	1.038	16.003
CO7	3720	5023.30	5023.30	3893.20	72	610.2
CO8	3721	16341.00	16341.00	13885.00	125	1363.00
CO9	3721	796.918	796.918	672.335	999999	66.104
CO10	3721	4602.73	4602.73	3258.01	75.48	999999
CO11	3721	2056.60	2056.60	1268.45	999999	999999
CO13	3721	416.841	416.841	247.834	999999	999999
CO14	3721	116.435	116.435	999999	999999	999999
CO15	3721	10273.00	10273.00	999999	96.9	999999
CO16	3721	12771.90	12771.90	10069.70	105.696	1828.60
CO17	3721	5608.40	5608.40	4760.30	46.8	551.7
CO20	3721	36.931	36.931	24.579	1.001	8.458
CO21	3724	46.87	46.87	24.933	0.5	8.719
CO22	3724	2643.97	2643.97	1926.49	999999	234.758
CO23	3724	371.413	371.413	259.906	15.72	70.338
CO24	3724	63.112	63.112	48.381	0.623	8.66
CO25	3724	3241.40	3241.40	2434.50	44.8	455.9
CO26	3724	572.065	572.065	472.339	6.295	52.372
CO27	3724	15669.10	15669.10	11891.40	193.5	3140.13
CO28	3728	455.179	455.179	356.714	999999	100.216
CO29	3728	142.781	142.781	30.924	1.995	999999
CO31	3728	93.38	93.38	71.655	1.496	7.721
CO32	3728	33.398	33.398	24.142	0.391	4.508
CO33	3728	663.405	663.405	562.2	10.3	34.012
CO34	3728	1433.94	1433.94	867.569	16	343.389
CO35	3728	214.182	214.182	140.552	3.8	39.837

TABLE DATA87(DMU, DATANAMES)

	SIC	SALE	REVT	COGS	EMP	XSGA
CO1	3720	5224.42	5224.42	731.133	41.216	999999
CO3	3720	4208.85	4208.85	3873.04	16.587	381.215
CO5	3720	2519.34	2519.34	1247.33	13.659	999999
CO6	3720	139.482	139.482	102.659	1.056	21.117
CO7	3720	5388.40	5388.40	4227.30	61	604.3
CO8	3721	15355.00	15355.00	13028.00	143.7	1617.00
CO9	3721	1103.89	1103.89	905.459	999999	102.476
CO10	3721	6679.90	6679.90	4088.26	86.8	999999
CO11	3721	2321.12	2321.12	1562.82	999999	999999
CO13	3721	575.286	575.286	345.696	999999	999999
CO14	3721	129.788	129.788	999999	999999	999999
CO15	3721	11321.00	11321.00	999999	99.3	999999
CO16	3721	13289.40	13289.40	10359.60	112.4	2013.30
CO17	3721	6052.50	6052.50	5110.90	48.2	527.6

CO20	3721	33.661	33.661	16.367	0.588	5.592
CO21	3724	43.161	43.161	27.168	0.5	10.325
CO22	3724	3375.19	3375.19	2437.55	42	301.62
CO23	3724	1132.66	1132.66	800.607	16.785	163.186
CO24	3724	66.736	66.736	51.057	0.549	8.865
CO25	3724	3216.80	3216.80	2363.30	44.4	446.4
CO26	3724	495.854	495.854	382.241	4.26	64.421
CO27	3724	17170.20	17170.20	12132.50	190	3338.80
CO28	3728	76.318	76.318	48.872	1.18	17.202
CO29	3728	208.227	208.227	48.241	2.414	999999
CO30	3728	12.744	12.744	5.941	0.306	2.61
CO31	3728	136.398	136.398	107.255	1.524	11.305
CO32	3728	38.728	38.728	28.238	0.563	6.5
CO33	3728	906.841	906.841	787.056	11	35.473
CO34	3728	1365.48	1365.48	832.951	14.2	331.714
CO35	3728	269.778	269.778	176.283	3.9	49.631
CO36	3728	241.885	241.885	31.533	999999	999999

TABLE DATA88(DMU, DATANAMES)

	SIC	SALE	REVT	COGS	EMP	XSGA
CO1	3720	6430.77	6430.77	712.96	39.898	999999
CO3	3720	5983.13	5983.13	5324.08	16.6	442.946
CO5	3720	1726.16	1726.16	1102.34	13.347	999999
CO6	3720	168.41	168.41	125.787	1.051	27.145
CO7	3720	7279.40	7279.40	999999	60	999999
CO8	3721	16962.00	16962.00	14316.00	154.2	1631.00
CO9	3721	1142.02	1142.02	999999	12.2	999999
CO10	3721	10044.86	10044.86	5789.29	133.6	999999
CO11	3721	2503.90	2503.90	1533.68	17.636	999999
CO13	3721	522.03	522.03	256.03	11.709	999999
CO14	3721	154.309	154.309	999999	999999	999999
CO15	3721	10590.00	10590.00	999999	86.8	999999
CO16	3721	15069.00	15069.00	11612.00	121.421	2118.00
CO17	3721	5797.10	5797.10	5016.80	44.6	514.3
CO19	3721	594.517	594.517	490.445	10.338	14.177
CO20	3721	26.558	26.558	20.839	0.467	4.619
CO21	3724	26.473	26.473	15.288	0.25	5.291
CO22	3724	3514.54	3514.54	2540.16	40.9	304.606
CO23	3724	1712.55	1712.55	1200.03	16.115	247.789
CO24	3724	61.975	61.975	46.105	0.517	9.421
CO25	3724	4522.69	4522.69	999999	43.8	999999
CO26	3724	400.444	400.444	304.489	3.768	51.374
CO27	3724	18087.80	18087.80	12775.30	186.8	3554.90
CO28	3728	59.812	59.812	41.27	0.99	14.818
CO29	3728	302.793	302.793	91.812	2.759	999999

CO30	3728	18.112	18.112	11.444	0.352	4.083
CO31	3728	170.646	170.646	132.335	1.549	14.411
CO32	3728	62.083	62.083	49.61	0.94	10.874
CO33	3728	1044.68	1044.68	904.934	12	39.863
CO34	3728	1477.29	1477.29	940.971	13.8	339.063
CO35	3728	323.589	323.589	216.005	4.9	59.13
CO36	3728	269.096	269.096	34.411	999999	999999

TABLE DATA89(DMU, DATANAMES)

	SIC	SALE	REVT	COGS	EMP	XSGA
CO1	3720	5323.79	5323.79	3313.02	36.899	999999
CO3	3720	6454.36	6454.36	5551.67	20.25	604.83
CO4	3720	11.325	11.325	9.19	999999	999999
CO5	3720	3377.48	3377.48	1750.59	27.471	999999
CO6	3720	204.524	204.524	146.804	1.081	30.989
CO7	3720	7430.50	7430.50	999999	58	999999
CO8	3721	20276.00	20276.00	17302.0	164.5	1766.00
CO9	3721	1770.94	1770.94	999999	22.5	999999
CO10	3721	14894.31	14894.31	9843.20	127.5	999999
CO11	3721	3166.62	3166.62	1451.94	16.327	999999
CO13	3721	1041.97	1041.97	248.986	11.69	999999
CO14	3721	185.639	185.639	999999	5	999999
CO15	3721	9891.00	9891.00	999999	82.5	999999
CO16	3721	14581.00	14581.00	11693.00	127.926	1965.00
CO17	3721	5248.40	5248.40	4471.30	41	533.2
CO19	3721	634.732	634.732	511.543	9.16	17.37
CO20	3721	24.183	24.183	16.798	0.485	4.32
CO21	3724	26.239	26.239	17.602	0.23	5.205
CO22	3724	4856.02	4856.02	3801.86	55.475	336.085
CO23	3724	1959.16	1959.16	1387.52	17.7	269.072
CO24	3724	68.134	68.134	49.801	0.566	9.557
CO25	3724	3531.20	3531.20	2652.40	43.2	505.9
CO26	3724	471.024	471.024	376.971	5.014	55.813
CO27	3724	19613.70	19613.70	13762.00	201.4	3767.40
CO28	3728	68.571	68.571	49.454	0.9	9.524
CO29	3728	333.638	333.638	103.323	2.723	999999
CO30	3728	22.516	22.516	15.337	0.289	4.138
CO31	3728	194.111	194.111	150.634	1.551	16.825
CO32	3728	71.923	71.923	55.422	0.747	10.447
CO33	3728	1078.71	1078.71	973.491	12	46.576
CO34	3728	1595.40	1595.40	947.917	13.7	330.273
CO35	3728	355.625	355.625	237.798	5.9	63.867
CO36	3728	327.414	327.414	38.51	999999	999999

TABLE DATA90(DMU, DATANAMES)

	SIC	SALE	REVT	COGS	EMP	XSGA
CO1	3720	6488.89	8648.31	4556.79	37.691	999999
CO2	3720	45.338	74.491	13.904	0.656	999999
CO3	3720	7270.02	8016.6	6193.54	20.59	707.059
CO4	3720	16.352	13.547	13.799	0.035	999999
CO5	3720	4333.53	4259.38	1235.96	27.868	999999
CO6	3720	211.807	236.334	150.582	1.091	33.045
CO7	3720	7915	7822.5	999999	54	999999
CO8	3721	27595	29314	23355	160.5	2032
CO9	3721	2433.74	2669.42	999999	25	999999
CO10	3721	18818.64	18691.25	10700.2	127.9	999999
CO11	3721	3064.9	3463.08	1175.69	15.714	999999
CO13	3721	1322.27	1763.38	371.986	12.925	999999
CO14	3721	205.595	232.463	999999	4.9	999999
CO15	3721	9958	9809	999999	73	999999
CO16	3721	16246	18432	13234	121.19	2073
CO17	3721	5489.8	5694.2	4561.1	38.2	450.5
CO18	3721	129.409	216.587	999999	999999	999999
CO19	3721	730.256	696.863	617.987	9.499	14.879
CO20	3721	15.437	20.06	14.322	0.39	4.065
CO21	3724	25.368	21.729	15.25	0.242	6.22
CO22	3724	6552.6	6220.39	5167.09	65.9	426.723
CO23	3724	2211.02	1878.79	1564.06	18.5	305.172
CO24	3724	65.326	57.605	49.813	0.577	9.688
CO25	3724	3445.8	3206.8	2678.4	33.2	529.9
CO26	3724	356.255	360.571	278.392	4.612	44.038
CO27	3724	21549.5	20953	15315.3	192.6	4115.2
CO28	3728	74.697	74.38	52.934	0.77	11.797
CO29	3728	156.352	274.496	35.813	1.408	999999
CO30	3728	27.523	32.224	16.87	0.399	3.969
CO31	3728	189.957	206.793	147.61	1.578	16.586
CO32	3728	64.434	51.015	46.253	0.587	8.838
CO33	3728	1385.09	1279.66	1210.56	11.5	46.223
CO34	3728	1599.8	1669.2	956.6	13	341.1
CO35	3728	441.133	479.537	287.913	5.86	84.815
CO36	3728	370.53	423.722	48.457	999999	999999

TABLE DATA91(DMU, DATANAMES)

	SIC	SALE	REVT	COGS	EMP	XSGA
CO3	3720	8016.60	8016.60	6920.47	21.215	771.875
CO6	3720	236.334	236.334	171.877	1.116	35.151
CO8	3721	29314.00	29314.00	23826.00	155.7	2708.00
CO16	3721	18432.00	18432.00	15267.00	109.123	1589.00

CO17	3721	5694.20	5694.20	4640.00	36.2	531.4
CO19	3721	696.863	696.863	575.463	9.601	17.294
CO20	3721	20.06	20.06	19.333	0.522	6.392
CO21	3724	21.729	21.729	12.823	0.245	6.478
CO22	3724	6220.39	6220.39	5123.19	61.4	391.097
CO23	3724	1878.79	1878.79	1396.59	15.75	263.893
CO24	3724	57.605	57.605	46.839	0.576	10.604
CO25	3724	3206.80	3206.80	2487.40	29.4	508.6
CO26	3724	360.571	360.571	293.905	3.852	49.084
CO27	3724	20953.00	20953.00	15623.00	185.1	4152.00
CO28	3728	74.38	74.38	51.079	0.762	13.234
CO30	3728	32.224	32.224	20.824	0.419	4.624
CO31	3728	206.793	206.793	165.633	1.604	17.131
CO32	3728	51.015	51.015	36.303	0.467	8.341
CO33	3728	1279.66	1279.66	1159.74	9.23	46.5
CO34	3728	1669.20	1669.20	974.8	12.8	395.5
CO35	3728	479.537	479.537	312.753	6.16	93.683

TABLE DATA92(DMU, DATANAMES)

	SIC	SALE	REVT	COGS	EMP	XSGA
CO1	3720	9895.72	9895.72	6017.61	999999	999999
CO2	3720	127.547	127.547	51.538	1.212	999999
CO3	3720	8745.97	8745.97	7500.00	22.222	866.552
CO4	3720	22.407	22.407	2.018	0.189	999999
CO5	3720	4324.83	4324.83	2129.77	999999	999999
CO6	3720	276.796	276.796	203.228	1.127	42.646
CO7	3720	8344.20	8344.20	999999	54	999999
CO8	3721	30184.00	30184.00	24105.00	142	3078.00
CO9	3721	3653.77	3653.77	999999	34.3	999999
CO10	3721	17612.40	17612.40	999999	999999	999999
CO11	3721	2830.35	2830.35	1379.66	14.909	999999
CO13	3721	2048.58	2048.58	624.573	12.606	999999
CO14	3721	270.969	270.969	999999	999999	999999
CO15	3721	10100.00	10100.00	999999	71.7	999999
CO16	3721	17373.00	17373.00	15156.00	87.377	1328.00
CO17	3721	5550.00	5550.00	4706.00	33.6	455
CO18	3721	258.719	258.719	999999	999999	999999
CO19	3721	846.821	846.821	719.997	9.24	11.233
CO20	3721	23.326	23.326	19.484	0.538	6.342
CO21	3724	25.882	25.882	16.309	0.27	7.477
CO22	3724	6288.00	6288.00	5654.26	999999	349.529
CO23	3724	1868.34	1868.34	1370.30	13.8	263.325
CO24	3724	51.897	51.897	41.469	0.565	12.209
CO25	3724	2887.60	2887.60	2164.10	23.8	528.8

CO26	3724	365.152	365.152	284.111	3.383	43.601
CO27	3724	22032.00	22032.00	16138.00	178	4550.00
CO28	3728	67.445	67.445	46.701	0.651	11.822
CO29	3728	264.187	264.187	61.335	2.375	999999
CO30	3728	32.027	32.027	20.357	0.434	4.913
CO31	3728	227.044	227.044	183.307	1.597	18.642
CO32	3728	47.602	47.602	43.651	0.397	8.628
CO33	3728	1175.15	1175.15	1107.46	6.5	43.8
CO34	3728	1672.70	1672.70	1004.70	12.3	381.9
CO35	3728	567.132	567.132	362.035	6.92	124.213
CO36	3728	492.006	492.006	999999	999999	999999

TABLE DATA93(DMU, DATANAMES)

	SIC	SALE	REVT	COGS	EMP	XSGA
CO1	3720	8990.79	8990.79	5770.19	999999	999999
CO2	3720	107.528	107.528	54.14	1.237	999999
CO3	3720	9931.98	9931.98	8244.43	17.404	1018.94
CO4	3720	25.755	25.755	3.123	0.163	999999
CO5	3720	3459.50	3459.50	1578.86	999999	999999
CO6	3720	277.42	277.42	200.909	1.126	47.47
CO7	3720	9074.60	9074.60	999999	56	999999
CO8	3721	25438.00	25438.00	19959.00	123	2763.00
CO9	3721	3689.67	3689.67	999999	36.5	999999
CO10	3721	16166.15	16166.15	999999	87.4	999999
CO11	3721	3104.94	3104.94	1461.05	999999	999999
CO12	3721	586.974	586.974	122.762	999999	1.535
CO13	3721	2327.60	2327.60	699.925	12.363	999999
CO14	3721	298.262	298.262	999999	999999	999999
CO15	3721	13071.00	13071.00	999999	83.5	999999
CO16	3721	14474.00	14474.00	12064.00	70.016	1061.00
CO17	3721	5063.00	5063.00	4145.00	29.8	485
CO18	3721	281.186	281.186	999999	999999	999999
CO19	3721	766.043	766.043	650.257	999999	999999
CO20	3721	30.91	30.91	25.341	0.528	8.596
CO21	3724	32.393	32.393	20.72	0.26	7.279
CO22	3724	5285.55	5285.55	4342.02	999999	291.471
CO23	3724	1696.97	1696.97	1278.46	10.25	272.145
CO24	3724	61.429	61.429	47.085	0.581	10.83
CO25	3724	2491.70	2491.70	1845.20	21	466.4
CO26	3724	438.293	438.293	349.392	6.43	53.516
CO27	3724	21081.00	21081.00	15460.00	168.6	3684.00
CO28	3728	64.541	64.541	43.96	0.527	11.121
CO29	3728	283.167	283.167	52.918	999999	999999
CO30	3728	35.221	35.221	22.361	999999	5.472
CO31	3728	266.408	266.408	207.293	1.827	25.391

CO32	3728	36.528	36.528	26.04	0.28	6.353
CO33	3728	918.141	918.141	807.936	4.9	28.352
CO34	3728	1383.10	1383.10	843.2	9.3	291.9
CO35	3728	666.796	666.796	432.908	8	140.965
CO36	3728	520.046	520.046	999999	999999	999999

TABLE DATA94(DMU, DATANAMES)

	SIC	SALE	REVT	COGS	EMP	XSGA
CO1	3720	8771.45	8771.45	5683.39	999999	999999
CO2	3720	100.88	100.88	43.797	999999	999999
CO3	3720	10790.06	10790.06	8885.85	17.243	1112.96
CO4	3720	22.385	22.385	2.368	0.156	999999
CO5	3720	3417.71	3417.71	1573.56	999999	999999
CO6	3720	309.08	309.08	230.395	1.133	48.525
CO7	3720	9681.00	9681.00	999999	53	999999
CO8	3721	21924.00	21924.00	16801.00	115	2830.00
CO9	3721	4327.10	4327.10	999999	37	999999
CO10	3721	10957.96	10957.96	999999	46.5	999999
CO11	3721	2350.22	2350.22	1039.60	999999	999999
CO12	3721	507.549	507.549	94.69	999999	1.292
CO13	3721	1992.80	1992.80	749.517	10.414	999999
CO14	3721	312.942	312.942	999999	999999	999999
CO15	3721	22906.00	22906.00	999999	999999	999999
CO16	3721	13162.00	13162.00	10762.00	65.76	981
CO17	3721	6711.00	6711.00	5208.00	42.4	753
CO18	3721	322.861	322.861	999999	999999	999999
CO19	3721	682.707	682.707	572.834	999999	999999
CO20	3721	32.098	32.098	26.604	0.512	7.1
CO21	3724	40.379	40.379	25.237	0.31	7.967
CO22	3724	4845.53	4845.53	3886.53	999999	318.643
CO23	3724	1419.55	1419.55	1060.77	9.2	215.058
CO24	3724	68.134	68.134	51.482	0.615	11.106
CO25	3724	2391.20	2391.20	1717.60	18	437.1
CO26	3724	525.833	525.833	431.648	5.41	69.768
CO27	3724	21161.00	21161.00	15539.00	171.5	3514.00
CO28	3728	61.738	61.738	40.836	0.653	12.141
CO29	3728	220.99	220.99	57.193	2.138	999999
CO30	3728	30.432	30.432	20.513	999999	4.856
CO31	3728	252.648	252.648	195.465	1.733	23.135
CO32	3728	35.806	35.806	24.638	0.309	7.098
CO33	3728	805	805	692.025	4	26.198
CO34	3728	1372.70	1372.70	854.9	9.2	279.8
CO35	3728	812.672	812.672	524.372	8.74	173.928
CO36	3728	595.158	595.158	999999	999999	999999

PARAMETERS

X(I,DMU)	Table of inputs for an arbitrary year
Y(R,DMU)	Table of all outputs for an arbitrary year
X0(I)	Inputs of DMU currently rated
Y0(R)	Outputs of DMU currently rated;

SCALAR

EPSILON	Archimedean infinitesmally small	/0.00000001/;

VARIABLES

OBJ	Value of objective function
THETA	Input contraction factor
EFFX(I)	Optimal inputs
EFFY(R)	Optimal outputs

POSITIVE VARIABLES

LAMBDA(DMU)	Weights
SLACKPLUS(I)	Input slacks
SLACKMINUS(R)	Output slacks;

EQUATIONS

DEFOBJ	defines objective function of dual program
BCC	states that sum of lambdas =E= one
DEFEFFY(R)	defines best practice outputs summing over DMU
OUTBAL(R)	output constraints
DEFEFFX(I)	defines best practice inputs summing over DMU
INBAL(I)	input constraints for discretionary inputs;

DEFOBJ..	OBJ =E= THETA - EPSILON*SUM(I, SLACKPLUS(I))
	- EPSILON*SUM(R,SLACKMINUS(R));
BCC..	SUM(DMU,LAMBDA(DMU)) =E= 1;
DEFEFFY(R)..	EFFY(R) =E= SUM(DMU, LAMBDA(DMU)*Y(R,DMU));
OUTBAL(R)..	EFFY(R) - SLACKMINUS(R) =E= Y0(R);
DEFEFFX(I)..	EFFX(I)=E= SUM(DMU, LAMBDA(DMU)*X(I,DMU));
INBAL(I)..	EFFX(I) + SLACKPLUS(I) =E= THETA*X0(I);

THETA.LO = 0.01;

MODEL DEABCC/DEFOBJ, DEFEFFY, OUTBAL, DEFEFFX, INBAL, BCC/;

```
PARAMETER
     RESULT(DMU,*)              Table with results from  DEA
     LAMBDAMATR(DMU,DMU)  Matrix of lambdas;

***Calculations for year Begin Here

ALIAS(DMU91,DMUALIAS);

X(I,DMU) = DATA91(DMU,I);
Y(R,DMU) = DATA91(DMU,R);

LOOP(DMUALIAS,

     X0(I) = X(I,DMUALIAS);
     Y0(R) = Y(R,DMUALIAS);
     EFFX.L(I) = X0(I);
     EFFY.L(R) = Y0(R);

     SOLVE DEABCC USING LP MINIMIZING OBJ;
     RESULT(DMUALIAS,"EFFNCY")      = THETA.L;
     RESULT(DMUALIAS,R)       = EFFY.L(R);
     RESULT(DMUALIAS,I)       = EFFX.L(I);
     LAMBDAMATR(DMUALIAS,DMU)      = LAMBDA.L(DMU);

     LAMBDA.L(DMU) = 0; LAMBDA.L(DMUALIAS) = 1;
     );
     DISPLAY "Results on the envelopment side for 1991", RESULT, LAMBDAMATR;
```

DATA USED IN CHAPTER 9, FIGURES 9.7-9.40

COMP	YEAR	SALE	EFFNCY	YEAR	CHNG SALE	EFFNCY	YEAR	ABS(CH SLS)	EFFNCY
CO2	1979	3392.973	0.967	1979		0.967	1979		0.967
CO2	1980	3376.701	0.960	1980	-16.272	0.960	1980	16.272	0.960
CO2	1981	3328.000	0.952	1981	-48.701	0.952	1981	48.701	0.952
CO2	1982	2936.000	0.939	1982	-392.000	0.939	1982	392.000	0.939
CO2	1983	2979.800	0.956	1983	43.800	0.956	1983	43.800	0.956
CO2	1984	3221.097	0.965	1984	241.297	0.965	1984	241.297	0.965
CO2	1985	4038.498	0.978	1985	817.401	0.978	1985	817.401	0.978
CO2	1986	5023.292	1.000	1986	984.794	1.000	1986	984.794	1.000
CO2	1987	5388.394	1.000	1987	365.102	1.000	1987	365.102	1.000
CO2	1988	5342.699	1.000	1988	-45.695	1.000	1988	45.695	1.000
CO2	1989	5282.097	1.000	1989	-60.602	1.000	1989	60.602	1.000
CO2	1990	5473.199	1.000	1990	191.102	1.000	1990	191.102	1.000
CO2	1991	5228.097	1.000	1991	-245.102	1.000	1991	245.102	1.000
CO2	1992	5620.000	1.000	1992	391.903	1.000	1992	391.903	1.000
CO2	1993	6275.000	1.000	1993	655.000	1.000	1993	655.000	1.000
CO2	1994	6680.000	1.000	1994	405.000	1.000	1994	405.000	1.000
COMP	YEAR	SALE	EFFNCY	YEAR	CHNG SALE	EFFNCY	YEAR	ABS(CH SLS)	EFFNCY
CO4	1979								
CO4	1980								
CO4	1981								
CO4	1982								
CO4	1983								
CO4	1984								
CO4	1985								
CO4	1986								
CO4	1987	2.889	0.726	1987		0.726	1987		0.726
CO4	1988	1.433	0.929	1988	-1.456	0.929	1988	1.456	0.929
CO4	1989	0.109	0.828	1989	-1.324	0.828	1989	1.324	0.828
CO4	1990	0.166	0.064	1990	0.057	0.064	1990	0.057	0.064
CO4	1991	0.722	0.430	1991	0.556	0.430	1991	0.556	0.430
CO4	1992	1.021	0.999	1992	0.299	0.999	1992	0.299	0.999
CO4	1993	1.000	0.210	1993	-0.021	0.210	1993	0.021	0.210
CO4	1994	1.000	0.618	1994	0.000	0.618	1994	0.000	0.618
COMP	YEAR	SALE	EFFNCY	YEAR	CHNG SALE	EFFNCY	YEAR	ABS(CH SLS)	EFFNCY
CO8	1979	8131.000	1.000	1979		1.000	1979		1.000
CO8	1980	9426.195	1.000	1980	1295.195	1.000	1980	1295.195	1.000
CO8	1981	9788.195	1.000	1981	362.000	1.000	1981	362.000	1.000
CO8	1982	9035.000	1.000	1982	-753.195	1.000	1982	753.195	1.000
CO8	1983	11129.000	1.000	1983	2094.000	1.000	1983	2094.000	1.000
CO8	1984	10354.000	1.000	1984	-775.000	1.000	1984	775.000	1.000
CO8	1985	13636.003	1.000	1985	3282.003	1.000	1985	3282.003	1.000
CO8	1986	16341.003	1.000	1986	2705.000	1.000	1986	2705.000	1.000
CO8	1987	15355.003	1.000	1987	-986.000	1.000	1987	986.000	1.000
CO8	1988	16962.000	1.000	1988	1606.997	1.000	1988	1606.997	1.000
CO8	1989	20276.000	1.000	1989	3314.000	1.000	1989	3314.000	1.000
CO8	1990	27595.000	1.000	1990	7319.000	1.000	1990	7319.000	1.000
CO8	1991	29314.000	1.000	1991	1719.000	1.000	1991	1719.000	1.000
CO8	1992	30184.000	1.000	1992	870.000	1.000	1992	870.000	1.000
CO8	1993	25438.000	1.000	1993	-4746.000	1.000	1993	4746.000	1.000
CO8	1994	21924.000	1.000	1994	-3514.000	1.000	1994	3514.000	1.000

COMP	YEAR	SALE	EFFNCY	YEAR	CHNG SALE	EFFNCY	YEAR	ABS(CH SLS)	EFFNCY
CO10	1979								
CO10	1980								
CO10	1981								
CO10	1982								
CO10	1983								
CO10	1984								
CO10	1985								
CO10	1986								
CO10	1987								
CO10	1988								
CO10	1989								
CO10	1990								
CO10	1991								
CO10	1992	5.916	0.423	1992		0.423	1992		0.423
CO10	1993	8.120	0.525	1993	2.204	0.525	1993	2.204	0.525
CO10	1994	7.619	0.561	1994	-0.501	0.561	1994	0.501	0.561
COMP	YEAR	SALE	EFFNCY	YEAR	CHNG SALE	EFFNCY	YEAR	ABS(CH SLS)	EFFNCY
CO14	1979	1455.448	0.860	1979		0.860	1979		0.860
CO14	1980	1476.010	1.000	1980	20.562	1.000	1980	20.562	1.000
CO14	1981	1729.336	1.000	1981	253.326	1.000	1981	253.326	1.000
CO14	1982	1915.528	1.000	1982	186.192	1.000	1982	186.192	1.000
CO14	1983	2003.243	1.000	1983	87.715	1.000	1983	87.715	1.000
CO14	1984	2220.162	1.000	1984	216.919	1.000	1984	216.919	1.000
CO14	1985	2557.806	1.000	1985	337.644	1.000	1985	337.644	1.000
CO14	1986	3048.520	1.000	1986	490.714	1.000	1986	490.714	1.000
CO14	1987	3440.125	1.000	1987	391.605	1.000	1987	391.605	1.000
CO14	1988	3325.061	1.000	1988	-115.064	1.000	1988	115.064	1.000
CO14	1989	3591.307	1.000	1989	266.246	1.000	1989	266.246	1.000
CO14	1990	3506.348	1.000	1990	-84.959	1.000	1990	84.959	1.000
CO14	1991	3990.385	1.000	1991	484.037	1.000	1991	484.037	1.000
CO14	1992	3963.492	1.000	1992	-26.893	1.000	1992	26.893	1.000
CO14	1993	3492.075	1.000	1993	-471.417	1.000	1993	471.417	1.000
CO14	1994	3224.535	1.000	1994	-267.540	1.000	1994	267.540	1.000
COMP	YEAR	SALE	EFFNCY	YEAR	CHNG SALE	EFFNCY	YEAR	ABS(CH SLS)	EFFNCY
CO17	1979	4057.600	0.999	1979		0.999	1979		0.999
CO17	1980	5395.695	1.000	1980	1338.095	1.000	1980	1338.095	1.000
CO17	1981	5175.800	1.000	1981	-219.895	1.000	1981	219.895	1.000
CO17	1982	5613.000	1.000	1982	437.200	1.000	1982	437.200	1.000
CO17	1983	6490.281	0.938	1983	877.281	0.938	1983	877.281	0.938
CO17	1984	8113.375	1.000	1984	1623.094	1.000	1984	1623.094	1.000
CO17	1985	9535.000	0.937	1985	1421.625	0.937	1985	1421.625	0.937
CO17	1986	10273.000	1.000	1986	738.000	1.000	1986	738.000	1.000
CO17	1987	11321.000	1.000	1987	1048.000	1.000	1987	1048.000	1.000
CO17	1988	10590.000	1.000	1988	-731.000	1.000	1988	731.000	1.000
CO17	1989	9891.000	0.980	1989	-699.000	0.980	1989	699.000	0.980
CO17	1990	9958.000	0.915	1990	67.000	0.915	1990	67.000	0.915
CO17	1991	9809.000	0.916	1991	-149.000	0.916	1991	149.000	0.916
CO17	1992	10100.000	0.929	1992	291.000	0.929	1992	291.000	0.929
CO17	1993	13071.000	1.000	1993	2971.000	1.000	1993	2971.000	1.000
CO17	1994	22906.000	1.000	1994	9835.000	1.000	1994	9835.000	1.000

COMP	YEAR	SALE	EFFNCY	YEAR	CHNG SALE	EFFNCY	YEAR	ABS(CH SLS)	EFFNCY
CO18	1979	5331.695	0.954	1979		0.954	1979		0.954
CO18	1980	6124.796	0.925	1980	793.101	0.925	1980	793.101	0.925
CO18	1981	7453.796	1.000	1981	1329.000	1.000	1981	1329.000	1.000
CO18	1982	7412.296	1.000	1982	-41.500	1.000	1982	41.500	1.000
CO18	1983	8242.398	1.000	1983	830.102	1.000	1983	830.102	1.000
CO18	1984	9819.296	1.000	1984	1576.898	1.000	1984	1576.898	1.000
CO18	1985	11617.699	1.000	1985	1798.403	1.000	1985	1798.403	1.000
CO18	1986	12771.902	1.000	1986	1154.203	1.000	1986	1154.203	1.000
CO18	1987	13289.402	1.000	1987	517.500	1.000	1987	517.500	1.000
CO18	1988	15069.000	1.000	1988	1779.598	1.000	1988	1779.598	1.000
CO18	1989	14581.000	0.998	1989	-488.000	0.998	1989	488.000	0.998
CO18	1990	16246.000	0.965	1990	1665.000	0.965	1990	1665.000	0.965
CO18	1991	18432.000	1.000	1991	2186.000	1.000	1991	2186.000	1.000
CO18	1992	17373.000	1.000	1992	-1059.000	1.000	1992	1059.000	1.000
CO18	1993	14474.000	1.000	1993	-2899.000	1.000	1993	2899.000	1.000
CO18	1994	13162.000	1.000	1994	-1312.000	1.000	1994	1312.000	1.000
COMP	YEAR	SALE	EFFNCY	YEAR	CHNG SALE	EFFNCY	YEAR	ABS(CH SLS)	EFFNCY
CO19	1979	1582.477	0.932	1979		0.932	1979		0.932
CO19	1980	1655.400	0.926	1980	72.923	0.926	1980	72.923	0.926
CO19	1981	1990.699	0.881	1981	335.299	0.881	1981	335.299	0.881
CO19	1982	2472.901	0.910	1982	482.202	0.910	1982	482.202	0.910
CO19	1983	3260.600	0.976	1983	787.699	0.976	1983	787.699	0.976
CO19	1984	3687.800	1.000	1984	427.200	1.000	1984	427.200	1.000
CO19	1985	5056.554	1.000	1985	1368.754	1.000	1985	1368.754	1.000
CO19	1986	5608.398	0.974	1986	551.844	0.974	1986	551.844	0.974
CO19	1987	6052.500	1.000	1987	444.102	1.000	1987	444.102	1.000
CO19	1988	5797.097	1.000	1988	-255.403	1.000	1988	255.403	1.000
CO19	1989	5248.398	0.997	1989	-548.699	0.997	1989	548.699	0.997
CO19	1990	5489.796	0.990	1990	241.398	0.990	1990	241.398	0.990
CO19	1991	5694.199	0.991	1991	204.403	0.991	1991	204.403	0.991
CO19	1992	5550.000	0.980	1992	-144.199	0.980	1992	144.199	0.980
CO19	1993	5063.000	0.977	1993	-487.000	0.977	1993	487.000	0.977
CO19	1994	6711.000	0.996	1994	1648.000	0.996	1994	1648.000	0.996
COMP	YEAR	SALE	EFFNCY	YEAR	CHNG SALE	EFFNCY	YEAR	ABS(CH SLS)	EFFNCY
CO21	1979								
CO21	1980								
CO21	1981								
CO21	1982								
CO21	1983								
CO21	1984								
CO21	1985								
CO21	1986	4.608	1.000	1986		1.000	1986		1.000
CO21	1987	18.173	0.821	1987	13.565	0.821	1987	13.565	0.821
CO21	1988			1988			1988		
CO21	1989	144.354	0.967	1989	126.181	0.967	1989	126.181	0.967
CO21	1990	133.648	0.950	1990	-10.706	0.950	1990	10.706	0.950
CO21	1991	137.248	0.883	1991	3.600	0.883	1991	3.600	0.883
CO21	1992	146.229	0.947	1992	8.981	0.947	1992	8.981	0.947
CO21	1993	169.868	0.987	1993	23.639	0.987	1993	23.639	0.987
CO21	1994	148.495	1.000	1994	-21.373	1.000	1994	21.373	1.000

COMP	YEAR	SALE	EFFNCY	YEAR	CHNG SALE	EFFNCY	YEAR	ABS(CH SLS)	EFFNCY
CO22	1979								
CO22	1980								
CO22	1981								
CO22	1982								
CO22	1983								
CO22	1984								
CO22	1985								
CO22	1986								
CO22	1987								
CO22	1988								
CO22	1989								
CO22	1990	2.499	0.864	1990		0.864	1990		0.864
CO22	1991	4.018	0.828	1991	1.519	0.828	1991	1.519	0.828
CO22	1992	3.575	0.767	1992	-0.443	0.767	1992	0.443	0.767
CO22	1993	3.457	0.780	1993	-0.118	0.780	1993	0.118	0.780
CO22	1994	3.280	0.714	1994	-0.177	0.714	1994	0.177	0.714
COMP	YEAR	SALE	EFFNCY	YEAR	CHNG SALE	EFFNCY	YEAR	ABS(CH SLS)	EFFNCY
CO24	1979	35.017	0.975	1979		0.975	1979		0.975
CO24	1980	45.554	1.000	1980	10.537	1.000	1980	10.537	1.000
CO24	1981	53.911	1.000	1981	8.357	1.000	1981	8.357	1.000
CO24	1982	63.084	1.000	1982	9.173	1.000	1982	9.173	1.000
CO24	1983	64.537	1.000	1983	1.453	1.000	1983	1.453	1.000
CO24	1984	63.277	1.000	1984	-1.260	1.000	1984	1.260	1.000
CO24	1985	55.721	1.000	1985	-7.556	1.000	1985	7.556	1.000
CO24	1986	36.931	0.793	1986	-18.790	0.793	1986	18.790	0.793
CO24	1987	33.661	1.000	1987	-3.270	1.000	1987	3.270	1.000
CO24	1988	26.558	0.878	1988	-7.103	0.878	1988	7.103	0.878
CO24	1989	24.183	0.920	1989	-2.375	0.920	1989	2.375	0.920
CO24	1990	15.437	0.967	1990	-8.746	0.967	1990	8.746	0.967
CO24	1991	20.060	0.634	1991	4.623	0.634	1991	4.623	0.634
CO24	1992	23.326	0.731	1992	3.266	0.731	1992	3.266	0.731
CO24	1993	30.910	0.743	1993	7.584	0.743	1993	7.584	0.743
CO24	1994	32.098	0.790	1994	1.188	0.790	1994	1.188	0.790
COMP	YEAR	SALE	EFFNCY	YEAR	CHNG SALE	EFFNCY	YEAR	ABS(CH SLS)	EFFNCY
CO28	1979								
CO28	1980								
CO28	1981								
CO28	1982								
CO28	1983	0.579			1983			1983	
CO28	1984	9.513	0.886	1984	8.934	0.886	1984	8.934	0.886
CO28	1985	32.513	0.775	1985	23.000	0.775	1985	23.000	0.775
CO28	1986	58.274	0.846	1986	25.761	0.846	1986	25.761	0.846
CO28	1987	55.052	0.872	1987	-3.222	0.872	1987	3.222	0.872
CO28	1988	61.928	0.963	1988	6.876	0.963	1988	6.876	0.963
CO28	1989	32.005	1.000	1989	-29.923	1.000	1989	29.923	1.000
CO28	1990	26.759	1.000	1990	-5.246	1.000	1990	5.246	1.000
CO28	1991	30.245	1.000	1991	3.486	1.000	1991	3.486	1.000
CO28	1992	26.287	1.000	1992	-3.958	1.000	1992	3.958	1.000
CO28	1993	16.184	0.846	1993	-10.103	0.846	1993	10.103	0.846
CO28	1994	20.461	0.912	1994	4.277	0.912	1994	4.277	0.912

COMP	YEAR	SALE	EFFNCY	YEAR	CHNG SALE	EFFNCY	YEAR	ABS(CH SLS)	EFFNCY
CO30	1979								
CO30	1980								
CO30	1981								
CO30	1982								
CO30	1983								
CO30	1984								
CO30	1985								
CO30	1986								
CO30	1987	41.170	0.848	1987		0.848	1987		0.848
CO30	1988	41.441	1.000	1988	0.271	1.000	1988	0.271	1.000
CO30	1989	27.924	1.000	1989	-13.517	1.000	1989	13.517	1.000
CO30	1990	27.958	0.989	1990	0.034	0.989	1990	0.034	0.989
CO30	1991	26.830	0.933	1991	-1.128	0.933	1991	1.128	0.933
CO30	1992	38.252	1.000	1992	11.422	1.000	1992	11.422	1.000
CO30	1993	29.331	0.977	1993	-8.921	0.977	1993	8.921	0.977
CO30	1994	22.239	0.915	1994	-7.092	0.915	1994	7.092	0.915
COMP	YEAR	SALE	EFFNCY	YEAR	CHNG SALE	EFFNCY	YEAR	ABS(CH SLS)	EFFNCY
CO31	1979	18.796	1.000	1979		1.000	1979		1.000
CO31	1980	21.603	1.000	1980	2.807	1.000	1980	2.807	1.000
CO31	1981	24.497	1.000	1981	2.894	1.000	1981	2.894	1.000
CO31	1982	24.850	1.000	1982	0.353	1.000	1982	0.353	1.000
CO31	1983	22.036	1.000	1983	-2.814	1.000	1983	2.814	1.000
CO31	1984	27.530	1.000	1984	5.494	1.000	1984	5.494	1.000
CO31	1985	32.313	1.000	1985	4.783	1.000	1985	4.783	1.000
CO31	1986	47.346	1.000	1986	15.033	1.000	1986	15.033	1.000
CO31	1987	46.870	1.000	1987	-0.476	1.000	1987	0.476	1.000
CO31	1988	43.161	1.000	1988	-3.709	1.000	1988	3.709	1.000
CO31	1989	26.473	1.000	1989	-16.688	1.000	1989	16.688	1.000
CO31	1990	26.239	0.945	1990	-0.234	0.945	1990	0.234	0.945
CO31	1991	25.368	1.000	1991	-0.871	1.000	1991	0.871	1.000
CO31	1992	21.729	0.985	1992	-3.639	0.985	1992	3.639	0.985
CO31	1993	25.882	0.955	1993	4.153	0.955	1993	4.153	0.955
CO31	1994	32.393	0.955	1994	6.511	0.955	1994	6.511	0.955
COMP	YEAR	SALE	EFFNCY	YEAR	CHNG SALE	EFFNCY	YEAR	ABS(CH SLS)	EFFNCY
CO32	1979	4.052	1.000	1979		1.000	1979		1.000
CO32	1980	4.285	1.000	1980	0.233	1.000	1980	0.233	1.000
CO32	1981	5.646	1.000	1981	1.361	1.000	1981	1.361	1.000
CO32	1982	5.705	1.000	1982	0.059	1.000	1982	0.059	1.000
CO32	1983	5.731	1.000	1983	0.026	1.000	1983	0.026	1.000
CO32	1984	6.157	1.000	1984	0.426	1.000	1984	0.426	1.000
CO32	1985	6.417	1.000	1985	0.260	1.000	1985	0.260	1.000
CO32	1986	6.192	1.000	1986	-0.225	1.000	1986	0.225	1.000
CO32	1987	7.068	1.000	1987	0.876	1.000	1987	0.876	1.000
CO32	1988	7.360	1.000	1988	0.292	1.000	1988	0.292	1.000
CO32	1989	7.326	1.000	1989	-0.034	1.000	1989	0.034	1.000
CO32	1990	8.225	1.000	1990	0.899	1.000	1990	0.899	1.000
CO32	1991	6.182	1.000	1991	-2.043	1.000	1991	2.043	1.000
CO32	1992	6.028	0.842	1992	-0.154	0.842	1992	0.154	0.842
CO32	1993	5.270	0.880	1993	-0.758	0.880	1993	0.758	0.880
CO32	1994	4.721	0.729	1994	-0.549	0.729	1994	0.549	0.729

COMP	YEAR	SALE	EFFNCY	YEAR	CHNG SALE	EFFNCY	YEAR	ABS(CH SLS)	EFFNCY
CO35	1979	468.748	1.000	1979		1.000	1979		1.000
CO35	1980	513.964	1.000	1980	45.216	1.000	1980	45.216	1.000
CO35	1981	598.776	1.000	1981	84.812	1.000	1981	84.812	1.000
CO35	1982	664.257	1.000	1982	65.481	1.000	1982	65.481	1.000
CO35	1983	746.609	1.000	1983	82.352	1.000	1983	82.352	1.000
CO35	1984	872.948	1.000	1984	126.339	1.000	1984	126.339	1.000
CO35	1985	883.864	1.000	1985	10.916	1.000	1985	10.916	1.000
CO35	1986	371.413	1.000	1986	-512.451	1.000	1986	512.451	1.000
CO35	1987	1132.660	1.000	1987	761.247	1.000	1987	761.247	1.000
CO35	1988	1712.552	1.000	1988	579.892	1.000	1988	579.892	1.000
CO35	1989	1959.155	1.000	1989	246.603	1.000	1989	246.603	1.000
CO35	1990	2211.024	1.000	1990	251.869	1.000	1990	251.869	1.000
CO35	1991	1878.787	0.981	1991	-332.237	0.981	1991	332.237	0.981
CO35	1992	1868.341	1.000	1992	-10.446	1.000	1992	10.446	1.000
CO35	1993	1696.968	0.941	1993	-171.373	0.941	1993	171.373	0.941
CO35	1994	1419.550	0.952	1994	-277.418	0.952	1994	277.418	0.952
COMP	YEAR	SALE	EFFNCY	YEAR	CHNG SALE	EFFNCY	YEAR	ABS(CH SLS)	EFFNCY
CO36	1979	49.876	0.975	1979		0.975	1979		0.975
CO36	1980	61.557	1.000	1980	11.681	1.000	1980	11.681	1.000
CO36	1981	64.871	0.978	1981	3.314	0.978	1981	3.314	0.978
CO36	1982	69.719	1.000	1982	4.848	1.000	1982	4.848	1.000
CO36	1983	54.959	0.905	1983	-14.760	0.905	1983	14.760	0.905
CO36	1984	56.008	0.881	1984	1.049	0.881	1984	1.049	0.881
CO36	1985	59.255	1.000	1985	3.247	1.000	1985	3.247	1.000
CO36	1986	61.323	0.931	1986	2.068	0.931	1986	2.068	0.931
CO36	1987	63.112	0.928	1987	1.789	0.928	1987	1.789	0.928
CO36	1988	66.736	1.000	1988	3.624	1.000	1988	3.624	1.000
CO36	1989	61.975	1.000	1989	-4.761	1.000	1989	4.761	1.000
CO36	1990	68.134	1.000	1990	6.159	1.000	1990	6.159	1.000
CO36	1991	65.326	0.920	1991	-2.808	0.920	1991	2.808	0.920
CO36	1992	57.605	0.841	1992	-7.721	0.841	1992	7.721	0.841
CO36	1993	51.897	0.799	1993	-5.708	0.799	1993	5.708	0.799
CO36	1994	61.429	0.894	1994	9.532	0.894	1994	9.532	0.894
COMP	YEAR	SALE	EFFNCY	YEAR	CHNG SALE	EFFNCY	YEAR	ABS(CH SLS)	EFFNCY
CO38	1979								
CO38	1980								
CO38	1981								
CO38	1982								
CO38	1983								
CO38	1984								
CO38	1985								
CO38	1986	4.637	1.000	1986		1.000	1986		1.000
CO38	1987	2.893	0.993	1987	-1.744	0.993	1987	1.744	0.993
CO38	1988	1.892	0.988	1988	-1.001	0.988	1988	1.001	0.988
CO38	1989	1.532	0.805	1989	-0.360	0.805	1989	0.360	0.805
CO38	1990	0.895	0.563	1990	-0.637	0.563	1990	0.637	0.563
CO38	1991	6.042	1.000	1991	5.147	1.000	1991	5.147	1.000
CO38	1992	7.498	1.000	1992	1.456	1.000	1992	1.456	1.000
CO38	1993	16.147	1.000	1993	8.649	1.000	1993	8.649	1.000
CO38	1994	17.559	0.817	1994	1.412	0.817	1994	1.412	0.817

COMP	YEAR	SALE	EFFNCY	YEAR	CHNG SALE	EFFNCY	YEAR	ABS(CH SLS)	EFFNCY
CO39	1979	2705.600	1.000	1979		1.000	1979		1.000
CO39	1980	2926.417	1.000	1980	220.817	1.000	1980	220.817	1.000
CO39	1981	3237.601	1.000	1981	311.184	1.000	1981	311.184	1.000
CO39	1982	2863.800	1.000	1982	-373.801	1.000	1982	373.801	1.000
CO39	1983	2979.000	1.000	1983	115.200	1.000	1983	115.200	1.000
CO39	1984	3494.299	1.000	1984	515.299	1.000	1984	515.299	1.000
CO39	1985	3256.200	1.000	1985	-238.099	1.000	1985	238.099	1.000
CO39	1986	3241.400	1.000	1986	-14.800	1.000	1986	14.800	1.000
CO39	1987	3216.800	1.000	1987	-24.600	1.000	1987	24.600	1.000
CO39	1988	4522.695	1.000	1988	1305.895	1.000	1988	1305.895	1.000
CO39	1989	3531.200	1.000	1989	-991.495	1.000	1989	991.495	1.000
CO39	1990	3445.800	0.934	1990	-85.400	0.934	1990	85.400	0.934
CO39	1991	3206.800	0.931	1991	-239.000	0.931	1991	239.000	0.931
CO39	1992	2887.600	0.989	1992	-319.200	0.989	1992	319.200	0.989
CO39	1993	2491.700	0.924	1993	-395.900	0.924	1993	395.900	0.924
CO39	1994	2391.200	0.953	1994	-100.500	0.953	1994	100.500	0.953
COMP	YEAR	SALE	EFFNCY	YEAR	CHNG SALE	EFFNCY	YEAR	ABS(CH SLS)	EFFNCY
CO40	1979	267.254	0.958	1979		0.958	1979		0.958
CO40	1980	259.566	0.926	1980	-7.688	0.926	1980	7.688	0.926
CO40	1981	259.428	0.896	1981	-0.138	0.896	1981	0.138	0.896
CO40	1982	346.681	0.915	1982	87.253	0.915	1982	87.253	0.915
CO40	1983	253.485	0.846	1983	-93.196	0.846	1983	93.196	0.846
CO40	1984	300.988	0.855	1984	47.503	0.855	1984	47.503	0.855
CO40	1985	352.927	0.866	1985	51.939	0.866	1985	51.939	0.866
CO40	1986	572.065	0.962	1986	219.138	0.962	1986	219.138	0.962
CO40	1987	495.854	1.000	1987	-76.211	1.000	1987	76.211	1.000
CO40	1988	400.444	1.000	1988	-95.410	1.000	1988	95.410	1.000
CO40	1989	471.024	0.936	1989	70.580	0.936	1989	70.580	0.936
CO40	1990	356.255	0.950	1990	-114.769	0.950	1990	114.769	0.950
CO40	1991	360.571	0.901	1991	4.316	0.901	1991	4.316	0.901
CO40	1992	365.152	0.995	1992	4.581	0.995	1992	4.581	0.995
CO40	1993	438.293	0.951	1993	73.141	0.951	1993	73.141	0.951
CO40	1994	525.833	0.907	1994	87.540	0.907	1994	87.540	0.907
COMP	YEAR	SALE	EFFNCY	YEAR	CHNG SALE	EFFNCY	YEAR	ABS(CH SLS)	EFFNCY
CO42	1979	9053.343	1.000	1979		1.000	1979		1.000
CO42	1980	12323.902	1.000	1980	3270.559	1.000	1980	3270.559	1.000
CO42	1981	13667.703	1.000	1981	1343.801	1.000	1981	1343.801	1.000
CO42	1982	13577.101	1.000	1982	-90.602	1.000	1982	90.602	1.000
CO42	1983	14669.203	1.000	1983	1092.102	1.000	1983	1092.102	1.000
CO42	1984	16331.703	1.000	1984	1662.500	1.000	1984	1662.500	1.000
CO42	1985	14991.601	1.000	1985	-1340.102	1.000	1985	1340.102	1.000
CO42	1986	15669.101	1.000	1986	677.500	1.000	1986	677.500	1.000
CO42	1987	17170.203	1.000	1987	1501.102	1.000	1987	1501.102	1.000
CO42	1988	18087.797	1.000	1988	917.594	1.000	1988	917.594	1.000
CO42	1989	19613.699	1.000	1989	1525.902	1.000	1989	1525.902	1.000
CO42	1990	21549.500	1.000	1990	1935.801	1.000	1990	1935.801	1.000
CO42	1991	20953.000	1.000	1991	-596.500	1.000	1991	596.500	1.000
CO42	1992	22032.000	1.000	1992	1079.000	1.000	1992	1079.000	1.000
CO42	1993	21081.000	1.000	1993	-951.000	1.000	1993	951.000	1.000
CO42	1994	21161.000	1.000	1994	80.000	1.000	1994	80.000	1.000

COMP	YEAR	SALE	EFFNCY	YEAR	CHNG SALE	EFFNCY	YEAR	ABS(CH SLS)	EFFNCY
CO46	1979								
CO46	1980								
CO46	1981								
CO46	1982								
CO46	1983								
CO46	1984								
CO46	1985								
CO46	1986								
CO46	1987	0.408	0.620	1987		0.620	1987		0.620
CO46	1988	0.880	0.955	1988	0.472	0.955	1988	0.472	0.955
CO46	1989	1.700	0.708	1989	0.820	0.708	1989	0.820	0.708
CO46	1990	3.497	0.800	1990	1.797	0.800	1990	1.797	0.800
CO46	1991	3.259	0.799	1991	-0.238	0.799	1991	0.238	0.799
CO46	1992	1.237	0.807	1992	-2.022	0.807	1992	2.022	0.807
CO46	1993	1.095	0.824	1993	-0.142	0.824	1993	0.142	0.824
CO46	1994	1.113	0.894	1994	0.018	0.894	1994	0.018	0.894
COMP	YEAR	SALE	EFFNCY	YEAR	CHNG SALE	EFFNCY	YEAR	ABS(CH SLS)	EFFNCY
CO49	1979	2.169	0.866	1979		0.866	1979		0.866
CO49	1980	2.893	0.808	1980	0.724	0.808	1980	0.724	0.808
CO49	1981	4.273	0.833	1981	1.380	0.833	1981	1.380	0.833
CO49	1982	4.585	0.834	1982	0.312	0.834	1982	0.312	0.834
CO49	1983	4.971	0.804	1983	0.386	0.804	1983	0.386	0.804
CO49	1984	2.952	0.682	1984	-2.019	0.682	1984	2.019	0.682
CO49	1985	3.843	0.756	1985	0.891	0.756	1985	0.891	0.756
CO49	1986	4.792	0.686	1986	0.949	0.686	1986	0.949	0.686
CO49	1987	5.156	0.723	1987	0.364	0.723	1987	0.364	0.723
CO49	1988	5.251	0.894	1988	0.095	0.894	1988	0.095	0.894
CO49	1989	6.103	0.872	1989	0.852	0.872	1989	0.852	0.872
CO49	1990	6.623	0.937	1990	0.520	0.937	1990	0.520	0.937
CO49	1991	5.326	0.748	1991	-1.297	0.748	1991	1.297	0.748
CO49	1992	9.453	0.866	1992	4.127	0.866	1992	4.127	0.866
CO49	1993	13.891	0.960	1993	4.438	0.960	1993	4.438	0.960
CO49	1994	9.071	0.833	1994	-4.820	0.833	1994	4.820	0.833
COMP	YEAR	SALE	EFFNCY	YEAR	CHNG SALE	EFFNCY	YEAR	ABS(CH SLS)	EFFNCY
CO50	1979								
CO50	1980								
CO50	1981								
CO50	1982								
CO50	1983								
CO50	1984								
CO50	1985								
CO50	1986								
CO50	1987								
CO50	1988								
CO50	1989								
CO50	1990								
CO50	1991	8.289	1.000	1991		1.000	1991		1.000
CO50	1992	10.010	1.000	1992	1.721	1.000	1992	1.721	1.000
CO50	1993	6.091	1.000	1993	-3.919	1.000	1993	3.919	1.000
CO50	1994	5.041	1.000	1994	-1.050	1.000	1994	1.050	1.000

COMP	YEAR	SALE	EFFNCY	YEAR	CHNG SALE	EFFNCY	YEAR	ABS(CH SLS)	EFFNCY
CO53	1979	325.200	1.000	1979		1.000	1979		1.000
CO53	1980	349.266	1.000	1980	24.066	1.000	1980	24.066	1.000
CO53	1981	189.452	1.000	1981	-159.814	1.000	1981	159.814	1.000
CO53	1982	223.488	1.000	1982	34.036	1.000	1982	34.036	1.000
CO53	1983	304.091	1.000	1983	80.603	1.000	1983	80.603	1.000
CO53	1984	451.135	1.000	1984	147.044	1.000	1984	147.044	1.000
CO53	1985	417.034	0.953	1985	-34.101	0.953	1985	34.101	0.953
CO53	1986	455.179	0.983	1986	38.145	0.983	1986	38.145	0.983
CO53	1987	76.318	0.886	1987	-378.861	0.886	1987	378.861	0.886
CO53	1988	59.812	0.923	1988	-16.506	0.923	1988	16.506	0.923
CO53	1989	68.571	0.972	1989	8.759	0.972	1989	8.759	0.972
CO53	1990	74.697	0.965	1990	6.126	0.965	1990	6.126	0.965
CO53	1991	74.380	0.953	1991	-0.317	0.953	1991	0.317	0.953
CO53	1992	67.445	0.985	1992	-6.935	0.985	1992	6.935	0.985
CO53	1993	64.541	0.991	1993	-2.904	0.991	1993	2.904	0.991
CO53	1994	61.738	0.965	1994	-2.803	0.965	1994	2.803	0.965
COMP	YEAR	SALE	EFFNCY	YEAR	CHNG SALE	EFFNCY	YEAR	ABS(CH SLS)	EFFNCY
CO55	1979								
CO55	1980								
CO55	1981								
CO55	1982								
CO55	1983								
CO55	1984								
CO55	1985								
CO55	1986								
CO55	1987								
CO55	1988								
CO55	1989	84.610	0.901	1989		0.901	1989		0.901
CO55	1990	51.970	0.879	1990	-32.640	0.879	1990	32.640	0.879
CO55	1991	48.253	0.960	1991	-3.717	0.960	1991	3.717	0.960
CO55	1992	43.167	0.996	1992	-5.086	0.996	1992	5.086	0.996
CO55	1993	54.710	0.972	1993	11.543	0.972	1993	11.543	0.972
CO55	1994	34.871	0.926	1994	-19.839	0.926	1994	19.839	0.926
COMP	YEAR	SALE	EFFNCY	YEAR	CHNG SALE	EFFNCY	YEAR	ABS(CH SLS)	EFFNCY
CO56	1979								
CO56	1980								
CO56	1981								
CO56	1982								
CO56	1983								
CO56	1984								
CO56	1985								
CO56	1986								
CO56	1987								
CO56	1988	1845.392	0.899	1988		0.899	1988		0.899
CO56	1989	3172.000	1.000	1989	1326.608	1.000	1989	1326.608	1.000
CO56	1990	3516.000	1.000	1990	344.000	1.000	1990	344.000	1.000
CO56	1991	1036.000	1.000	1991	-2480.000	1.000	1991	2480.000	1.000
CO56	1992	1566.000	0.996	1992	530.000	0.996	1992	530.000	0.996
CO56	1993	1871.000	1.000	1993	305.000	1.000	1993	305.000	1.000
CO56	1994	704.000	1.000	1994	-1167.000	1.000	1994	1167.000	1.000

COMP	YEAR	SALE	EFFNCY	YEAR	CHNG SALE	EFFNCY	YEAR	ABS(CH SLS)	EFFNCY
CO57	1979								
CO57	1980								
CO57	1981								
CO57	1982								
CO57	1983								
CO57	1984								
CO57	1985								
CO57	1986								
CO57	1987								
CO57	1988								
CO57	1989								
CO57	1990	300.210	1.000	1990		1.000	1990		1.000
CO57	1991	314.635	1.000	1991	14.425	1.000	1991	14.425	1.000
CO57	1992	295.490	1.000	1992	-19.145	1.000	1992	19.145	1.000
CO57	1993	277.107	1.000	1993	-18.383	1.000	1993	18.383	1.000
CO57	1994	226.131	1.000	1994	-50.976	1.000	1994	50.976	1.000
	YEAR	SALE	EFFNCY						
CO58	1979								
CO58	1980								
CO58	1981								
CO58	1982								
CO58	1983								
CO58	1984								
CO58	1985								
CO58	1986								
CO58	1987								
CO58	1988								
CO58	1989								
CO58	1990	22.786	1.000	1990		1.000	1990		1.000
CO58	1991	9.620	1.000	1991	-13.166	1.000	1991	13.166	1.000
CO58	1992			1992			1992		
CO58	1993	11.612	0.996	1993	1.992	0.996	1993	1.992	0.996
CO58	1994	14.824	0.914	1994	3.212	0.914	1994	3.212	0.914
COMP	YEAR	SALE	EFFNCY	YEAR	CHNG SALE	EFFNCY	YEAR	ABS(CH SLS)	EFFNCY
CO60	1979								
CO60	1980								
CO60	1981								
CO60	1982								
CO60	1983								
CO60	1984								
CO60	1985	1141.846	0.955	1985		0.955	1985		0.955
CO60	1986	1952.885	1.000	1986	811.039	1.000	1986	811.039	1.000
CO60	1987	2258.523	1.000	1987	305.638	1.000	1987	305.638	1.000
CO60	1988	2520.619	1.000	1988	262.096	1.000	1988	262.096	1.000
CO60	1989	2520.682	1.000	1989	0.063	1.000	1989	0.063	1.000
CO60	1990	2163.765	0.923	1990	-356.917	0.923	1990	356.917	0.923
CO60	1991	2009.344	0.881	1991	-154.421	0.881	1991	154.421	0.881
CO60	1992	1961.255	0.923	1992	-48.089	0.923	1992	48.089	0.923
CO60	1993	2285.246	1.000	1993	323.991	1.000	1993	323.991	1.000
CO60	1994								

COMP	YEAR	SALE	EFFNCY	YEAR	CHNG SALE	EFFNCY	YEAR	ABS(CH SLS)	EFFNCY
CO62	1979								
CO62	1980								
CO62	1981								
CO62	1982								
CO62	1983								
CO62	1984								
CO62	1985	27.445	0.935	1985		0.935	1985		0.935
CO62	1986	33.398	0.914	1986	5.953	0.914	1986	5.953	0.914
CO62	1987	38.728	0.834	1987	5.330	0.834	1987	5.330	0.834
CO62	1988	62.083	0.866	1988	23.355	0.866	1988	23.355	0.866
CO62	1989	71.923	0.916	1989	9.840	0.916	1989	9.840	0.916
CO62	1990	64.434	0.986	1990	-7.489	0.986	1990	7.489	0.986
CO62	1991	51.015	0.940	1991	-13.419	0.940	1991	13.419	0.940
CO62	1992	47.602	0.759	1992	-3.413	0.759	1992	3.413	0.759
CO62	1993	36.528	1.000	1993	-11.074	1.000	1993	11.074	1.000
CO62	1994	35.806	0.932	1994	-0.722	0.932	1994	0.722	0.932
COMP	YEAR	SALE	EFFNCY	YEAR	CHNG SALE	EFFNCY	YEAR	ABS(CH SLS)	EFFNCY
CO63	1979	392.643	1.000	1979		1.000	1979		1.000
CO63	1980	517.128	1.000	1980	124.485	1.000	1980	124.485	1.000
CO63	1981	543.918	1.000	1981	26.790	1.000	1981	26.790	1.000
CO63	1982	565.880	1.000	1982	21.962	1.000	1982	21.962	1.000
CO63	1983	569.134	1.000	1983	3.254	1.000	1983	3.254	1.000
CO63	1984	613.933	1.000	1984	44.799	1.000	1984	44.799	1.000
CO63	1985	607.139	1.000	1985	-6.794	1.000	1985	6.794	1.000
CO63	1986	626.124	1.000	1986	18.985	1.000	1986	18.985	1.000
CO63	1987	663.405	1.000	1987	37.281	1.000	1987	37.281	1.000
CO63	1988	906.841	1.000	1988	243.436	1.000	1988	243.436	1.000
CO63	1989	1044.677	1.000	1989	137.836	1.000	1989	137.836	1.000
CO63	1990	1078.712	0.968	1990	34.035	0.968	1990	34.035	0.968
CO63	1991	1385.086	1.000	1991	306.374	1.000	1991	306.374	1.000
CO63	1992	1279.656	0.988	1992	-105.430	0.988	1992	105.430	0.988
CO63	1993	1175.152	1.000	1993	-104.504	1.000	1993	104.504	1.000
CO63	1994	918.141	1.000	1994	-257.011	1.000	1994	257.011	1.000
COMP	YEAR	SALE	EFFNCY	YEAR	CHNG SALE	EFFNCY	YEAR	ABS(CH SLS)	EFFNCY
CO66	1979	842.630	1.000	1979		1.000	1979		1.000
CO66	1980	926.026	1.000	1980	83.396	1.000	1980	83.396	1.000
CO66	1981	1045.687	1.000	1981	119.661	1.000	1981	119.661	1.000
CO66	1982	961.573	1.000	1982	-84.114	1.000	1982	84.114	1.000
CO66	1983	909.318	1.000	1983	-52.255	1.000	1983	52.255	1.000
CO66	1984	1041.948	1.000	1984	132.630	1.000	1984	132.630	1.000
CO66	1985	1284.141	1.000	1985	242.193	1.000	1985	242.193	1.000
CO66	1986	1433.940	1.000	1986	149.799	1.000	1986	149.799	1.000
CO66	1987	1365.482	1.000	1987	-68.458	1.000	1987	68.458	1.000
CO66	1988	1477.289	1.000	1988	111.807	1.000	1988	111.807	1.000
CO66	1989	1595.398	1.000	1989	118.109	1.000	1989	118.109	1.000
CO66	1990	1599.800	1.000	1990	4.402	1.000	1990	4.402	1.000
CO66	1991	1669.200	1.000	1991	69.400	1.000	1991	69.400	1.000
CO66	1992	1672.700	1.000	1992	3.500	1.000	1992	3.500	1.000
CO66	1993	1383.100	1.000	1993	-289.600	1.000	1993	289.600	1.000
CO66	1994	1372.700	1.000	1994	-10.400	1.000	1994	10.400	1.000

COMP	YEAR	SALE	EFFNCY	YEAR	CHNG SALE	EFFNCY	YEAR	ABS(CH SLS)	EFFNCY
CO67	1979	66.791	0.952	1979		0.952	1979		0.952
CO67	1980	78.501	0.945	1980	11.710	0.945	1980	11.710	0.945
CO67	1981	103.220	0.952	1981	24.719	0.952	1981	24.719	0.952
CO67	1982	111.689	1.000	1982	8.469	1.000	1982	8.469	1.000
CO67	1983	129.341	0.951	1983	17.652	0.951	1983	17.652	0.951
CO67	1984	153.311	0.963	1984	23.970	0.963	1984	23.970	0.963
CO67	1985	171.816	0.933	1985	18.505	0.933	1985	18.505	0.933
CO67	1986	214.182	0.981	1986	42.366	0.981	1986	42.366	0.981
CO67	1987	269.778	1.000	1987	55.596	1.000	1987	55.596	1.000
CO67	1988	323.589	1.000	1988	53.811	1.000	1988	53.811	1.000
CO67	1989	355.625	0.993	1989	32.036	0.993	1989	32.036	0.993
CO67	1990	441.133	0.978	1990	85.508	0.978	1990	85.508	0.978
CO67	1991	479.537	0.992	1991	38.404	0.992	1991	38.404	0.992
CO67	1992	567.132	1.000	1992	87.595	1.000	1992	87.595	1.000
CO67	1993	666.796	0.957	1993	99.664	0.957	1993	99.664	0.957
CO67	1994	812.672	0.965	1994	145.876	0.965	1994	145.876	0.965

Bibliography

Abetti, P. A. and C. W. LeMaistre (1987). "RPI as a "role model" promoting industrial innovation, manufacturing productivity, and regional economic development." In *Industrial Innovation, Productivity, and Employment*. P. A. Abetti, C. W. LeMaistre and R. W. Smilor, Eds. Austin: The University of Texas at Austin, the IC2 Institute: 63-79.

Agility Forum (1994). *Agile Customer-Supplier Relations*. Report Series on Agility. Bethlehem: Agility Forum.

Agility Forum (1994). *Exploring Ways Agile Competition and Virtual Companies Impact Your Company's Bottom Line*. 3rd Annual Conference/Workshop Proceedings, Austin, Texas: Agility Forum.

Albrecht, T. L. and V. A. Ropp (1984). "Communication about innovation in networks of three U.S. organizations." *Journal of Communication* (Summer): 79-91.

American Productivity & Quality Center (1993). *The Benchmarking Management Guide*. Portland, OR: Productivity Press.

Amos, J. W. and D. V. Gibson (1995). *An exploratory model of agility: Key facilitators and performance metrics*. Agility Forum Fourth Annual Conference Proceedings, J. J. Barker, Ed. Atlanta, GA: Agility Forum.

Amos, J. W., D. V. Gibson and T. K. Sung (1996). "Exploratory Model for Agile Manufacturing." *Journal of Industrial Studies* 7: 245-262.

Applegate, L. M., J. I. Cash, Jr. and D. Q. Mills (1988). "Information Technology and Tomorrow's Manager." *Harvard Business Review* 66(6): 128-136.

Argyris, C. (1994). "Good communication that blocks learning." *Harvard Business Review* 72(4): 77-85.

Asava, R. G. and R. L. Engwall (1994). *Key Need Areas for Integrating the Agile Virtual Enterprise*. Working paper. Bethlehem, PA: Iococca Institute, Agility Forum.

Avery, C. (1989). *Organizational communication in technology transfer between R&D consortium and its shareholders: The case of the MCC*. Dissertation. Austin: College of Communication, The University of Texas at Austin.

Bacharach, S. B. (1989). "Organizational Theories: Some Criteria for Evaluation." *The Academy of Management Review* **14**(4): 496-515.

Badaway, M. K. (1991). "Managing Human Resources." *Resource Technology Management*: 19-35.

Bahrami, H. (1992). "The Emerging Flexible Organization: Perspectives from Silicon Valley." *California Management Review* **34**(4): 33-52.

Baroudi, J. J. and W. J. Orlikowski (1989). "The Problem of Statistical Power in MIS Research." *MIS Quarterly* (March): 87-106.

Barrington, H. A. (1986). "Continuous Development: Theory and Reality." *Personnel Review* **15**(1): 27-31.

Batt, W. L., Jr. and E. Weinberg (1978). "Labor-management cooperation today." *Harvard Business Review* (Jan-Feb): 96-104.

Becker, H. S. (1970). *Sociological Work*. Chicago: Aldine.

Benbasat, I. (1984). "An Analysis of Research Methodologies." In *The Information System Research Challenge*. F. W. McFarlan, Ed. Boston: Harvard Business School Press: 47-85.

Benbasat, I., D. K. Goldstein and M. Mead (1987). "The Case Research Strategy in Studies of Information Systems." *MIS Quarterly* (Sep): 369-386.

Benjamin, R. I. and E. Levinson (1993). "A Framework for Managing IT-Enabled Change." *Sloan Management Review* (Summer): 23-33.

Blackburn, J. (1990). "The Time Factor." *National Productivity Review* **9**(4): 395-408.

Blalock, H. M., Jr., Ed. (1980). *Sociological Theory and Research: A Critical Approach*. New York: Macmillan Publishing.

Blonkvist, C. L. and S. C. Goble (1994). "Reengineering isn't the only answer." *Manufacturing Systems* **12**(2): 52-56.

Bluestone, B., P. Jordan and M. Sullivan (1981). *Aircraft Industry Dynamics, An Analysis of Competition, Capital and Labor*. Boston: Auburn House.

Bonfeld, P. (1995). "Building international agility." *Chief Executive* (100). 50-53.

Booth, R. (1996). "Manifesto for ABM." *Management Accounting-London* **74**(2). Feb: 32.

Borthick, A. F. and H. P. Roth (1993). "Accounting for time: reengineering business process to improve responsiveness." *Cost Management* (Fall 1993): 4-13.

Bowen, H. K., K. B. Clark, et al. (1994). "Regaining the Lead In Manufacturing." *Harvard Business Review* **72**(5): 108-109.

Bowen, H. K., K. B. Clark, et al. (1994). "Development projects: The engine of renewal." *Harvard Business Review* **72**(5): 110-120.

Bowen, H. K., K. B. Clark, et al. (1994). "Make Projects the School for Leaders." *Harvard Business Review* **72**(5): 131-140.

Bowen, H. K., K. B. Clark, et al. (1994). "Make projects the school for leaders." *Harvard Business Review* **72**(5): 131-140.

Bowyer, J. (1973). *History of Building*. London: Crosby Lockwood, Stables.

Boynton, A. C., B. Victor and B. J. Pine, II (1993). "New competitive strategies: Challenges to organizations and information technology." *IBM Systems Journal* **32**(1): 40-64.

Braithwaite, A. (1992). "Integrating the global pipeline: Logistics systems architectures." *Logistics Information Management* **5**(3): 8-18.

Burgess, T. F. (1994). "Making the Leap to Agility: Defining and Achieving Agile Manufacturing Through Business Process Redesign and Business Network Redesign." *International Journal of Operations & Production Management* **14**(11): 23-34.

Burt, D. N. (1989). "Managing Suppliers Up to Speed." *Harvard Business Review* **67**(4): 127-135.

Buzacott, J. A. (1995). "A perspective on new paradigms in manufacturing." *Journal of Manufacturing Systems* **14**(2): 118-125.

Byrne, J. A. (1992). "Paradigms for Postmodern Managers." *Business Week* (Special Issue). 62-63.

Candadai, A., S. Champati, et al. (1993). *Information Needs In Agile Manufacturing*. Working Papers. College Park, MD: Department of Mechanical Engineering and Institute for Systems Research, University of Maryland.

Carter, P. L., S. A. Melnyk and R. B. Handfield (1995). "Identifying the basic process strategies for time-based competition." *Production & Inventory Management Journal* **36**(1): 65-70.

Cash, J. I., Jr. and B. R. Konsynski (1985). "IS Redraws Competitive Boundaries." *Harvard Business Review* (Mar-Apr): 134-142.

Chambers, S. (1992). "Flexibility in the context of manufacturing strategy." In *Manufacturing Strategy Process and Content*. C. A. Voss, Ed. London: Chapman & Hall: 283-296.

Charnes, A., W. Cooper, et al., Eds. (1994). *Data Envelopment Analysis: Theory Methodology & Application*. Norwell: Kluwer Academic Publishers.

Chase, R. B. and D. A. Garvin (1989). "The Service Factory." *Harvard Business Review* **67**(4): 61-69.

Cheng, J. L. C. and J. McKenney (1983). "Toward an Integration of Organization Research and Practice: A Contingency Study of Bureaucratic Control and Performance in Scientific Settings." *Administrative Science Quarterly* **28**: 85-100.

Cowan, H. J. (1977). *The Master Builders: A History of Structural and Environmental Design from Ancient Egypt to the Nineteenth Century*. New York: Wiley.

Cunningham, J. B. (1983). "Gathering Data in a Changing Organization." *Human Relations* **36**(5): 403-420.

Daft, R. L. (1983). "Learning the Craft of Organizational Research." *Academy of Management Review* **8**(4): 539-546.

Daft, R. L. and R. H. Lengel (1984). "Information richness: A new approach to manager information processing and organizing design." In *Research in Organizational Behavior, Vol. 5*. B. Straw and L. Cummings, Eds. CT: JAI Press.: 121-233.

Daft, R. L. and R. H. Lengel (1986). "Organizational information requirements, media richness and structural design." *Management Science* **32**(5): 554-571.

Daft, R. L. and N. B. Macinstosh (1990). "Can Organization Studies Begin to Break Out of the Normal Science Straitjacket? An Editorial Essay." *Organization Science* **1**(1): 1-10.

Davenport, T. H. (1993). *Process Innovation: Reengineering Work Through Information*. Boston: Harvard Business School Press.

Davenport, T. H. (1994). "Saving IT's Soul: Human-Centered Information Management." *Harvard Business Review* **72**(5): 119-131.

Davidson, W. H. (1993). "Beyond re-engineering: The three phases of business transformation." *IBM Systems Journal* **32**(1): 65-79.

Davis, S. and J. Botkin (1994). "The coming of knowledge-based business." *Harvard Business Review* **72**(5): 165-170.

Davis, S. M. (1987). *Future Perfect*. Reading, MA: Addison-Wesley.

D'Cruz, J. R. and A. M. Rugman (1993). "Developing international competitiveness: The five partners model." *Business Quarterly* **58**(2): 60-72.

De Meyer, A. (1992). "An empirical investigation of manufacturing strategies in European industry." In *Manufacturing Strategy Process and Content.* C. A. Voss, Ed. London: Chapman & Hall: 222-238.

Dion, P., P. M. Banting and L. M. Hasey (1990). "The Impact of JIT on Industrial Marketers." *Industrial Marketing Management* **19**: 41-46.

Doll, R. (1981). "Information Technology and Its Socioeconomic and Academic Impact." *On-line Review* **5**(1): 37-46.

Doll, W. J. and M. A. Vonderembse (1992). "The evolution of manufacturing systems: towards the post-industrial enterprise." In *Manufacturing Strategy Process and Content.* C. A. Voss, Ed. London: Chapman & Hall: 353-370.

Dove, R. (1994a). "The meaning of life & the meaning of agile." *Production Magazine* (November).

Dove, R. (1994b). "Plumbing the agile organization." *Production* **106**(12). Dec: 14-15.

Dove, R. (1995a). "Agile benefits: Viability and leadership." *Production* **107**(4). Apr: 20-21.

Dove, R. (1995b). "Agile cells and agile production." *Production* **107**(10). Oct: 16-18.

Dove, R. (1995c). "Agility engineering: Lego lessons." *Production* **107**(3). Mar: 12-14.

Dove, R. (1995d). "Design principles for agile production." *Production* **107**(12). Dec: 16-18.

Dove, R. (1995e). "Introducing principles for agile systems." *Production* **107**(8). Aug: 14-16.

Dove, R. (1995f). "Loose change adds up to big money." *Production Magazine* (February).

Dove, R. (1995g). "Measuring Agility: The Toll of Turmoil." *Production Magazine* **107**(1). Jan: 12-14.

Dove, R. (1995h). "Mobilizing knowledge with agility audits." *Production* **107**(5). May: 18-20.

Dove, R. (1995i). "The power of agile examples." *Production* **107**(6). Jun: 18-20.

Drucker, P. (1992). "The New Society of Organizations." *Harvard Business Review*(Sep-Oct).

Drucker, P. F. (1990). "The Emerging Theory of Manufacturing." *Harvard Business Review* **68**(3): 94-102.

Drucker, P. F. (1995). "The information executives truly need." *Harvard Business Review* **73**(1): 54-62.

Dumaine, B. (1989). "How Managers Can Succeed Through Speed." Editorial. *Fortune.* Feb 13.

Earls, A. R. (1995). "Incubators of Agility." *Computerworld* **29**(4). Jan. 23: 81-82.

Eisenhardt, K. M. (1989). "Building Theories from Case Study Research." *Academy of Management Review* **14**(4): 532-550.

Eisenhardt, K. M. (1990). "Speed and Strategic Choice: How Managers Accelerate Decision Making." *California Management Review* **32**(3): 39-54.

Eisenhardt, K. M. (1992). "Speed and Strategic Choice: Accelerating Decision-Making." *Planning Review* **20**(5): 30-32.

Eisenhardt, K. M. and B. J. Westcott (1988). "Paradoxical Demands and the Creation of Excellence: The Case of Just-In-Time Manufacturing." In *Paradox and Transformation: Toward a Theory of Change in Organization and Management*. R. E. Quinn and K. S. Cameron, Eds. Cambridge: Ballinger: 169-203.

Emory, C. (1985). *Business Research Methods*. Homewood, IL: Richard D. Irwin, Inc.

Ettlie, J. E. (1992). "Agility: The $500,000 Answer?" *Production*. October 1992: 14.

Evans, J. S. (1991). "Strategic Flexibility for High Technology Manoeuvres: A Conceptual Framework." *Journal of Management Studies* **28**(1): 69-89.

Evans, W. M. and P. Olk (1991). "R&D consortia: A new organizational form." *Sloan Management Review* **31**(3): 37-46.

Farrell, M. J. (1957). "The Measurement of Productive Efficiency." *Journal of the Royal Statistical Society, Series A* **120**(3): 253-290.

Fausfeld, H. I. and C. S. Haklish (1985). "Cooperative R&D for competitors." *Harvard Business Review* **63**: 60-76.

Filstead, W. J., Ed. (1971). *Qualitative Methodology*. Chicago: Markham Publishing.

Fisher, M. and A. Raman (1992). "Reducing the cost of demand uncertainty through accurate response to early sales." Working Paper. *Operations Research, special issue: New Directions for Operations Management Research*.

Fisher, M. L., J. H. Hammond, et al. (1994). "Making Supply Meet Demand in an Uncertain World." *Harvard Business Review* (May-Jun).

Flaig, L. S. (1992). "The "Virtual Enterprise": your new model for success." *Electronic Business*. March 30: 153-155.

Flanagan, P., C. Bilby and C. Meisl (1991). "Process-Based Analysis in a Hierarchical Modeling Framework." In *Modeling and Simulation of Advanced Space Programs*. C. Bilby and G. Kozmetsky, Eds. Austin: IC2 Institute, The University of Texas at Austin: 353-370.

Forcese, D. P. and S. Richer (1970). *Stages of Social Research—Contemporary Perspectives*. Englewood Cliffs, NJ: Prentice-Hall, Inc.

Ford, H. (1926). "Mass Production." In *Encyclopaedia Britannica, 13th Edition*. Vol. 2: 821-823.

Forrester, J. W. (1958). "Industrial Dynamics: a major breakthrough for decision makers." *Harvard Business Review* **36**(4): 37-66.

Galbraith, J. K. (1958). *The Affluent Society*. Boston: Houghton Mifflin.

Gansler, J. (1982). *The Defense Industry*. Cambridge: MIT Press.

General Accounting Office (1993). *NASA Aeronautics: Efforts to preserve US leadership in the aeronautics industry are limited*. GAO Report. Washington: GPO.

Gibson, D. and E. M. Rogers (1991). *Synergy on Trial: Texas High Tech and MCC*. Working papers. Austin: IC2 Institute, The University of Texas at Austin.

Gibson, D. V., G. Preuss, et al. (1990). "MCC: The Packaging and Interconnect Program." *Harvard Business Review* (4): 1-23.

Gibson, D. V. and E. M. Rogers (1994). *R & D Collaboration on Trial: The Microelectronics & Computer Technology Corporation*. Boston: Harvard Business School Press.

Gibson, D. V. and R. W. Smilor (1991). "Key Variables in Technology Transfer: A Field-Study Based Empirical Analysis." *Journal of Engineering & Technology Management* **8**(3,4): 287-312.

Giffi, C., A. Roth and G. Seal (1990). *Competing in world-class manufacturing: America's 21st century challenge / National Center for Manufacturing Sciences*. Homewood, IL: Business One Irwin.

Ginzberg, M. J. and R. L. Schultz (1987). "The Practical Side of Implementation Research." *Interfaces* **17**(3): 1-5.

Glaser, B. G. (1978). *Theoretical Sensitivity: Advances in the methodology of Grounded Theory*. Mill Valley, CA: Sociology Press.

Glaser, B. G. and A. L. Strauss (1967). *The Discovery of Grounded Theory*. New York: Aldine.

Glaser, B. G. and A. L. Strauss (1970). "Discovery of Substantive Theory: A Basic Strategy Underlying Qualitative Research." In *Qualitative Methodology*. W. J. Filstead, Ed. Chicago: Markham Publishing: 288-301.

Glick, W. H., G. P. Huber, et al. (1990). "Studying changes in organizational design and effectiveness: retrospective event histories and periodic assessments." *Organization Science* 1(3): 293-312.

Goldman, S. (1996). *Keynote Address to PICS Conference*. Picture the Future: Competing through Agile Manufacturing and Logistics in Virtual Organisations, R. Van Landeghem, Ed. Brussels: PICS.

Goldman, S. L. (1993). *Agile Manufacturing: a new production paradigm for society*. Bethlehem, PA: Agile Manufacturing Enterprise Forum, Iococca Institute.

Goldman, S. L. (1994). "Agile Competition and Virtual Corporations, The Next "American Century"?" *National Forum* **LXXIV, 74**(2): 43-47.

Goldman, S. L. (1994). *Illustrations of Agile Competitive Behavior*. Working Paper. Bethlehem, PA: Lehigh University.

Goldman, S. L., Ed. (1995). *Agility Initial Survey—Results of a Pilot Study to Identify Core Parameters of an Agile Manufacturing Enterprise and Their Impact on Cycle Time, Quality, and Cost*. Agility Reports. Bethlehem: Lehigh University.

Goldman, S. L. and R. N. Nagel (1993). "Management, technology and agility: the emergence of a new era in manufacturing." *International Journal of Technology Management* 8(1/2): 18-38.

Goldman, S. L., R. N. Nagel and K. Preiss (1995). *Agile Competitors and Virtual Organizations: Strategies for Enriching the Customer*. New York, NY: Van Nostrand Reinhold.

Governor's Task Force on Economic Transition (1993). *Defense Transition: Economic Promise for Texas*. AWR 91-9. Report. February, Austin: Governor's Office of Economic Transition, State of Texas.

Grates, G. F. (1994). "The subtlety and power of communications in corporate renewal initiatives." *Public Relations Quarterly* 39(1): 40-43.

Groover, M. P., M. Meixell, et al. (1995). *Initial experience with the development of agility measures and audits in manufacturing operations*. Creating The Agile Organization: Models, Metrics and Pilots, J. J. Barker, Ed. Atlanta, GA: Agile Manufacturing Enterprise Forum.

"Grumman Pensions Problems." (1985) *Journal of Buyouts and Acquisitions* 3(2). January: 29-34.

Gupta, A., C. Hahn and S. Rehmus (1991). "Transaction Skills: Foundation for Success in Risk Business." *Bank Management* 67(6). Jun: 12-18.

Gupta, D. (1989). "A Framework for Understanding Manufacturing Flexibility." *Journal of Manufacturing Systems* **8**: 89-97.

Gupta, D. (1993). "On Measurement and Valuation of Manufacturing Flexibility." *International Journal of Production Research* **31**: 2947-2958.

Gupta, D. and J. A. Buzacott (1994). "A 'goodness test' for operational measures of manufacturing flexibility." *Manuscript*.

Haeckel, S. H. and R. L. Nolan (1993). "Managing by wire." *Harvard Business Review* **71**(5): 122-132.

Hall, D. and J. Jackson (1992). "Speeding Up New Product Development." *Management Accounting* **74**(4): 32-36.

Hamel, G. and C. K. Prahalad (1994). "Competing for the future." *Harvard Business Review* **72**(4): 122-128.

Hamilton, S. and B. Ives (1982). "MIS Research Strategies." *Information and Management* **5**: 339-347.

Hammer, M. (1990). "Reengineering Work: Don't Automate, Obliterate." *Harvard Business Review* **68**(4): 104-112.

Hammer, M. and J. Champy (1993). *Reengineering the Corporation: A Manifesto for Business Revolution*. New York: Harper Business.

Handy, C. (1992). "Balancing Corporate Power: A New Federalist Paper." *Harvard Business Review* **70**(6): 59-72.

Harland, C., D. Williams and L. Fitzgerald (1993). "Supply chain methodology." *Human Systems Management* **12**(1): 17-23.

Hatch, M. (1987). "Physical barriers, task characteristics, and interactions activity in research development firms." *Administrative Science Quarterly* **32**: 387-399.

Hayes, R. H. and R. Jaikumar (1988). "Manufacturing's Crisis: New Technologies, Obsolete Organizations." *Harvard Business Review* (Sep-Oct).

Hayes, R. H. and G. P. Pisano (1994). "Beyond world-class: The new manufacturing strategy." *Harvard Business Review* **72**(1): 77-84+.

Hayes, R. H. and R. W. Schmenner (1978). "How should you organize manufacturing?" *Harvard Business Review* **56**(1): 105-118.

Hayes, R. H. and S. C. Wheelwright (1984). *Restoring Our Competitive Edge: Competing Through Manufacturing*. New York: John Wiley & Sons, Incorporated.

Hayward, K. (1994). *The World Aerospace Industry: Collaboration and Competition*. London: Duckworth & RUSI.

Hazelhurst, R. J., B. J. Bradbury and E. N. Corlett (1969). "A Comparison of the Skills of Machinists on Numerically-Controlled and Conventional Machines." *Occupational Psychology* **43**(3,4): 169-182.

Henderson, J. C. (1990). "Plugging into Strategic Partnerships: The Critical IS Connection." *Sloan Management Review* **31**(3): 7-18.

Henderson, J. C. and N. Venkatraman (1993). "Strategic alignment: Leveraging information technology for transforming organizations." *IBM Systems Journal* **32**(1): 4-16.

Hill, T. (1989). *Manufacturing Strategy: Text and Cases*. Homewood, IL: Irwin.

Hill, T. J. (1992). "Incorporating manufacturing perspectives in corporate strategy." In *Manufacturing Strategy Process and Content*. C. A. Voss, Ed. London: Chapman & Hall: 3-12.

Hirschman, A. O. (1958). *The Strategy of Economic Development*. New Haven: Yale University Press.

Hounshell, D. A. (1984). *From The American System to Mass Production 1800-1932*. Baltimore: Johns Hopkins University Press.

Howard, R., Ed. (1993). *The Learning Imperative: Managing People for Continuous Innovation*. The Harvard Business Review Book Ser. Boston: Harvard Business School Press.

Howes, T. (1994). Interview by Jeff Amos. Texas Instruments. December 12, 1994.

Huber, G. H. and R. L. Daft (1987). "Information environments." In *Handbook of Organizational Communication*. F. Jablin, L. Putman, K. Roberts and L. Porter, Eds. Beverly Hills, CA: Sage.

Hughes, E. C. (1960). "Introduction: The Place of Field Work in Social Science." In *Field Work: An Introduction to the Social Sciences*. B. H. Junker, Ed. Chicago: University of Chicago: iii-xiii.

Hum, S. H. (1992). "Competition Strategies—Implications for Singapore Managers." *Singapore Management Review* **14**(2).

Hum, S. H. (1995). "Time-based competition: Some empirical data from Singapore." *Asia Pacific Journal of Management* **12**(2): 123-131.

Inman, B. R. (1987). "Commercializing technology and U.S. competitiveness." *High Technology Market Review* **1**(2): 83-98.

Irving, J. C., J. L. George, et al. (1995). *Labor/management partnership: A roadmap to organized labor in the agile age*. Creating The Agile Organization: Models, Metrics and Pilots, J. J. Barker, Ed. Atlanta, GA: Agile Manufacturing Enterprise Forum.

Ives, B., S. Hamilton and G. B. Davis (1980). "A Framework for Research in Computer-Based Management Information Systems." *Management Science* **26**(9): 910-934.

Ives, B., S. L. Jarvenpaa and R. O. Mason (1993). "Global business drivers: Aligning information technology to global business strategy." *IBM Systems Journal* **32**(1): 143-161.

Ives, B. and G. P. Learmonth (1984). "The Information System as a Competitive Weapon." *Communications of the ACM* **27**(12): 1193-1201.

Jaikumar, R. (1986). "Postindustrial Manufacturing." *Harvard Business Review* **64**(6): 69-76.

Johnston, H. R. and M. R. Vitale (1988). "Creating Competitive Advantage with Interorganizational Information Systems." *MIS Quarterly* **12**(2): 153-165.

Jones, D. T. (1992). "Beyond the Toyota production system: the era of lean production." In *Manufacturing Strategy Process and Content*. C. A. Voss, Ed. London: Chapman & Hall: 189-210.

Kaplan, R. S. (1984). "Yesterday's Accounting Undermine Production." *Harvard Business Review* (Jul-Aug).

Karmarkar, U. (1989). "Getting Control of Just-In-Time." *Harvard Business Review* (Sep-Oct).

Katz, D. and R. L. Kahn (1966). *The Social Psychology of Organization*. New York: Wiley.

Kendrick, D. A. (1983). "A Mathematical-Computer Language for Linear Programming Problems." In *Dynamic Modeling and Control of National Economies*. R. Basar and L. F. Pau, Eds. Oxford: Pergamon Press Ltd.

Kidd, P. (1995). "Agile Marketing & Logistics Practices Meeting, October 17-18." Viewgraphs. Westport, CT.

Kidd, P. T. (1994). *Forging New Frontiers: The Quest for Agile Manufacturing*. Reading, PA: Addison-Wesley.

Kiechel, W., III (1993). "How we will work in the year 2000." *Fortune* **127**(10). May 17: US 38-52; Asian 30-37.

Kinni, T. B. (1994). "Measuring Up: benchmarking can be critical, but it doesn't have to be expensive." *Industry Week*. December 5.

Kirk, J. and M. L. Miller (1986). *Reliability and Validity in Qualitative Research*. Beverly Hills: Sage.

Kivenko, K. (1995). "Leading your organization to reduced cycle time and increased agility." *Cost & Management* **69**(5). Jun: 4.

Klein, J. A. (1989). "The Human Costs of Manufacturing Reform." *Harvard Business Review* (Mar-Apr).

Knuth, D. (1995). "Chrysler shifts to overdrive at dealer help desk." *Communications News* **32**(7). Jul: 16.

Konsynski, B. R. (1993). "Strategic control in the extended enterprise." *IBM Systems Journal* **32**(1): 111-142.

Kotha, S. (1994). *Mass Customization: Implementing the Emerging Paradigm for Competitive Advantage.* Working papers. Sep, New York: New York University.

Kotler, P. (1989). "From Mass Marketing to Mass Customization." *Planning Review* **17**(5). September/October: 10-13, 47.

Kotter, J. P. (1995). "Leading change: Why transformation efforts fail." *Harvard Business Review* **73**(2): 59-67.

Kozmetsky, G. (1987). "The Impact of Engineering Education on Local Industry and Economic Development." In *Industrial Innovation, Productivity and Employment.* P. A. Abetti, C. W. LeMaistre and R. W. Smilor, Eds. Austin: IC2 Institute, The University of Texas at Austin: 81-102.

Kozmetsky, G. (1988). *The challenge of technology innovation in the coming economy.* 13th Annual Symposium on Technology Transfer, Oregon: Technology Transfer Society.

Kozmetsky, G. (1988). "Commercializing technologies: The next steps." In *Federal Lab Technology Transfer: Issues and Policies.* G. R. Bopp, Ed. Praeger, NY: 171-182.

Kozmetsky, G. (1993). "Regionally Based Learning-Teaching Factories". Speech: Speech presented to the First Annual Boarder Conference on Manufacturing and Environment: Progress Through Manufacturing Excellence The University of Texas at El Paso, IC2 Institute. May 24, 1993.

Krafcik, J. F. (1988). "Triumph of the Lean Production System." *Sloan Management Review* **30**(1): 41-52.

Kresa, K. (1995). *Northrop Grumman—Future Look.* Company literature. December 12, 1994, Hawthorne, CA: Northrop Grumman.

Kubinski, R. (1995). Interview by Jeff Amos. 3M. January 8.

Kuhn, R. L., Ed. (1985). *Frontiers in Creative & Innovative Management.* New York: Harper Business.

Kuhn, R. L. and S. Nozette, Eds. (1987). *Commercializing SDI Technologies.* Westport: Greenwood Publishing Group, Incorporated.

Kumar, A. and J. Motwani (1995). "A methodology for assessing time-based competitive advantage of manufacturing firms." *International Journal of Operations & Production Management* **15**(2): 36-53.

Kuznets (1965). *1965 Economic Growth and Structure: Selected Essays.* New York: W.W. Norton.

Larson, E. W. and D. H. Gobeli (1987). "Matrix Management: Contradictions and Insights." *California Management Review* **29**(4): 126-138.

Leavitt, H. J. and T. L. Whisler (1958). "Management in the 1980's." *Harvard Business Review* **36**(6): 41-48.

Lee, A. S. (1989). "A Scientific Methodology for MIS Case Studies." *MIS Quarterly* (March): 33-50.

Lee, J. Y., R. Jacob and M. Ulinski (1994). "Activity-Based Costing and Japanese Cost Management Techniques: A Comparison." *Advances In Managing Accounting* **3**: 179-196.

Leonard-Barton, D., H. K. Bowen, et al. (1994). "How to integrate work and deepen expertise." *Harvard Business Review* **72**(5): 121-130.

Likert, R. (1958). "Measuring Organizational Performance." *Harvard Business Review* **36**(2): 41-50.

Lillrank, P. (1995). "The transfer of management innovations from Japan." *Organization Studies* **16**(6): 971-989.

Limerick, D. and B. Cunnington (1993). *Managing the New Organization: A Blueprint for Networks and Strategic Alliances.* San Francisco: Jossey-Bass.

Lincoln, Y. S. and E. G. Guba (1985). *Naturalistic Inquiry.* Newbury Park, CA: Sage Publications.

"LTV Files Bankruptcy." (1991) *Aviation Week and Space Technology* **135**(1). July 8: 75.

Luftman, J. N., P. R. Lewis and S. H. Oldach (1993). "Transforming the enterprise: The alignment of business and information technology strategies." *IBM Systems Journal* **32**(1): 198-221.

Malone, M. S. (1995). "Pennsylvania guys mass customize." *Forbes* (ASAP Supplement): 82-85.

Manoochehri, G. H. (1984). "Suppliers and the JIT Concept." *Journal of Purchasing and Materials Management* (Winter): 16-21.

Markides, C. C. and N. Berg (1988). "Manufacturing Offshore is Bad Business." *Harvard Business Review* (Sep-Oct).

Marquardt, M. (1996). *Building the Learning Organization.* New York: McGraw-Hill.

Marx, K. (1932). *Capital, the Communist Manifesto and Other Writings.* New York: Random House Publishing.

Maskell, B. H. (1991). *Performance Measurement for World Class Manufacturing: A Model for American Companies*. Portland: Productivity Press.

"MCC To Develop National Agile Manufacturing Network." (1994) *Industrial Engineering* (March):10-11.

McDaniel, S., J. G. Ormsby and A. B. Gresham (1990). "The Effect of JIT on Distributors." *Industrial Marketing Management* 21: 145-149.

Merrifield, D. B. (1987). "Driving Forces of Change in the U.S. Economy: Their Impact on Productivity and Industrial World Leadership." In *Industrial Innovation, Productivity and Employment*. P. A. Abetti, C. W. Lemaistre and R. W. Smilor, Eds. Austin: IC2 Institute, The University of Texas at Austin: 23-44.

Merrills, R. (1989). "How Northern Telecom Competes on Time." *Harvard Business Review* 67(4): 108-114.

Merton, R. K., M. Fiske and P. L. Kendall, Eds. (1956). *The Focused Interview*. Glencoe, IL: The Free Press.

Miller, J. A. (1995). *Achieving agile performance through reengineering the product definition process*. Creating the Agile Organization: Models Metrics and Pilots, J. J. Barker, Ed. Atlanta, GA: Agile Manufacturing Enterprise Forum.

Miller, J. G. and T. E. Vollman (1985). "The Hidden Factory." *Harvard Business Review* (Sep-Oct).

Mintzberg, H. (1979). "An emerging strategy of "direct" research." *Administrative Science Quarterly* 24(December): 582-589.

Mintzberg, H. (1983). "An Emerging Strategy of 'Direct Research'." In *Qualitative Methodology*. J. Van Maanen, Ed. Beverly Hills: Sage Publications: 105-116.

Mintzberg, H. (1989). *Mintzberg on Management—Inside our Strange World of Organizations*. New York: The Free Press.

Misterek, S. D. A. (1992). "The nature of the link between manufacturing strategy and organizational culture." In *Manufacturing Strategy Process and Content*. C. A. Voss, Ed. London: Chapman & Hall: 331-352.

Moore, L. B. (1958). "How to Manage Improvement." *Harvard Business Review* 36: 75-84.

Murphy, W. J., III (1987). *Cooperative action to achieve competitive strategic objectives: A study of MCC*. Dissertation. Cambridge: Harvard University, School of Business.

Nagel, R. and D. Allen (1993). "Virtual winners." *International Management* 48(5, Europe Edition): 64.

Nagel, R. N. (1992). *Performance Capabilities of the Next Generation Manufacturing Enterprise*. Report. May 7, Bethlehem, PA: Lehigh University.

Nagel, R. N. B. P. (1994). "Agility: The Ultimate Requirement for World-Class Manufacturing Performance." *National Productivity Review* 13(3): 331-340.

National Center for Manufacturing Sciences (1991). "World Class Manufacturing Operating Principles for the 1990s and Beyond." In *Concurrent Life Cycle Management*. F. Y. Phillips, Ed. Austin: IC2 Institute, The University of Texas at Austin: 3-12.

National Research Council (1993). *Breaking the Mold: Forging a Common Defense Manufacturing Vision*. Washington, D.C.: National Academy Press.

Nevison, J. M. (1994). "Up to speed: The cost of learning on a white-collar project." *Project Management Journal* 25(2): 11-15.

Newman, J. W. (1978). "Working with behavioral scientists." *Harvard Business Review* 56(4): 67-74.

Noble, B. P. (1993). "Reinventing labor: An interview with union president Lynn Williams." *Harvard Business Review* 71(4): 114-123+.

Nohria, N. and R. G. Eccles (1994). *Networks and Organizations*. Cambridge: Harvard Business School Press.

Nolan, R. L. (1973). "Managing the computer resource: a stage hypothesis." *Communications of the ACM* 16(7): 399-405.

Nolan, R. L. (1979). "Managing the Crises in Data Processing." *Harvard Business Review*: 115-126.

Nolan, R. L. and D. C. Croson (1995). *Creative destruction: a six stage process for transforming the organization*. Boston: Harvard Business School Press.

Noyes, D. (1995). "Sentient Technology: Toward Knowledge Based Engineering." Presentation. Bethlehem, PA, Cogito, Inc.

O'Connor, B. and C. Bilby (1991). "An Activity-Based Lunar Surface Operations Cost Analysis." In *Modeling and Simulation of Advanced Space Programs*. C. Bilby and G. Kozmetsky, Eds. Austin: IC2 Institute, The University of Texas at Austin: 371-384.

O'Grady, P. J. (1988). *Putting the Just-In-Time Philosophy into Practice*. East Brunswick: Nichols Publishing Company.

O'Sullivan, L. and J. M. Geringer (1993). "Harnessing the power of your value chain." *Long Range Planning* 26(2): 59-68.

Pandiarajan, V. and R. Patun (1994). "Agile manufacturing initiatives at Concurrent Technologies Corp." *Industrial Engineering* 26(2): 46-49.

Parthasarthy, R. and S. P. Sethi (1992). "The Impact of Flexible Automation on Business Strategy and Organizational Structure." *Academy of Management Review* **17**(1): 86-111.

Pascale, R. (1984). "Perspectives on Strategy: The Real Story Behind Honda's Success." *California Management Review* **26**(3): 47-72.

Peters, T. (1994). "Re-Inventing Civilization." *Future Outlook 94/95*. 16-18.

Peters, T. J. and R. H. Waterman (1982). *In Search of Excellence: Lessons from America's Best Run Companies*. New York: Harper and Row.

Pettigrew, A. (1973). *The Politics of Organizational Decisions making*. London: Tavistock.

Pilling, D. L. (1989). *Competition in Defense Procurement*. Washington, D.C.: Brookings Institute.

Pine, B. J., II, B. Victor and A. C. Boynton (1993). "Making mass customization work." *Harvard Business Review* **71**(5): 108-111+.

Pine, J. B., II and S. M. Davis (1993). *Mass Customization: The New Frontier in Business Competition*. Boston: Harvard Business School Press.

Pinkston, J. T. (1989). "Technology Transfer: Issues for Consortia." In *Entrepreneurial Management: New Technology and New Market Development*. K. D. Walters, Ed. Boston: Ballinger: 143-149.

Pint, E. and R. Schmidt (1994). *Financial Condition of U.S. Military Aircraft Prime Contractors*. Santa Monica, CA: Rand Corporation Report.

Pisano, G. P. (1994). "Knowledge, integration, and the locus of learning: An empirical analysis of process development." *Strategic Management Journal* **15**(Special Issue): 85-100.

Pisano, G. P. and R. H. Hayes, Eds. (1995). *Manufacturing Renaissance: A Harvard Business Review Book*. Business Review Bks. Boston: Harvard Business School Press.

Pollalis, Y. A. (1994). *Strategic Alignment and Information Technology-based Coordination: Lessons from the U.S. Banking Industry*. Working Paper. Oct 25. New York: Syracuse University.

Port, O. (1992). "Moving Past the Assembly Line." *Business Week* (Special Issue). 177-180.

Port, O. and J. Carey (1991). "This is what the US must do to stay competitive: make factories 'agile', link them by computer-and collaborate." *Business Week* (Dec 16): 92-94.

Porter, M. E. (1985). *Competitive Advantage: Creating and Sustaining Superior Performance*. New York: The Free Press.

Porter, M. E. (1990). *The Competitive Advantage of Nations*. New York: The Free Press.

Pozos, A. (1995). "American Productivity & Quality Center: International Benchmarking Clearinghouse". Benchmarking presentation. Feb 18. Automation and Robotics Research Institute: UT Arlington Workshop on Agility.

Preiss, K. and S. L. Goldman, Eds. (1991). *Twenty-First Century Manufacturing Enterprise Strategy: Vol. 1: An Industry-Led View*. Bethlehem: Lehigh University.

Preiss, K. and S. L. Goldman, Eds. (1991). *Twenty-First Century Manufacturing Enterprise Strategy: Vol. 2: Infrastructure*. Bethlehem: Lehigh University.

Preiss, K. and S. L. Goldman (1994). *Agile Competitors & Virtual Organizations: Strategies for Enriching the Customer*. New York: Van Nostrand Reinhold.

Presley, A., M. Johnson and D. H. Liles (1994). *Enterprise excellence: continuous enterprise improvement and the small manufacturer*. 2nd Industrial Engineering Research Conference: Institute of Industrial Engineers.

Quigley, P. J. (1990). "The Coming of the Rabbiphant: Toward Decentralized Corporations." *Executive Speeches* **5**(2). Sep: 8-12.

Rabbitt, J. T. and P. A. Bergh (1993). *The ISO 9000 Book: A Global Competitor's Guide to Compliance & Certification*. New York: Quality Resources.

Raia, E. (1986). "Just-In-Time USA: Industry Giants Meet New Arrival JIT—With Success." *Purchasing* (Feb). February 13: 48-71.

"Republic Steel." (1985) *Iron Age* **228**(4). February 15: 43-44.

Rhodes, E. (1978). *Data Envelopment Analysis and Approaches for Measuring the Efficiency of Decision-Making Units with an Application to Program Follow-through in U.S. Education*. Ph.D. dissertation. Pittsburgh, PA: School of Urban & Public Affairs, Carnegie Mellon Univ.

Richardson, H. L. (1995). "Make time an ally." *Transportation & Distribution* **36**(7): 46-50.

Richardson, H. L. and P. A. Trunick (1995). "Breakthrough thinking in logistics." *Transportation & Distribution* **36**(12). Dec: 34-46.

Rios, J. P. (1993). "Investment in new production capacity under uncertain market conditions." *Industrial Engineering* **25**(6): 31-34.

Roach, T. (1992). *Effective Systems Development in Complex Organizations: A Field Study of Systems Development and Use in the United Stated Army Medical Department*. Ph.D. dissertation. September 1992, Austin: University of Texas at Austin.

Robb, C. S. (1986). "A New Progressive Agenda for an Era of Economic Change: Basic Values and Principles." *Vital Speeches of the Day* **52**(22). Sep 1: 678-682.

Rockart, J. F. and F. L. S. (1983). "The Management of End User Computing." *Communications of the ACM* **26**(10): 776-784.

Roe, J. W. (1916). *English and American Tool Builders*. New Haven: Yale University Press.

Roe, M. A., B. Fossum and H. B. Dorsey, Eds. (1993). *Teaching Factories: A Strategy for World Class Manufacturing Regional Deployment of Manufacturing Application and Education Networks*. IC2 Institute Monograph series. Austin: The University of Texas at Austin, the IC2 Institute.

Rogers, D. (1989). "Entrepreneurial approach to accelerate technology commercialization." In *Entrepreneurial Management: New Technology and New Market Development*. K. D. Walters, Ed. Boston: Ballinger: 3-15.

Rogers, E. M. (1986). *Communication Technology*. New York: Free Press, The.

Rogers, E. M. and D. L. Kincaid (1982). *Communication Networks: A New Paradigm for Research*. New York: Free Press.

Rosenberg, N., Ed. (1969). *The American System of Manufactures*. Edinburgh: Edinburgh University Press.

Rostow, W. W. (1991). "Towards a New World Economic Order in an Era of Global Federalism." In *Concurrent Life Cycle Management*. F. Y. Phillips, Ed. Austin: IC2 Institute, The University of Texas at Austin: 245-266.

Rostow, W. W. (1993). "The American Administrative Style: A Costly Inheritance." In *Generating Creativity and Innovation in Large Bureaucracies*. R. L. Kuhn, Ed. Westport, CT: Quorum Books. **4**: 21-49.

Rostow, W. W. (1994). *The United States and the World: The First Half of the 21st Century*. #94-06-3. Photocopy. Austin: IC2 Institute, The University of Texas at Austin.

Roth, A. V. and C. A. Giffi (1991). *Manufacturing Futures Factbook, The 1988 North American Manufacturing Futures Survey*. Boston: Boston University School of Management Manufacturing Roundtable.

Roth, A. V., C. A. Giffi and G. M. Seal (1992). "Operating strategies for the 1990s: elements comprising world-class manufacturing." In *Manufacturing Strategy Process and Content*. C. A. Voss, Ed. London: Chapman & Hall: 89-120.

Schein, E. (1993). "On dialogue, culture and organizational learning." *Organizational Dynamics* (Autumn): 40-51.

Schine, E. (1991). "Northrop's Biggest Foe May Have Been Its Past." *Business Week* (3212-Industrial/Technology Edition). May 6: 30-31.

Schmenner, R. W. (1988). "The Merit of Making Things Fast." *Sloan Management Review* **30**(1): 11-17.

Scott, W. R. (1965). "Field Methods in the Study of Organizations." In *Handbook of Organizations*. J. G. March, Ed. Chicago: Rand McNally: 261-304.

Seiford, L. M. (1994). "A DEA Bibliography (1978-1992)." In *Data Envelopment Analysis: Theory Methodology & Application*. A. Charnes, W. Cooper, A. Y. Lewin and L. M. Seiford, Eds. Norwell: Kluwer Academic Publishers: 437-479.

Senate Committee on Banking Finance and Urban Affairs (1989). *Hearings on " Internationalization of the Aerospace Industry"*. Washington: GPO.

Senate Committee on Government Operations (1992). *Hearings on " Federal Support for U.S. Aeronautics Industry"*. Washington: GPO.

Senge, P. (1990). *The Fifth Discipline*. New York: Doubleday.

Shapero, A. (1971). *An Action Program for Entrepreneurship*. ORC TA 68-29 (NEG). Report. April, Austin: Multi-Disciplinary Research, Inc.

Shapiro, H. J. and T. Cosenza (1987). *Reviving Industry in America: Japanese Influences on Manufacturing & the Service Sector*. New York: Harper Business.

Sheridan, J. H. (1993). "Agile Manufacturing: A New Paradigm." *Technology Productivity Journal* **1993**(11): 39-48.

Sheridan, J. H. (1993). "Agile manufacturing: Stepping beyond lean production." *Industry Week* **242**(8). April 19: 30-46.

Sheridan, J. H. (1994). "Reengineering isn't enough." *Industry Week* **243**(2): 61-62.

Short, J. E. and N. Venkatraman (1992). "Beyond Business Process Redesign: Redefining Baxter's Business Network." *Sloan Management Review* **34**(1): 7-20.

Skinner, W. (1958). "Manufacturing—missing link in corporate strategy." *Harvard Business Review* **47**(3): 136-145.

Skinner, W. (1969). "Manufacturing—Missing Link in Corporate Strategy." *Harvard Business Review*(May-June): 136-145.

Skinner, W. (1974). "The Decline , Fall, and Renewal of Manufacturing Plants." *Industrial Engineering* (October).

Skinner, W. (1974). "The Focused Factory." *Harvard Business Review* (May-Jun).

Skinner, W. (1985). *Manufacturing: the Formidable Competitive Weapon.* New York: John Wiley.

Skinner, W. (1986). "The Productivity Paradox." *Harvard Business Review* (Jul-Aug).

Skinner, W. (1992). "Missing the links in manufacturing strategy." In *Manufacturing Strategy Process and Content.* C. A. Voss, Ed. London: Chapman & Hall: 13-25.

Smilor, R. and D. Gibson (1990). "R&D consortia and technology transfer: initial lessons from MCC." *Journal of Technology Transfer* **14**(2): 11-22.

Smith, A. (1776). *An Inquiry Into the Nature and Causes of the Wealth of Nation's.* Rpt. 1976. Classic Book Series. New York: The Modern Library.

Smith, A. (1994). "Interview". Presentation: Jeff Amos, Author Anderson. November 20, 1994.

Smytka, D. L. and M. W. Clemens (1993). "Total cost supplier selection model: A case study." *International Journal of Purchasing & Materials Management* **29**(1): 42-49.

Spanner, G. E., J. P. Nuno and C. Chandra (1993). "Time-based strategies— Theory and practice." *Long Range Planning* **26**(4): 91-101.

Spekman, R. E. (1988). "Strategic Supplier Selection: Understanding Long-Term Buyer Relationships." *Business Horizons* **31**(4): 75-81.

Spira, J. S. and B. J. Pine, II (1993). "Mass customization." *Chief Executive* (83). Mar: 26-29.

St John, C. H. and K. C. Heriot (1993). "Small suppliers and JIT purchasing." *International Journal of Purchasing & Materials Management* **29**(1): 11-16.

Stalk, G., Jr. (1988). "Time—The Next Source of Competitive Advantage." *Harvard Business Review* **66**(4): 41-51.

Stalk, G., Jr. (1992). "Time-Based Competition and Beyond: Competing on Capabilities." *Planning Review* **20**(5). Sep/Oct: 27-29.

Stalk, G., Jr. and T. M. Hout (1990). *Competing Against Time: How Time-Based Competition is Reshaping Global Markets.* New York: Free Press, The.

Stalk, G., Jr. and T. M. Hout (1990). "How Time-Based Management Measures Performance." *Planning Review* **18**(6): 26-29.

Stalk, G., Jr. and T. M. Hout (1990). "Redesign Your Organization for Time-Based Management." *Planning Review* **18**(1): 4-9.

Stalk, G., Jr. and A. M. Webber (1993). "Japan's dark side of time." *Harvard Business Review* **71**(4): 93-102.

Stata, R. (1989). "Organizational Learning—The Key to Management Innovation." *Sloan Management Review* **30**(3): 63-74.

Sullivan, K. (1991). "Inventing the Future: New Approaches to Management, Compensation, and Learning at Apple Computer." *Employment Relations Today* **18**(4). Winter: 417-424.

Taguchi, G. and D. Clausing (1990). "Robust Quality." In *Manufacturing Renaissance*. G. P. Pisano and R. h. Hayes, Eds. Cambridge: Harvard Press: 173-188.

Tankha, S. and J. Amos (1995). *White Paper on Aerospace Industry and Agility*. White Paper. Austin: IC2 Institute, The University of Texas at Austin.

Taylor, F. W. (1911). *The Principles of Scientific Management*. Rpt: 1967, c1947. New York: Norton.

Tedlow, R. S. and G. Jones (1993). *The Rise and Fall of Mass Marketing*. London: Routledge.

Teece, D. J. (1992). "Competition, Cooperation, and Innovation: Organizational Arrangements for Regimes of Rapid Technological Progress." *Journal of Economic Behavior & Organization* **18**(1): 1-25.

Teledyne Systems Corporation (1955). *System Effectiveness and Cost Effectiveness for the Integrated Helicopter Avionics System (IHAS)*. Hawthore, CA: Teledyne Systems Corp.

Thomas, J. (1994). "The secret to supply chain excellence." *Distribution* **93**(10). Sep: 6.

Udo, G. J. (1993). "The impact of telecommunications on inventory management." *Production & Inventory Management Journal* **34**(2): 32-37.

Udo, G. J. and T. Grant (1993). "Making EDI pay off: The Averitt Express experience." *Production & Inventory Management Journal* **34**(4): 6-11.

Underwood, J. (1994). Interview by Jeff Amos. AT&T Power Systems. December 11.

Utterback, J. M. (1994). *Mastering the Dynamics of Innovation: How Companies Can Seize Opportunities in the Face of Technological Change*. Boston: Harvard Business School Press.

Vadas, D. (1995). "Aerospace after the Cold War: A Blueprint for Success." *Aerospace America*. October: 29.

Van Maanen, J. (1979). "Reclaiming Qualitative Methods for Organizational Research: A Preface." *Administrative Science Quarterly* **24**: 520-526.

Van Maanen, J. (1983). *Qualitative Methodology*. Beverly Hills, London, New Delhi: Sage Publications.

Vasilash, G. S. (1993). "Manufacturing Agility: The Conference." *Production* **105**(4). Apr: 58-63.

Vastag, G., J. D. Kasarda and T. Boone (1994). "Logistical Support for Manufacturing Agility in Global Markets." *International Journal of Operations & Production Management* **14**(11): 73-85.

Vesey, J. (1990). "Meet the New Competitors: They Think in Terms of Speed-To market." *Industrial Engineering* (Dec).

Vollman, T. E., R. S. Collins, et al. (1992). "A conceptual framework for manufacturing restructuring." In *Manufacturing Strategy Process and Content*. C. A. Voss, Ed. London: Chapman & Hall: 57-88.

Voss, B. (1994). "A new spring for manufacturing." *Journal of Business Strategy* **15**(1): 54-57.

Voss, C. A. (1992). "Manufacturing strategy formulation as a process." In *Manufacturing Strategy Process and Content*. C. A. Voss, Ed. London: Chapman & Hall: 121-132.

Voss, C. A., Ed. (1992). *Manufacturing Strategy Process and Content*. London: Chapman & Hall.

Wandmacher, R. R. (1994). *Information management as a key to agile manufacturing*. Working paper. October 24: General Motors North American Operations, Management Information Systems.

Want, J. H. (1993). "Managing radical change." *Journal of Business Strategy* **14**(3): 20-28.

Weick, K. (1984). "Theoretical Assumptions and Research Methodology Selection." In *The Information Systems Research Challenge*. F. W. McFarlan, Ed. Boston: Harvard Business School Press: 111-132.

Weick, K. (1989). "Theory Construction as Disciplined Imagination." *The Academy of Management Review* **14**(4): 516-531.

Weick, K. (1990). "Technology as equivoque: Sense-making in new technologies." In *The Information Systems Research Challenge*. F. W. McFarlan, Ed. Cambridge: HBR Press: 143-149.

West, E. G. (1969). *Adam Smith*. New Rochelle: Arlington House.

Wheelwright, S. C. (1978). "Reflecting corporate strategy in manufacturing decisions." *Business Horizens*(February): 57-66.

Wheelwright, S. C. and R. H. Hayes (1985). "Competing Through Manufacturing." *Harvard Business Review*(Jan-Feb).

Whetten, D. A. (1989). "What Constitutes a Theoretical Contribution?" *The Academy of Management Review* **14**(4): 490-495.

Williams, F. and D. Gibson (1990). *Technology Transfer: A Communication Perspective*. Beverly Hills, CA: Sage Publishing.

Womack, J. P. and D. T. Jones (1994). "From lean production to the lean enterprise." *Harvard Business Review* **72**(2): 93-103.

Womack, J. P., D. T. Jones and D. Roos (1990). *The Machine the Changed the World.* New York: Rawson Macmillan.

Yin, R. K. (1981). "The Case Study Crisis: Some Answers." *Administrative Science Quarterly* **26**: 58-65.

Youssef, M. A. (1992). "Agile Manufacturing: A Necessary Condition for Competing in Global Markets." *Industrial Engineering* **24**(12). Dec: 18-20.

Index